Blind Handshake

Blind Handshake

DAVID HUMPHREY

Periscope Publishing

Published by
Periscope Publishing, Ltd.
Gloria Kury, Director

Distributed by Prestel Publishing
900 Broadway, Suite 603, New York, NY 10003
Phone 212 995 2720
Fax 212 995 2733
sales@prestel-usa.com

Editors: Chelsea Weathers and Nell McLister
Design: Geoff Kaplan/General Working Group

The designer and author of this book collaborated on every phase of
its development. It extends the dyamic of art writing to book design
and production.

Typeset in Univers designed by Adrian Frutiger

ISBN 978-1-934772-32-4
Library of Congress Control Number: 2009935570

Image on the cover:
David Humphrey, *Plein Air*, 2008

ART WRITING + ART
1990 – 2008

David Humphrey, *Made for Each Other,* 2009

David Humphrey, *Roman Nocturne,* 2008 (next page)

David Humphrey, *Witness*, 2008

Favorite Things: David Humphrey

Seeing comes before words; the child looks and recognizes before it can speak.
John Berger, 1972

IT SOUNDS TRUE, DOESN'T IT? The famous opening of John Berger's "Ways of Seeing" stakes a terse, and apparently unassailable claim. Generations of art students have read those words and felt heartened: seeing is the primordial experience! Poetry, political philosophy, standup comedy, art criticism—all happen in the secondary realm of language; visual art registers in some, deeper precinct of the brain. But, alas, the situation is more complicated than Berger wished. Apart from faces, infants aren't good at recognizing much. They *are* marvelous linguists though. As adults, we are shaped mostly by things we hear our fellow humans say. We live in language.

So we should resign ourselves to the fact that sight is, in social terms, a second-class sense. Pictures are inefficient and faulty communication platforms. Their inadequacy makes them infinite grist for everything verbal—for glossing, explaining, communing, disagreeing. Their semi-silence keeps us talking. Artists, knowing how grotesquely powerful words are, tend to be undertalkers—at least about their own work. They don't want to constrain (or dam) the burgeoning word-current that will determine their own reputations. Instead, most of the time, they talk about *other* people's artworks. A flood of diverted verbiage spills into neighboring channels. That rechanneling is art talk—the live, unpublished, bar-and-studio version of art criticism. And art talk is what, essentially, you are about to read.

Of course, David Humphrey's sentences don't always read like talk, at least not in any ordinary sense. When Humphrey says that Lucian Freud's paintings "persecute his subjects into existence," or describes the "tangled geodesics" of Ellen Altfest's painted tumbleweeds, we're struck by how apt and evocative, not how colloquial, these phrases are. At one point, in an essay about beauty, Humphrey launches into an impromptu personal credo that sounds, at first, as if it could have been written by an avant-garde psychiatrist:

> The dissolving of identity, the discovery of unconscious material in the real, a thralldom of the senses underwritten by anxiety, are a few of my favorite things.

It's the ghostly appearance of Julie Andrews in the final phrase that flicks the switch, magically transforming a relatively dense idea sequence into karaoke. Text becomes performance; earnestness shifts toward wryness. That transition is typical of Humphrey, both on the page and live in person. To stand next to him at an art opening is to hear an accelerating fusillade of choice anecdotes, movie tie-ins, literary allusions, and sly judgments, often prefaced with a laughing, personalized invitation: "Wait—you are going to *love* this." Humphrey's art talk is special—in being volatile, funny, unapologetically book-fed, and openhanded. But the fact that his writing captures the way he speaks is not its only claim to the status of art talk, or at least, not its most important one.

When Humphrey began writing, around 1990, the art world's momentum, after the boom of the eighties, was freshly uncertain. In New York, identity issues were ascendant, while criticism seemed largely partisan or bland, in either case unhelpful. There was, in retrospect, plenty of room for someone as unbeholden as Humphrey, someone with an equal appetite for psychoanalytic theory and for punk rock, for *October* magazine and for *Zap Comix*. In the regular column he began writing for LA's *Art issues* magazine, Humphrey set out to write the kind of criticism he wanted to read. He would pick three shows, not necessarily the ones he liked best, but ones from which he thought he could tease "a little thematic arc." Each column, in other words, would be both an idea talk and a gallery walk; the idea was to integrate the two, to reconnect ideas and objects. In the face of so much faux empiricism, he wanted to keep in mind the way artists speak in one another's studios. During studio visits, ideas are welcome, pronouncements less so. Typically, the visitor talks as he looks, cataloguing impressions, making distinctions, parsing tone. The aim is to offer the host artist a kind of constructive, synthesizing attentiveness.

That's the essence of Humphrey's writing. His voice has the animated, collegial spirit of a studio visitor. He has a great, greedy, omnivorous eye, and he loves registering what it sees. He moves eagerly from general observations back to description. He also quotes readily from whatever he's reading (Stanley Cavell, Michael Baxandall, Adam Phillips, James Elkins, Jacques Attali). His allusions feel impulsive—they are offered, not insisted upon. Like a talker, Humphrey the writer is happy to switch gears, to digress, to go long or short. Sometimes there's a summation; sometimes just a quip. One of the entries here is a single sentence, like a comment made in passing a friend's open studio door. A major hallmark of periodical criticism—the dutiful mapping out of influence, debts, and

stylistic affiliation— Humphrey largely avoids. An even bigger omission: Humphrey doesn't give or recognize grades. He ignores the whole apparatus of artworld status. You will never read him say that X is among the greatest artists of his generation. Censure, the mainstay of nervous and cocksure critics alike, is also notably absent. Even writing about the bathos of Odd Nerdrum, Humphrey keeps his eyes on the pictures, admirably conjuring the "defoliated excremental earth" of Nerdrum's dour landscapes. Only a few stray word choices, delivered with no special emphasis, hint at what the writer might say if he were asked to buy one. In Humphrey's patience and flexibility, you can feel his freedom—the permission given by the fact that reviewing was always a sideline. "This wasn't writing," Humphrey remembers telling himself. "This was just studio practice put into words."

While Humphrey remains far better known as a painter (not to mention a sculptor, curator, and teacher), his "sideline"

is now almost two decades old, and it belies Humphrey's own modesty. There are plenty of other painter-critics, but few can match the sheer literary panache of, for instance, "Fizzy Nimbus," Humphrey's seductive reverie on the paintings of Julie Heffernan. Few are as gifted in phrasemaking, either—beginning with the two-word poem of this volume's title. And few are as funny—although Humphrey's humor is often clothed in the camouflage of serious diction, as in this observation, from "Hair Piece":

> While defecating is periodic and inspired, hair growth is continuous and involuntary.

Will the word "inspired" ever sound quite the same again? Nuggets of dry precision like that, offered in passing, are typical Humphrey. In writing about his own bawdy Surrealist variations of Dwight Eisenhower's paintings, Humphrey suggests that

> My attentions constitute a form of contact, intimacy within a context of extreme detachment.

The accelerating (homo)eroticism of the words "attentions," "contact," and "intimacy" sets up the delicately ambivalent payoff. If you assume that Humphrey is mocking the Presidential Sunday painter, "extreme detachment" reads as a sardonic understatement, a euphemism for feelings that might be less than polite. But on second thought, the phrase is also accurate, and even weirdly touching. So many decades after Ike's death, none of us has any investment in liking or disliking him. Humphrey is goosing a ghost. But you can feel his sympathy as well. We are all headed, sooner or later, for "a context of extreme detachment." We'll be lucky, half a century hence, if someone like Humphrey chooses to goose us.

Art issues folded in 2000. Since then, Humphrey has been contributing reviews to *Art in America*, as well as writing catalogue essays for other artists, and for the group shows he often curates. *Blind Handshake* is a kind of mid-career retrospective—a fairly selective one, representing roughly half of Humphrey's output. The sequence is not chronological, nor do the pieces necessarily appear in their original form. Most of the *Art issues* columns ("originally titled "New York Fax" and, later, "New York Email") have been broken out of their original groupings, stripped of their connective commentary, and left to stand on their own. The range of subjects, though, is representative. There is a sprinkling of patriarchs: Matisse, Magritte, de Kooning. There are a few older luminaries: Chuck Close, Jörg Immendorf, Richard Prince. There are campy detours to tattoo parlors and kitsch meccas. About one of these— Arizona's Wickenburg Desert Caballeros Museum—Humphrey owns up to a certain nepotism, since it turns out that his grandfather was a passionate benefactor. (How did Humphrey come by his taste for kitsch? Now we know.)

The vast majority of Humphrey's subjects, however, are peers: artists from the tail end of the baby boom, most now in their forties. Among these Humphrey is not quite ecumenical. Though he has a weakness for language-based art (as you might expect),

most of his choices are painters, like himself, and most of these work in some kind of figurative idiom, ranging from the fine-brush naturalism of Altfest and Heffernan, to the antic, cartoon-inflected near-abstraction of Amy Sillman, Barnaby Furnas, James Esber, and Inka Essenhigh. Several of the artists covered here (myself included) are acquaintances or friends—an inevitability in the New York art world, especially for an artist as ardently social as Humphrey. If, from a non–New York perspective, that sounds nettlesome, let me testify to the fact that Humphrey is remarkably even-handed. Writing about his own exceptionally inclusive circle, he is neither tougher nor gentler, but always his curious, conscientious, infectiously caffeinated self.

The result is a generational group portrait, written by its most open-eyed and articulate central player. The theme-clusters that link the book's individual sections represent most of our major talking points over these last two decades. Humphrey and his editor, Nell McClister, have

arranged these into a lightly detectable sequence. Two opening essays function as introductions, the first ("My Summer of Solitude") autobiographical, the second ("Hi My Name is Artwork") casually theoretical. After that, clusters of varying length follow on themes of fantasy, narrative, religion, sex, deception, self-portraiture, and so on. The penultimate cluster, on trash and plastic, leads to a standalone finale, "Describable Beauty," which begins autobiographically: "One of the reasons I became an artist," Humphrey confesses, "was to avoid writing."

As far as I can tell, this book doesn't offer any "rosebud" to Humphrey's own art. No secret aversions or predilections are inadvertently revealed. Probably, if such secrets exist, they are sitting in plain sight, painted into the gleeful stylizations of Humphrey's paintings. What *Blind Handshake* offers instead is exactly what its title promises: *contact*, a virtual handshake, immersing you, the reader, in a singularly sharp-minded, generous, and energetic temperament. Nobody expects you to read this at one sitting. In the pages ahead are more than a hundred gallery shows, comprising a virtual art fair on paper. As in a real art fair, ambling is the norm. As you amble, conversations—that is to say, words—will surround you. Words, *pace* Berger, come before, during, and after pictures. The question is, what words are helpful? What words make looking more fun, and blindness less normal? You are holding the answer in your hands.

Alexi Worth

Attainable Freedom

DAVID HUMPHREY IS A consummate viewer. In his art writing—a longtime "sideline" to his career as a highly accomplished, inventive painter—he approaches his subjects with a genius for the particular that only an active practitioner can possess. He allows the works to speak in their own language, directly to him.

Reading these texts is like paying a series of studio visits to each of the artists. Even when institutionalized within MFA programs, the studio visit remains a tentative, delicate and highly collaborative social form, potentially awkward at its best, and Humphrey's essays are perfect examples of this. The viewer enters an artist's studio prepared to leave all preconceptions, and the day's mental clutter, behind. There's necessarily a long stretch of silence involved. You walk back and forth. It often takes a long time to make that mental shift, to enter the world of the work. You know that eventually your job is to speak, but it's important never to force it. Speak too soon, and you risk never *seeing* the work. Eventually details, or color, or some mental sweep in the work will emerge… and these are the clues. As you begin describing the clues, the work draws you further in… patterns no longer contained within the frame of the work begin to seep out, and this is *excitement*…

Humphrey, a great fan of psychoanalysis, wisely recognizes that while surmising the artist's intentions can be useful, the goal of this particular form of detective work is to never, exactly, conclude. Throughout these texts, he begins with a simple, direct observation of what's in front of his face: the subject's "upward-turning eyes" in Frank Holiday's *Iris* (1999); the "checkered floor [that] points in perspective to a vanishing point" in Gillian Carnegie's *Cemetery Gate* (2006). Reportage of physical fact is used as a gateway to something more… metaphysical. In each of these viewings, Humphrey uses the essay to tease out the artist's intentions and arrive at a possible truth about the work's meaning. As the works fall into focus in Humphrey's mind, they accrue a hallucinatory power. His writings transcribe heightened experience. It's no coincidence that his literary sources dip back into early 20th century surrealism and its celebration of *wasted time* as art's primary material. "Artists," writes Humphrey in his short text on Sally Ross' *Untitled* (1998), "are gods over their fabricated worlds… they remind us that play can exercise the best part of our hardworking selves."

It is a paradoxical fact that "being an artist" is one of the most often-cited vocational goals of American youth, yet "visiting an art museum or gallery" does not even rank within the top ten American pastimes. Illusions of freedom… no one knows how to look at art! I'm reminded of Jean-Luc Godard's remarkable film *Sympathy for the Devil*, chronicling the development of that Rolling Stones song in a recording studio over six days in June 1968, and the way in which art is refined into cultural product, how "the artist" is unwittingly cast to the fans as an exemplar of unattainable freedom. Yet freedom is right here: "Art works help us to imagine what freedom looks like," observes Humphrey.

Refusing the R & D branding and marketing role the art world assigns to its critics, Humphrey shies away from polemics, never presuming to invent any new movements or trends. One could almost (falsely) perceive him as being deeply conservative, in his reluctance to link works of visual art with conclusions arrived at through critical theory. Yet this reluctance stems from not only his fidelity to the work but also the openness and rigor of his thinking.

In his 1996 essay "Describable Beauty," for instance, Humphrey asserts a refreshing ambivalence towards the abstract noun that became a rallying cry of one of the culture wars of that decade. While other *Art issues* writers like Dave Hickey and David Pagel championed "beauty" in opposition to content-based work they disliked, Humphrey persuasively argues that the concept of "beauty" needs to be "reinvented over and over… within each person or group. "Beauty's problem," he writes, "is the uses to which it is put." Rather than conflating beauty with formalism, he reaches for something more dangerous, less definable: "Beauty is psychedelic, a derangement of recognition, a flash of insight or a pulse of laughter… analogic or magical thinking embedded in… desire."

Reading these texts together, it becomes apparent that Humphrey's writings do not simply propose, they *enact* a utopian space… a lost world of leisure, in which the world outside stops for a while, and the world inside the artwork lives through him. "My goal," Humphrey writes, recalling his early years in New York, "was to build a studio in my head and treat the world as a hallucination."

I can't think of another practicing artist besides the late Fairfield Porter who has written as prolifically about visual culture as Humphrey. Many artists produce texts advancing their aesthetic cause in a parallel medium, but Humphrey's art-writing project is much more elusive. Does his writing ultimately narrate his art practice? Yes — but in the largest possible sense. Humphrey gives equally serious and knowing consideration to the portraits of Lucien Freud, the tattoo art of Don Ed Hardy and the shopping-surveillance photographs of Merry Alpern. In his willingness to travel so far as a critic beyond Humphrey-the-Painter's conceptual orbit, he advances a "motivational fiction" that narrates art-making itself: a willingness to encounter experience with alertness and presence.

The closest he comes here to discussing his own studio practice is in the wonderful essay *Wet Clay*, written ostensibly in the defense of the pariahs of contemporary art, ceramicists – whose medium brings them uncomfortably close to the (female, suburban) domain of craft pottery. Scavenging yard sales and flea markets for kitsch figurines that he'll render as plump sphinxes within candy-drenched landscapes, Humphrey confesses: "My work seeks the unexpectedly expressive within the ultra-conventional." To him, these forlorn 'pre-loved' objects are "as full as a pair of lungs, breathing in the feelings people project." As he concludes, "'Clay history' speaks only if we care to listen and have the imagination to speak back." This is what Humphrey achieves in this book as a viewer and critic of visual culture.

Chris Kraus

Joel Meyerowitz, *Crowd on Street, New York City*, 1976

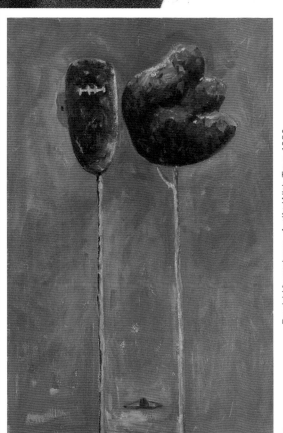

David Humphrey, *Artist With Tree*, 1980

My Summer
of
Solitude

New York in 1976 was much darker than it is now, especially downtown. Black clothes seemed blacker then. The municipal government was broke and nights in my neighborhood were lit by the regular torching of abandoned buildings and stripped cars. I moved to the city that aggressively cold winter, dazzled by the activities of people making new art in big cheap industrial spaces. I was twenty and attracted by what I imagined was solitude en masse; it was my existential/romantic notion of the urban artist/loner. I remember entering the determined tides of work-bound people each day to realize, months later, that I had never recognized a single person I had passed previously.

Independence Day that year was the Bicentennial. New York hosted a proud and very fancy Disney/Macys's celebration with fireworks at the bottom of the island. Purposeless curiosity and loneliness propelled me that day from my home in the East Village down Broadway into the enveloping dusk. A slow trickle of people thickened with each southward block to become a crawling density at the recently completed World Trade Center. I don't think the streetlights were working—I remember the space becoming less and less discernible, slightly disorienting, even threatening. Thousands of us eventually impacted to a complete halt in the dim canyons just below the towers. A collective sense of frustration nearly boiled over as the first booms of the fireworks rolled over us with the realization that we would miss the show. A slow surge forward squeezed away personal space we thought had already been surrendered. There was no way to get out. The anticipated ecstatic fusion with the national television audience and cheering crowds who limned the harbor never happened. We missed the biggest pyrotechnical entertainment spasm in history. Ten thousand pleasure boats had joined the massive fleet of tall ships watching from the water along with hundreds of thousands of people on shore. Marines, the Coast Guard, and the Army Corps of Engineers took orders from a command center in the Trade Center's south tower. We, the blocked ones, could only hear the countless shells and mortar fusillades launched from barges and islands. The next day's newspaper informed us that we also missed patriotic music, celebrity readings, and a helicopter pulling a giant flag across the sky. That same paper also contained news of an almost simultaneous raid by Israeli commandos to free hostages held at Entebbe airport in Uganda.

Thousands of us had been cut off. We were failed witnesses, clotted and stagnant, blinded by the buildings meant as a backdrop for the TV audience relaxing safely at home. It was an indignity for us to be smeared against the very cause of our frustration. We were an inconvenience to each other and to the crowd-control authorities. I naively hated those people. They were the others, the ones art was happy to offend or confuse. They were the undifferentiated ones we artists needed to frame our absurd singularity. My conception of this artworld we, however, was a fantasy, as I had yet to obtain even the tiniest milieu. I was as cut off as that Independence Day crowd. My goal was to build a studio in my head and treat the world as a hallucination. I was proud to imagine myself as socially unintegrated.

The crowd and I were an unhappily fused horde of grumbling consumers—hungry sheep unconsciously obeying nebulous orders. We wanted a big show, but our frustration had made us stale and viscous, not volatile like the blackout rioters of the next summer, the anti-war demonstrators of last summer, or the rock audiences I had joyously merged with as a teenager. We eventually dispersed into an ebb tide of aversion and disappointment. On the long walk home, however, the throng atomized into fellow New Yorkers: attractive, eccentric, and driven people, neighbors, proto-friends, colleagues, and lovers.

2002

David Humphrey, *Self Portrait*, 2000

Hi, My Name is Artwork

ARTWORKS CAN BE INCONVENIENT, often making conspicuous efforts to go against the grain. Other times they are more sociable, working hard to insinuate or ingratiate. Whether they adopt postures of detachment or engagement, an ineradicable quotient of ambiguity intensifies their vitality. They are, often happily, only human.

The artist's signature, along with the work's material characteristics, inflects the way it navigates and adapts to a future of unanticipated circumstances, much as we do. Alternating positions of resistance, assimilation, and participation help us thrive in different situations. This applies to the course of a day as well as the arc of a lifetime. We assimilate in order to study unfamiliar situations and to learn how things work. Sometimes we don't want to be noticed. Resistance builds strength and sharpens our sense of distinction, while participation rewards us with a connection to others. Who doesn't want to be successful? Freedom from necessity is a recurring dream, and art is good at exercising a vision of this freedom. Artworks help us to imagine what freedom looks like and consequently help us to resist the status quo.

New art, for a very long time, has caused things to mean what they hadn't meant previously. It can conjure fresh meanings from familiar forms and render the perceived world like a hallucination. Art can symbolize or symptomatize contradictions and tensions in the culture and can juggle various ratios of conformity and deviance. New art has also thrived on its ability to produce confusion, sometimes for progressive ends and sometimes in the service of mayhem and disorder. Works based on deviant attitudes adapt well to the latter while eventually, perhaps, helping to serve the ever-fluctuating use of style to sell consumer products. Art objects still address only one person at a time, and are lucky if they can produce confusion or any strong reaction whatsoever with their shocks and postures.

We artists should not underestimate the importance of the stories we tell ourselves about how art will make a difference. These motivational fictions describe the ways a work might interact with the world to justify our extravagant, and potentially narcissistic, labors: that our art has transformational potential. A work might be understood as being critical of society or sanctuary from it, for instance, or a Trojan horse sent to the enemy as a nasty gift to unsettle their deeply entrenched frames of mind. We need renewable encouragement to make fresh work year after year in the face of uncertain rewards. Political art glows with these motivational fictions, no matter how much we may agree or disagree with the content. Paranoia provides one of the most effective sources of motivation. That's why the "spectacle" has been so engaging for artists in the last few decades. The spectacle is described in theory as everywhere, with no boundary to its insidiously embracing circumference. It can replace deity as the ubiquitous and invisible force that catches us in its address and through which our public utterances are addressed. It neither confirms nor denies our ascriptions but compels us to continue undermining its grand perniciousness.

I don't think artists are reliable, however, at making their work socially useful. Some will be more responsible than others, but the work's capacity to survive depends on its ability to produce engaging interpretations whenever and wherever it finds itself. Do we want to be good citizens or servants of a system we may or may not approve of? The inconvenience that artworks present to pragmatic or utilitarian attitudes provokes both resentment and, hopefully, unanticipated insight.

The meaning of an artwork is promiscuously slippery, ambiguous, and, like artists, not very dependable. Contexts come and go while attitudes within the work often seem to evaporate or shift. The U.K. has recently been embracing new art as an instrument of public policy to promote "diversity, access, relevance, civic pride, community innovation and social inclusion." A recent exhibition at the Met of Renaissance art from Delft had many examples of astonishingly beautiful art that beamed with unambiguous civic pride. Does collectively embraced new art necessarily satisfy an appetite to feel good about ourselves? Works we love often seem to aid insights that come from us, not necessarily about ourselves but issuing from our best self. These special works seem to have significance above the others by virtue of their capacity to bring us a heightened sense of our singularity on the shared plane of culture. Some works almost seem to reorganize themselves as we change over the years; they grow with us and share our power to resist or assimilate.

I feel the artwork's relative uselessness is one source of its enduring value. Maybe that's my motivational fiction. If we can't be outside the spectacle, at least our metaphors will continue the always-unfinished job of imagining and desiring an outside, that perhaps things are more mutable than we thought.

1998

David Humphrey, *Thanks!*, 2004

David Humphrey, *Studio,* 1996

On Flirtation

The paradox that... might be integral to fantasies of success (the attainment of ideals)—is that fanta- sies are reliable because they cannot be achieved; that the person and his or her ideal may fear being exhausted by complete attainment.

Dana Schutz

DANA SCHUTZ CUT eight blob-shaped holes into two of the fourteen paintings in her series *Stand By Earth Man*. The variously sized holes disperse across the nude figures of *Male Model* and *Female Model* (all works 2007) and seem fathomless because of the black velvet behind. *Day Dreamer* is uncut but features the same disrupting black shapes, this time as stains from a leaking pen in the pocket of a reclining man's shirt. Schutz's blobs disturb the repose of her pictures while articulating a recurring theme of productive rupture. *How we would give birth* hilariously depicts a blank-eyed newborn making a bloody mess as he or she squeezes out of the mother's vagina. Mother, meanwhile, stares into an Alfred Bierstadt landscape on the wall behind. (Is she noticing the tiny waterfall spilling as if from between the legs of mountains in the distance?) Mother and child are making a big stain-painting on the sheets while a floral pink box of Kleenex waits absurdly on the dresser.

Shutz applies prodigious descriptive powers to the imagination of possibilities. She paints conjectures as if they were conclusions, as if she were painting from life. Gravity, light, space, and living people are vividly conjured with a sense that they could also, perhaps, collapse back into undifferentiated brushwork... abstraction. Shutz blends description and speculation to suggest a comic world encumbered by weight and mass, threats and rewards, pasts and futures. The phrase "How we would" that begins the title of these paintings suggests qualities of contingency at odds with the assertive presence of her depicted objects. Shutz characterizes her new work as "miscues to the future," which is perhaps what all artworks are, but she folds her imagination of that future into the narrative. *Dad* pictures the upside-down word "DAD" inscribed, as if with a finger, in the sand near the water's edge. *Dad*'s now-dry paint anticipates the washing away of both word and man.

How we cured the plague, at ten by twelve feet, is a big and ambitious painting. A naked male, with outstretched arms and many tumors, stands on a pedestal in a large room surrounded by cages of monkeys, flying birds, a shark, doctors, and nude people milling about or lying on cots. Fluids play an important role, collecting in plastic i.v. bags, flowing between species through inserted tubes, or forming puddles on the floor. *How we cured the plague* is a science-fiction history painting infused with anxieties about biological boundaries and group dynamics. Schutz employs painting as a strenuous solitary activity that registers the stresses and longings of a life among others.

2007

James Esber, R. Crumb, and Peter Saul

THE FLESHY FORMS in James Esber's paintings are wrinkled and seem obscene even when they are depicting an innocent bunny or piece of clothing. Both *The New Yorker* and the *New York Times* cite R. Crumb and Peter Saul as Esber's precursors, but all three are part of a tradition of the grotesque that threads its way from the faux grottos of Nero's palace to the fantastic ornamental wall painting in Italian Renaissance palazzi to British eighteenth-century caricature and Surrealism. Esber's images of a woman flashing her breasts, a hobo roasting a hot dog, and an entangled cluster of figures are rendered with a vigor and lewdness that conforms to Mikhail Bakhtin's definition of the grotesque as "ordinary life turned into amusing and ludicrous monstrosities." Like Crumb and Saul, Esber is a practiced stylist with an illustrator's eye for emphatic details and corpulent idiosyncrasy.

Unlike them, however, Esber makes images that are not so easy to recognize; his bodies are tangles of intersecting fragments and subdivisions that strain against coherence. They are catastrophes whose disorder and incompleteness challenge our ability to describe what is going on. Conventions, stereotypes, and habits of seeing are engaged and undermined by shifts, subdivisions, and exaggerations within Esber's depictions. His very American imagery is folksy, as if imagined pornographically by Norman Rockwell. *Hobo*, 2000 is, in fact, derived from Rockwell's *Hobo*, 1928. Cuteness, innocence, and lovability are mercilessly burlesqued. Esber's bodies are engaged in a civil war with themselves; each part is rendered separately, drawn as a differently colored autonomous region. His people are patch-jobs of heterogeneous parts, composites held together by tight nests of hatched lines and a

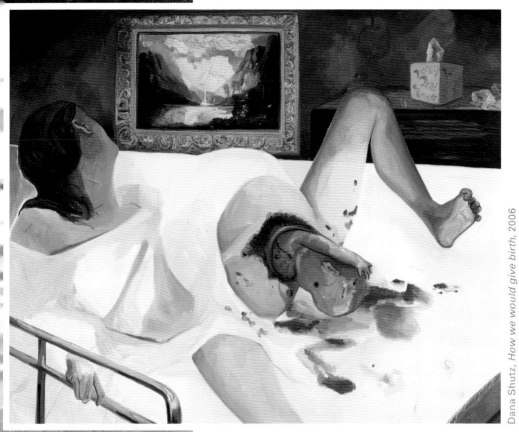

Dana Shutz, *How we would give birth*, 2006

R. Crumb, *Quissac, Nov. 13, '03*, 2003

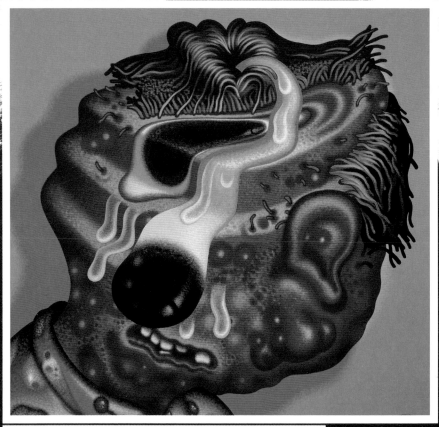

Peter Saul, Man Looking for a Bathroom, 1999

James Esbe, *Self Portrait of the Artist as a Foursome*, 2000

BLIND HANDSHA

constraining contour. The composite, almost cutout image floats like a decal on its bruised or stained background. Other works, like *Biggy Small*, 2000, dispense with the background altogether. These images are rendered in colored plasticine dabbed and smeared directly on the wall. The abundant interior of the figures, with their puckered and bulging volumes, becomes an island world surrounded by the milky blankness of the gallery wall. These denser works don't subdivide themselves like the paintings but more insistently dramatize the incongruity between their methodical hand-wrought rendering and woozily distorted image.

. The painting *Self Portrait of the Artist as a Foursome*, 2000, pictures a boy with his tongue out in absorbed concentration as he draws on the back of another, who is having sex with a third, while a fourth boy is ambiguously attached from behind. Viewers must mentally untangle the images, pry them apart and reassemble them, in order to construct their sense. Like all monsters, this one is erratic and unwhole in ways that resemble our fluctuating self-image. The inconsistencies of seeing, being seen, wanting, doing, and making are knotted into a great copulatory cluster.

R. CRUMB has been living in France and doing drawings on restaurant placemats. He is a deft observer of personality and character type; a noticer of how haircuts are always slightly ridiculous. Crumb can render a person's disposition and style of dress with hilarious economy. His characteristic cross-hatched line gives all his characters a lumpy shagginess that seems to express both affection and mockery. With his restaurant drawings, Crumb can perform the social trick of establishing contact while keeping people at a distance. One gets the feeling that the activity of drawing, for Crumb, is a form of compulsive behavior that

helps him inhabit a world that is never quite comfortable for him. This work feels habitual and automatic, as though doodling were not a matter of choice, which is not to diminish their charm and accomplished wit.

Crumb alternates between drawing the people or places around him and exercising his well-rehearsed comic-book skills. He's exerted an impressive and sustaining influence on gallery and comic-book artists for decades and now seems to be enjoying himself, and why not? He returns again and again to the sexual preoccupations, narcissistic or paranoid anxieties, social observation, and worship of favorite musicians that fans expect from him. These restaurant drawings are sometimes stained with food or torn casually from larger sheets, but their public address is confirmed by carefully placed captions and dates. Crumb's drawings fulfill another of Bakhtin's definitions of the grotesque: "the lowering of all that is high, spiritual, ideal, abstract; it is a transfer to the material level, to the sphere of earth and body." These drawings seem to savor such a fall, but Crumb arrests the placemat's final passing into garbage with his signature ink stains.

PETER SAUL's paintings respect very little but the ability of a picture to arrest attention. His flamboyant language of mockery and exaggeration howls for a response. The paintings are spatially vehement; pneumatic forms aggressively swell to the limits of the picture and push toward the viewer. The flat pictures seem to barely contain Saul's hyperbolic bodies, which insist so strongly on provoking laughs or outrage. His paintings of heads sustain the goofy ferocity that has characterized his work for almost forty years without the heavy machinery of narrative. The familiar genre of portraiture highlights the unpredictable and elastic character of his inventions.

The unruly abundance of Saul's individuals strains against the methodical way they are painted. Saul has developed a dabbing mark, a fuzzy dot, with which he builds form in small increments toward their glowing highlights. His manner of painting is caring and careful; a finely wrought radiance and deft articulation paradoxically supports the image's pushy vulgarity. The swollen heads behave like endomorphic goo as insides incontinently squeeze out in the form of sweat, drool, and pimples. Orifices migrate across faces with mutilating freedom while tidy marks make sure everything is properly located. Saul shepherds the obedient little daubs into their supporting roles within the exaggerated depictions. Saul works hard on these paintings, and his devotional labors perplex the aversion his images seem intent on provoking. *The Man Looking for a Bathroom*, 1999, is about to burst while urine oozes from the top of his head. The guy depicted in *I'm Wrong/So What*, 1999, sports a shit-eating grin on his cuboid tooth-sprouting face. He's the uncool Mr. Cool with a two-tone haircut, mouse-turd facial hair, and suave plaid jacket. A fried egg–like eye drips over his hard–cornered brow. He could stand for the belligerently independent artist who affects not to give a damn what critics have to say.

Hugh Kenner writes, "A grotesque is an energy which aborts, as if to express its dissatisfaction with available boundaries." Esber, Crumb, and Saul emphatically celebrate their maladjusted boy-selves as a blow to the status quo. They need a certain amount of familiar conventions in their work, available boundaries, to be pulverized in order to exercise their dereliction, irresponsibility, and emphatic acts of creation.

2000

Amy Sillman I

AMY SILLMAN'S PAINTINGS are populated by heterogeneous objects composed into persuasive unities by the charm and rigor of her strong painterly personality. The eccentric vividness of her images is a protest against the unconsidered and taken-for-granted. Her work performs with the radiant sadness of a wounded love song and expresses a consciousness shaped by passions and anxieties. The wind in *Blizzard*, 1997, blows leaves centrifugally from the compressed scramble of an oversize head, as if to encourage its emotional coming apart. The diminutive torso holds this composite-head like a golf tee, while the breast of a snout-nosed woman within the head-ball expresses a line of drips that stream down her spine, between her legs and under her feet to form a pool.

Sillman's paintings dramatize the complicated burden of imagination, its ability to picture anticipated threats or losses as well as the fulfillment of wishes and longings. She employs processes of stripping-down, erasing, and burying as well

as stacking, listing, and layering. The broad yellow band across the middle of *Miniature Illinois*, 1997, hums with a complicated blankness; its density of pentimenti suggests a succession of images proposed and rejected. Sillman renders vision under the influence of emotion, but entangled in historic painting languages. Her forms bear their load of associations with the self-accepting smile of an impaired person; she writes, "Like a fatso, my paintings are built for comfort not speed." Sillman fuses the mutant dynamism of cartooning with the formal architecture of abstract painting to achieve compositions that hold together with hilariously ad-hoc ingenuity; her figures are composed with the imminent possibility that they will unravel.

1997

Amy Sillman II

I DON'T KNOW what they mean, but *blassive* and *glisstic*, *bloculate* and perhaps *indevalent* are good words to describe Amy Sillman's paintings. Her *cranic* images are very *phoughty*. The words are from a list she painted down the center of a painting called *Shield*, 1997. They are hand-printed with proud singularity along with more words like *fadgy*, *neglitive*, *poetile*, and *appuded* in a stack from the top of the painting to the bottom, their prefixes estranged from the suffixes by the shield's green and yellow halves. The expressive strangeness and comic indefinability of the words are felicitous. Describing Sillman's paintings is a peculiar challenge because her images are unlikely hybrids with many idiosyncratic details. They feel tender and vulnerable while paradoxically resisting description. That *Shield*'s neologisms have a protective function is suggested by the carefully lettered insults, like *coward*, *hypocrite*, *cutesy*, and *daft*, covering the background.

Her new paintings promote rangy analogies with people, maps, gardens, and diagrams in swoony alternation. They are ravishing, wounded, and raving while retaining a high degree of poised formality. Narratives are kindled from the assembled elements; paint daubs accumulate with mosaic density to blossom into foliage, architecture, or crowds of former lovers. Sillman's paintings have a strong personality expressed by a loquacious jocularity and confessional intimacy. A radiant brightness saturates her painted atmospheres as horizons curl onto themselves and hapless protagonists are imprinted by anxieties and longings.

Calling ourselves Team SHaG, Elliott Green and I made collaborative paintings with Amy. We were able to enter each other's painted worlds and do things that ordinary spectators can only do imaginatively. We came to know how Sillman's paintings emphatically invite engaged participation in their generous and habitable spaces, that their pervasive subjectivity is buoyantly inviting. It is an accomplishment of style for a painting to suggest what comes more naturally to literature, a sense of living in someone else's mind. The mind of these paintings is singular and clusterfucked, splendid and demented. Sillman's work encourages us to marvel at the ways we can be a fascinating stranger, even to ourselves.

1998

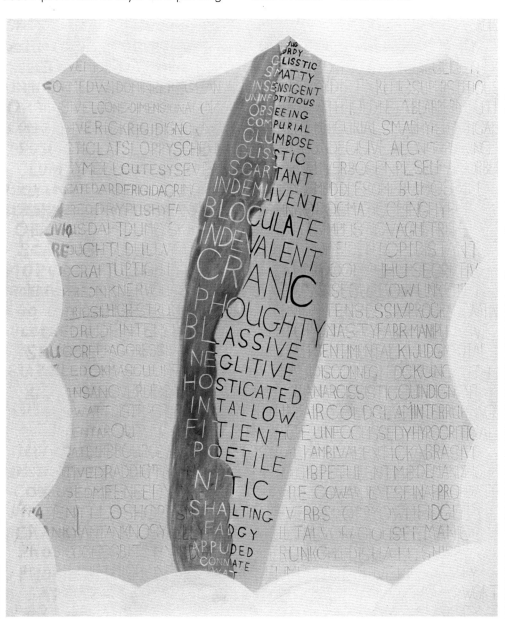

Amy Sillman, *Shield*, 1997

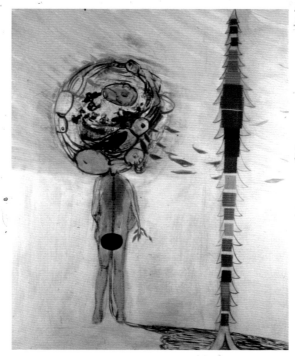

Amy Sillman, *Blizard*, 1997

Team SHaG, *Lonley Dog*, 2002

Team SHaG, *All But*, 2002

Life and Limb

THE WORLD IS LOUSY with threats and dangers! It's amazing that we aren't paralyzed with dread. We're good, though, at telling stories that both assuage and kindle our fears.

Narrative can be purveyed by almost any substance in an astonishing variety of genre. Narrative is deep, like brain function; we don't understand anything without connecting cause to effect, before to after. A story uses memory and imagination to organize these pasts and futures into sense. Narrative/figurative art spreads across history, from prehistoric cave paintings to the digital messages beamed by eccentric scientists into space to fish for intelligent life. Children everywhere are told stories that influence their pictures. Because figurative artworks can only represent a narrative fragment, the spectator must imagine what occurred before and after. The narrative artwork simultaneously tells a story about its own making and about an artist who made decisions and performed these actions for our consideration.

Engulfment anxieties, conflicted feelings of resistance, surrender, and sexual longing drive narrative. Some artists picture a sanctuary from these conditions while others dive straight into them; some adopt a comic stance while others are deadly serious. The spectator is thematically anticipated in many works as agent/actor but other works pretend we don't exist.

2005

Henry Darger, *Untitled (Calmaminia Strangling Children for Revenge of Defeat in Battle)*,

Kerry James Marshall, *Everything Will Be Alright I Just Know It Will,* 2004

Dana Hoey

DANA HOEY USES THE GENRE of fiction photography to illuminate the psychologically dense space between women. She stages moments charged with the consequences of what came before and pregnant with what will come. Hoey's preferred subjects are group activities like meals, walks, or conversations. She captures the evolved conventions and subtle choreographies people employ to improvise their social presence. Hoey emphasizes various signs and anomalies within those occasions to charge them with off-beat difficulties, unfinished negotiations, embarrassments, and awkward intimacies. **Her work is neither faux-documentary nor faux-movie-still but operates, instead, with what the novelist Don DeLillo describes as a "deep density of convention that allows us to accept highly stylized work as true to life."**

1995

Richard Onyango

KENYAN ARTIST Richard Onyango chronicles, with a series of paintings, his life-altering and sometimes dramatic eight-year relationship with Dr. Souzy Drosie, an expatriate English woman. An erotic charge animates the story as it travels through carefully and tenderly detailed locations. Some paintings grouped together as *Drosie and Me* and *The Salambo Night*, 1990–91, act out scenes described by him in his autobiographical essay, *The Rise and Fall of Richard*. Onyango first met his Drosie at a nightclub where he played drums. After a couple of inconclusive and awkward encounters at local beach hotels, he finally visits Drosie's hotel room. He writes, "She acted like a lion in fury when she's angry. And Lo! She held my shirt with her two hands and cut all the buttons from A–Z. She turned to my trousers and did the same waaa!!!! I now sensed danger because she pressed me down hard and her eyes were red like fire and she was stronger than me." The painting that depicts this scene tells us with a sign on the wall that this moment happened in the Banburi Beach Sea Lodge; another sign over the bed reads "MAINTAIN SILENCE PLEASE *Thanks*," while a painting of an ocean cruiser on the wall playfully interprets what is happening on the bed's watery sheets. Drosie died before these works were painted, so they are simultaneously images

of fulfillment and loss, memories saturated with feeling. Onyango's story is myth-like in the way it organizes details and priorities, crises and resolutions. It keeps alive a past nearly sacred to him, dramatizing the constitution of his current identity.

Like much popular and vernacular painting across Africa, Onyango's work carries a strong sense of local culture. He also paints portraits of pop stars, transportation vehicles, historic and religious images. These hybrid genres, with their liberal accumulation of specific consumer products and local décor, reflect the complex evolution of post-colonial African idioms. Onyango's Drosie becomes symbolic of the promise of exhibiting his work in the commercial world of international contemporary art. **He is the passionately adaptable actor, director, and writer on these stages.** Drosie, in the details of her class, size, and gender, is figured as something overpowering and completely other. *Drosie in the Hotel Intercontinental*, 1990, depicts the two lovers embracing on a swing with a smiling Onyango looking proudly back from behind a massively luminous Drosie dressed in bra and panties. He seems eager to show off his bountiful fortunes while a wave breaks in the swimming pool right behind their loins.

1993

Odd Nerdrum

THE NORWEGIAN artist Odd Nerdrum makes paintings that appear to sustain traditional European Old Master values. His retro-historical style taps ethno-cultural memory and pictures stories in an oracular, visionary mode. His paintings, while straining for universal symbolic effect (a picture of a man, for instance, becomes a hallowed image of mankind), project a strong, deeply Northern sense of place. His corpulent, Rembrandtesque figures are hunter-warriors surviving at a precarious limit of civilization, very close to a defoliated excremental earth. Nerdrum's heavy viscous paint links his nomadic protagonists to their habitat by embodying both dirt and flesh.

Many figures are pictured either blind or with eyes closed; sleeping, dead, or dormant. In *Blind Wanderer*, 1992, a recumbent, open-mouthed couple in chrysalis-like garb signals their allegorical role with two ritually held twigs. This earth-bound Adam and Eve display evidence of their fertility in

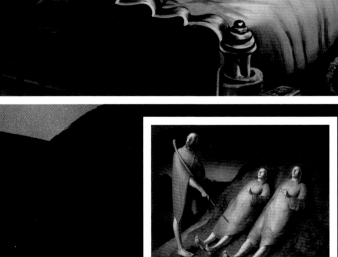

the direction of a mysterious off-frame light source. Their inwardly turned vision declares its autonomy from our gaze. In the manner of plants, this couple is indifferent to our attention as they absorb the radiant light. Nerdrum's storytelling vision refuses to admit any

trappings of a modernity he apparently despises. The painted figures, however, don't enjoy the liberating consolation one might expect from their return to Eden; they seem imprisoned within, even deformed by, the overbearing artifice of Nerdrum's art-historical references.

1993

juxtaposes a shiny metal personal accessory with a body. In this case a hand, seen from the point of view of its owner, places an ornamented mirror between her own knees to capture the image of a red cardinal with outspread wings backlit against a leafy tree and cloudless sky. The bird, seen from below, is made to fly from between her legs in a skewed variation of the Annunciation. But how did Murphy do it? My guess is taxidermy, but it doesn't matter as the fiction is compelling and the choreography of durations and directional looking is brilliant. We look ponderously down to catch the sight of something fleeting above.

Catherine Murphy

JESUS HANGS ON the cross while the cross hangs from a woman's neck into the shadowed space between her breasts. The details in Catherine Murphy's larger-than-life-size depiction *Pendant*, 2005, matter because the artist has articulated them with such labored precision and because the combined public display of cleavage and faith is perplexingly common. Murphy's tightly cropped image pictures the large pendant in the center while the woman's neck and face are off-frame. The golden arms of the Christian accessory press into her softly veined mammaries while the cross's central beam is suspended between them. Since Murphy's emergence in the '70s, her paintings have braided a psychologically dense formality with a high-resolution observation of objects. The V shape of the pendant's chain at the top of the painting is echoed by Jesus's upraised arms and again by the plunging neckline of the tight-fitting garment that frames the lower edge of the image.

This exhibition of four drawings and six paintings includes work from 2005 to 2008 and could be seen as an essay on cruciformity: Each work finds an unexpected way to reflect on the intersection of vertical and horizontal. The creases of an unfolded tablecloth, blankets hanging from a clothesline, magazine images pinned to a wall, or the four parts of a multi-panel snowscape find ways to embed this simple compositional device within works committed to **extended acts of sacramental looking**. Murphy's process requires that she make the work by directly observing her motif. At the same time high levels of artifice and sly reflexivity support these efforts. The paintings convince us with their non-photographic verisimilitude that she looked at what was before her for an extended period of time even when that would seem to be an impossibility. *Hand Mirror*, 2008, like *Pendant*,

Murphy's paintings frequently reflect on their condition as pictures, sometimes by means of analogies to windows, mirrors, or other pictures within the image, and always with light-handed wit. *Spill*, 2007, is a drawing of the shards of a broken glass on a round wooden tabletop flooded by a milky spill. The dry graphite paradoxically conjures wetness while the broken glass playfully refers to the off-frame unbroken window reflected in the spill and the glass under which this drawing is framed. Murphy's law, though, is to forbid gratuitous acts of show-off rendering; she leaves almost no evidence of markmaking and imbues her images with a contemplative detachment porous to associations. Is *Spill*, with the puddle's anthropomorphic shape, its quality of ritual trauma and encrypted admonition to not cry (over spilt milk), another version of the crucifixion?

2008

Chris Ofili 2

CHRIS OFILI'S NEW PAINTINGS ARE STRAIGHT, both in the sense of having no collaged elements and in their heterosexual preoccupations. Stylized couples, in a few paintings, intertwine on dance floors enveloped by tropical nightclub atmospheres and spiritual overtones. In *Confession (Lady Chancellor)*, 2007, a magenta nude woman with a halo and orange hair receives a sacrament-like cocktail from a man's hand coming into the picture from above. Her genitals peek out from below, her hands reach in opposite directions, and, refracted in the cocktail, a crisp abstraction connects sky and hands while promising an evening of intoxicating pleasure.

The hetero of heterosexual is hyperbolic in Ofili's sculptures. The male is dark and roughly

Catherine Murphy, *Pendant*, 2005

articulated while the female is light and mirror-polished. The male sprouts wings as the couple variously interpenetrates each other in a burlesque of the Christian Annunciation. Their metalized bodies awkwardly exaggerate the opposing qualities of gnarly priapic angel-man and hyper-available android-woman. The monstrosity of these sculptures is both a caricature of cheesy bronze fanciness and a wily exercise of Ofili's prerogatives as an international superstar.

Where Ofili's earlier paintings, set on ornamented dung-ball feet, had the hieratic authority of giant playing cards, the new, equally oversize paintings are less protected, more willing to adopt the vulnerable posture of a provisional, easily modified, image. They're

painted with an unfussy, almost spontaneous directness that supports his playfully comic tone. In at least five paintings the reanimated Lazarus of Christian myth reclines under a tree with a hard-on. The paintings seem more interested in promiscuous thematic play than in purveying edifying sacred imagery. Ofili applies vitality to these traditional images with injections of style and potential irreverence, as though, like parents, the images can be mistreated without losing their status. **Ofili complicates a rhetoric of ecstatic immanence with Caribbean public-art stylizations and Picabia-like obfuscations about his intentions.**

Ofili's afro-futurist love gods are not individuals but idiosyncratic symbol-types, articulated in the amped-up hybrid vernacular of poster art or contemporary Shona stone carving. He both reverses and scrambles the way modern artists interpreted traditional African forms by applying their Europeanized formal inventions to third-world pop idioms. The musicologist Michael E. Veal has noted that the music of Dub articulates post-colonial culture's disposition toward "diasporic tropes of exile and nostalgia." Ofili's work similarly possesses a sense of longing and displacement exercised as a triumphalist history of spiritualized sex.

2008

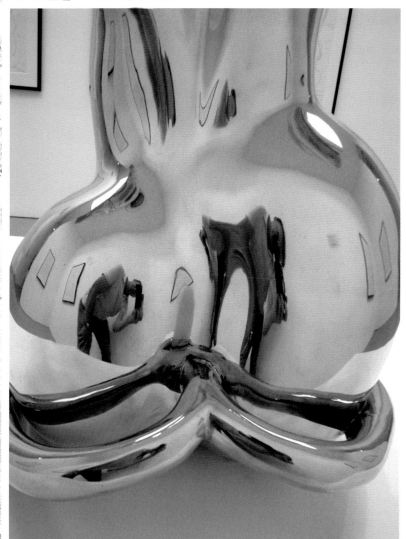

Chris Ofili, *Confession (Lady Chancellor)*, 2007

Nineteen Penises

THE NAMES SPREAD across many cultures: Wang, Dong, Schlong, Dick, Peter, Willie, Johnson, Rod. Some names have punch, like Schmuck, Prick, Pecker, and Cock. Others bust out with spicy associations: Wiener Schnitzel, Pink Torpedo, Bald Monkey, Weeping Jesus. We will never finish the task of renaming the penis, because we can never finish the task of understanding it.

From the possessor's point of view, the penis is a double agent, both one's own and separate, private and public, a tool and an independent actor. It can be a source of embarrassment or pride, vulnerability or power. A penis is the little part that preoccupies; its incessant re-proportioning attracts disproportionate attention. It is a shape-shifting troublemaker.

Artists and non-artists alike have been depicting the penis for most of recorded time, in spite of the sometimes ferocious prohibition against its representation. This selection of artworks from the Frank Moore archive charts a circuitous itinerary through the vast continent of penis. Some of the members included here have been fashioned by hand, others are documented photographically, and all were emphatically made to be looked at. Whether the artist's purpose was to arouse, protest, explain, or provoke, each work testifies to an irrepressible desire to look at what we've been told over and over should not be seen in public.

2004

Like a Man

I ATTENDED A PANEL in 1993 at Exit Art misleadingly called "Libido." The panelists spoke on a variety of loosely related subjects at various distances from the all-women show on exhibition there. Afterward, among friends, I was asked how I felt about the panel "as a man." It felt very strange to speak from the point of view of my maleness or to speak for other men. Perhaps the question was asked to determine my relation, as a theoretical beneficiary, to a clearly despised patriarchal order. If I am not always, in some way, speaking as a man, then, perhaps, I could propose a version: to feel it as a role. Should this relate to my preferences or appetite? What kind of sex do I like? What kind of art?

Different ways of speaking of "pleasure" and "desire" were in the air at that panel. The mobile identifications that occur in masquerade and performance were valued by a couple of the speakers as positive feminist procedures. The process of identifying with others and making representations, however, has also been seen as somewhat troubled by a historically colonizing or acquisitive male gaze. I think the critiques, while rendering negative judgments on some practices, have also reanimated the imaginative potential for the way people picture themselves and others. The dynamics of power that operate in that space become illuminated. The stakes are raised. Artworks thrive in this anxious and potentially dangerous interzone. But what really motivates people to make art? It is certainly not new to believe that libido is a big part of it, sublimated or de-sublimated. An excitable and renewable drive is helpful to overcome the generalized social indifference and lack of support for art. Sexual politics and the politics of having or representing sex liberally flows here. A notion that identity is constructed seems productive, and understandably popular, for artists. So let's construct! Maybe that's not so easy. Having the artist's name attached to his or her work already initiates the production of a fictional, theatrical, identity in the rhetorics of presentation. But psychological and social restrictions persist.

Perhaps the association of madness and art is a cliché, but it has productive features. Artists can be lunatics in the way their passions are figured in their work. The extraordinary elaborations, evasions, circuitous representations, and embarrassingly straightforward declarations give some work a crazy radiance. I completely enjoy encountering the supernatural exuberance or ferocity of these works. Artists and viewers can travel out of themselves. The artist can be both an other and him- or herself. Artists perform this othering for the delectation and interpretation of others. The works provide occasions for what Nietzsche calls "the joy of understanding what another means." Nietzsche notes, however, that artists play a "desperate game" because, in a sense, they do without the present. The artist encounters others only at a remove. Nietzsche describes the artist's suffering as exaggerated "because their ambition and envy are so great." We proceed from estrangement. Appropriately, the artworld is itself often felt as a community of estrangements.

1993

David Humphrey, *Bear Boy*, 2006

Michael Harwood, *Barberini Faune, Glyptothek*, 1988

Michael Mitchell, *Untitled*, 1999

David Humphrey, *Preoccupied*, 1998

David Humphrey, *Poure Bol*, 1998

45

Nikki S. Lee

WHEN DOES SOCIABILITY BECOME SOCIOPATHOLOGY? How does adaptation to social context affect the self's coherence, or its authenticity? There is a smooth gradient from empathetic identification to fraud. When Nikki S. Lee has herself photographed while working as a stripper, she splits her address. Of course, it doesn't matter to the strip-club clients that Lee is simultaneously practicing a genre of contemporary art; for them, her naked-ness is what matters. Lee has successfully adapted to this role, but in *Exotic Dancer's Project*, 2000, which follows her and her colleagues as they hang out backstage and perform their onstage routines, it is her acceptance by the club co-workers that receives more attention.

Many writers on Lee are compelled to show that no one has been deceived. Lee's crafty powers of empathy and adaptation, though, have earned her admission to and cooperation from groups alien to her experience; they seem to embrace her. How else could she capture those moments of casual intimacy and convincing esprit de corps? The unseen person behind her camera surely had an important role, but the camera snips off everything that came before or happened after. We are left with the absorbing task of following Lee through her chameleon adventures. **Her various subjects have a chance to play themselves in her fiction while she plays a copy without an original.** Lee's shifting masquerades have the effect of rendering contexts extra vivid; stereotypes are variously reinforced and illuminated, created and dissolved by her presence.

Do we possess or borrow our multiple selves? Our powers of assimilation and deception are surely honed by evolution and experience. Nietzsche observed that "part of the terrifying and questionable character of existence" is that "lies are necessary in order to live."

2002

Elmgreen & Dragset

THE COLLABORATIVE TEAM Elmgreen & Dragset often plays practical jokes that are extremely impractical. They placed a large sign at the entrance to the Tanya Bonakdar Gallery announcing "Opening Soon: PRADA." It efficiently deterred visitors from entering their show while making a sly allusion to the still unopened Prada store in Soho that was to replace the downtown Guggenheim Museum. The joke is sweetly at Elmgreen & Dragset's expense. Of course, if you are an informed gallery-goer, the sign is not a deterrent but rather an eloquent spatial and institutional dislocation, a clever intervention into lower Manhattan's never-ending drama of upwardly mobile real estate. It is also a bald-faced lie of the type advocated by Oscar Wilde, who admired the liar's "frank, fearless statements, his superb irresponsibility." Wilde thought lying was an art with "secrets of form and color" and "craft mysteries" that require "careful study, the most disinterested devotion."

But perhaps Elmgreen & Dragset's Prada sign is only guilty of misrepresentation. This lesser crime is, after all, victimless and can be justified by its capacity to prompt edifying insights about the constructed-ness of social spaces or the economic forces turning Chelsea into the new Soho. Elmgreen & Dragset's lively use of dissembling and artifice in the Prada sign also serves as an introduction to a dysfunctional clock installed as the sole object within the gallery. *Cornered Clock, Powerless Structure fig. 244*, 2001, is folded into the corner so that its hands can never proceed beyond 1:30. The stopped clock is powerless against time but effectively arrests our attention with its straight-faced surreality and superclean design. People can breeze past toward their next destination, disoriented by Elmgreen & Dragset's playful readjustments.

2001

Tom Friedman

FOR TOM Friedman, thresholds and limits provide organizing principles. He demonstrates, for instance, the maximum number of garbage bags that can be stuffed into one garbage bag, as well as the maximum length a particular piece of wire can be and still stand upright on its own when secured to the floor. The dopey simplicity of these occupations bespeaks a sustained discipline, and a guileless aplomb. Three apparently empty pedestals demonstrate the deceptiveness of appearances. On one is placed a barely noticeable 1/2-millimeter ball of the artist's feces. On another a piece of paper, perfectly matched in color and size to the top surface, rests almost invisibly. Above the empty third pedestal, the checklist informs us, is an eleven-inch sphere of "space which has been cursed."

Such demonstrations conventionally serve detached theoretical speculation but in Friedman's hands become living experiments that test our own spectatorial modes of attention. We can choose to believe that the artist carefully fashioned his fecal ball as well as cursed the larger ball of air. But our trust in what Friedman does in solitude must coexist with our knowledge of the untrustworthiness he demonstrated in *Hot Balls*, 1992, which is made of variously colored recreational balls "the artist stole from stores." Friedman gently rewards those who accept his fragile contract with comic beauty. His solitary crimes are memorialized by the multicolored hot property organized by diminishing sizes in a radiating pattern on the gallery floor.

1992

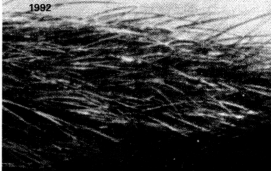

Nikki S. Lee, *The Exotic Dancers Project*, 2000

Elmgreen and Dragset, *Prada Marfa*, 2005

Tom Friedman, *Hot Balls*, 1992

Merry Alpern

IN THE SPRING OF 1997 Merry Alpern equipped her purse with a hidden security camera and videotaped shopping excursions to women's clothing stores. Photographs printed from these tapes provide clandestine peeks into this extremely public form of intimate behavior. Her purse-eye view scans vertiginously down escalators, into mirrors, and up the skirts of women in changing rooms. Some photographs observe women studying themselves with the practiced efficiency of lifelong shoppers; others capture the reflective and well-lit spaces that encourage them. Alpern catches the routine self-absorption with which these shoppers assess the worthiness and transformational potential of various products. The soft realities of imperfect flesh meet the cool solicitousness of mirrored retail architecture. The glass that covers Alpern's photos harmonizes with retail architecture's rhetorics by incorporating the viewer's reflection. Spectators become absorbed with the shoppers in a universe of looking, assessing, and wanting.

Alpern herself is presumably "undercover" among the shoppers and in the changing rooms, **so her voyeurism is slyly complicated by an inconspicuous exhibitionism.** Her reputation as a sneaky documentarian was already established by a series of photos from 1993 in which she covertly photographed activities in the bathroom of a sex club from a neighboring window. Alpern is now among her observed subjects but continues to raise similar questions about the propriety of her activities. These stolen glances quietly resonate with the sexual dimensions of shoplifting; her purse snatches unguarded images from the unsuspecting. **1998**

Shizuka Yokomizo

SHIZUKA YOKOMIZO WRITES LETTERS to her prospective portrait subjects with the anonymous salutation "Dear Stranger." Artworks address us the same way with their mute requests for time and attention. Yokomizo's form letter, though, asks people to stand alone by a window in their home for ten minutes on a designated evening so she can take their picture without making their acquaintance. Closed curtains signal their unwillingness to cooperate.

Yokomizo remains as much a stranger to her subjects as they are, and she is, to us. We trust that she never met these portrait subjects just as they trusted that Yokomizo is a bona-fide artist. We have less to lose than her strangers, though, as they had to temporarily surrender some of their privacy. It's not obvious why they consented to the arrangement but **their dispositions all seem watchful.** Nobody smiles but each posing stranger looks straight into the camera. They model with highly individuated self-possession as if to acknowledge a connection to unknown viewers while constructing a protective barrier. Yokomizo's photographs deftly capture this split between openness and defense in a choreography of anonymous regards. **2001**

Kevin Landers

KEVIN LANDERS MADE PHOTO-GRAPHS of attractive women he convinced to expose themselves in public. The works are trophies of his successes but suggest little of the coercive charms he must have employed to achieve them. However, there is nothing clandestine about the images. The women are willing participants even as they pretend not to notice that their breasts are showing while they mail a letter, play a video game, or do their laundry. Tits, usually, are the point, but spread legs and panties also make appearances. The work testifies to Landers's ability to persuade strangers to participate in this potentially embarrassing project as well as his own willingness to expose embarrassing preoccupations. The shameless artifice of pulling down a bra or bending over in a short skirt has the comically flagrant gratuitousness of a biker-chick magazine photo.

Blatant flesh, though, soon exhausts itself. Other subjects emerge. Elements in

the environ-
ment become
unlikely sub-
jects: shelved
Pedigree brand
dog food, an
oversize tire, a
space-age video
game, or a
    bank of blue

mailboxes with
top-mounted
red signs. These
peripheral
objects have
an offbeat,
pop-minimalist,
sculptural
beauty. Their
unsubliminal

seductions
lead us to a
consideration
of urban
sculptural
form; the
women
are red
herrings.
Could Landers
be protecting
his love for
product dis-
play structures
and brightly
colored
objects behind
a naughty
sexuality?
1999

Shizuka Yokomizo, *Stranger,* 2005

Merry Alpern, *Shopping #36,* 1999

Kevin Landers,
Untitled, 1999

Kevin Landers, *Untitled (McDougal is Dead)*, 1999

Eugene Von Bruenchenhein

OBSESSION, the leitmotif of much so-called outsider art, is often characterized by the ritual-like repetition of certain behaviors. The self-taught Eugene Von Bruenchenhein (1910–1983) made thousands of photographs of his wife Marie during their forty-year marriage. Along with his vast output of visionary paintings, sculpture, and writing, these photographs testify to emphatic compulsions. In the photos Von Bruenchenhein gift-wraps Marie's nakedness with his adoration. He fashioned sets of crowns—some out of tin cans and glittery Christmas ornaments, others of brightly colored ceramic—to highlight her status as the object of his total devotion. Marie appears wrapped in the conventions of period pin-up photography as well as the pearls, flowers, and ornamental drapes provided by her husband. Some pictures are hand colored, evidently with brushes made from Marie's hair. Her persona in these images is extraordinarily constant; neither concealed nor revealed, but rather held still in a moment of detached simplicity. It remains unclear whether Von Bruenchenhein wanted these images to be made public, but everything about their detail and organization suggests at least a fantasy of their public life. **Von Bruenchenhein and his wife clearly wanted her image to be delectable to others, while they possess each other alone, over and over.**

Whether understood as gifts or commodities, artworks are wrapped up in themselves and perhaps can only be truly opened at the risk of their destruction.

1994

Amy Adler

THE PRESS RELEASE STATES unambiguously that Amy Adler's exhibition "Once in Love With Amy" consists of "color photographs of the artist at 19 taken by an older woman," even though the exhibition's nine objects are not photos by the "older woman" but images assembled in a computer. It looks as though the "taking" here is by Adler and not her shutterbug admirer. The older woman, however, deserves a great deal of credit; she initiated what would become a sequence of repetitions, copies, and reversals that Adler now presents for our delectation.

Adler made large drawings of her own figure from the original photos and then digitally plugged them back into the originals. Her earnest renderings introduce a different genre to the older woman's amateur softcore pictures. Adler employs a devotional mode of drawing, a practice well rehearsed by star-struck teenagers, in which the labor of a saccharine depiction is used to establish contact with the adored and unreachable subject. In this case, however, that remote subject is the artist's younger body, whose image had been taken by another woman. Adler reconscripts that idealized image for updated purposes. The currency of the decade-old exchange between Adler and the older woman is converted for use in this more public economy of contemporary art. In one series of images, the young Adler lies spread-eagle across an antique wooden table. Her submission before the camera is represented for us in a newly configured consensuality in which she shares with us her reclaimed image.

The drawn figures are blended and colored just enough to be convincing within the fiction of the photos. Adler's deft employment of software cloning tools highlights the drawing's handmade distinction from the photo-smooth world of background interiors while carving out a space within them. The two modes of representation animate a desire to reconnect the figure with the alienated location on new terms. **Adler acts the role of herself inside a representation of the past.** In the largest piece, a naked Amy semi-reclines before a smoldering fireplace, her stiff impassivity telling little of what is going on or what she feels. The drawing, however, shows that much time and effort was spent returning this new Amy to that living room. Adler's teen years are not the only things lost here; the gallery assures us that the drawings scanned for these works have been destroyed.

1997

Amy Adler, *Once in Love With Amy*, 1997

Fizzy Nimbus

IT'S HARVEST TIME in many
Julie Heffernan paintings. Grand
cornucopias of edible bounty pile
up around solitary protagonists
while fires tint the autumnal mood.
These ultra-fecund landscapes and
smoldering Old World interiors
speak of things long ago or far away,
but with such vivid urgency as to
draw them within arm's reach. The
practice of painting, for some, has
passed into a very late season in
which historic recollection is the
only yield. But Heffernan's work
acknowledges no such limitation
as she moves with vigorous ease
between technically challenging
historic modes of depiction and
elaborate flights of imagination.

Heffernan's sitters seem the
possessors of colorful secrets that
could be revealed with attentive
close looking. She titles most of
her works *Self-Portrait*, augmented
variously with *as Netherworld, as
Demi-God, as Great Scout Leader, as
Soft Target*. But we can't automatically assume that Heffernan is talking
about herself. The women in her
pictures present an impassive
demeanor calmly adapted to their
extraordinary circumstances, while
the iconographically thick surroundings seem to speak effusively of
longings and anxieties. Heffernan
paints the interpenetration of
these composed surrogate-
selves and their worlds,
infusing them with a vitality
that seems to acknowledge
off-frame entanglements
and inner compulsions. The
paintings are almost diagrams of how
unruly emotions and powerful sensa-
tions are wrapped in a seamlessly
enveloping consciousness. They
are pictures of a volatile subjectivity arguing with an accomplished
self-possession. Heffernan's selves

Julie Heffernan, *Self Portrait as Radiant Host, 2000*

multiply, radiate, and metastasize into all types of objects.

In some paintings, such as *Self-Portrait as Stone Woman*, 2003, our heroine's body is nearly atomized. She comes apart within the disciplined terms of briskly applied paint, as though the brush were trying to keep up with rapidly unfolding phenomena. Heffernan builds her fictional picture-spaces in the traditional role of a hired master whose task is to celebrate someone who matters, a goddess or a wealthy patron. Corollas fizz and sparkle to crown these sovereign, unfazed subjects enveloped by bewildering circumstances.

Heffernan assumes more roles in the paintings than is indicated by the simple "as" in her titles. In addition to being the portrait subject and artist, she plays the commissioner of the portrait, the gardener, the architect, the wardrobe designer, and the interior decorator, as well as the painter of the other works hanging on interior walls. Imperial fanciness and fanatically elaborated passages of paint give her subtly shifting voice a manic authority. Who is this apparent traditionalist and slyly reserved exhibitionist to herself but a set of extravagant others? She accepts the venerable challenge of passionately inhabiting a subject while maintaining a detached perspective. Skill is employed to focus the painter's explosively hyperactive sensibility, while the conventionalized formats, of landscape, portrait or still life, anchor her ardent assertions of problematic and ecstatic subjecthood. The self in her work is staged as an operation, something performed in acts of dressing up or make-believe, not singular but rather an animate congestion, a nimbus of brushstrokes masquerading as butterflies or birds caged within the picture-object's four sides. The container is another Heffernan stand-in, this time bearing her signature, as when we say, "I have a great Heffernan in my collection!" The paintings invite us to travel through circuitously interconnected regions for the adventure of going to an unfamiliar place and meeting an appealing stranger.

Her undressing is also a costume, suggesting a sexuality up for grabs. Nakedness, though, is partial; genitals are never depicted. Instead they are extravagantly displaced and refigured everywhere. In *Self-Portrait as Radiant Host*, 2000, a striped lizard noses a sliced peach in the zone where her vagina would be if it were not hidden behind an oversize pile-up of fruit. Numerous streams flow suggestively in and out of geologic orifices in the background landscape. The outdoors is anatomical, irrigated by abundant associations with bodily fluids and nether parts. The grand binarism of above and below the waist is invoked as Heffernan metaphorically lifts her skirts to reveal magic and a playful dread of uncontainable forces, while above the sky, ceiling or trees act the role of mind. Heffernan's spaces, whether indoors or out, are corporeal. She carves deep picture-cavities that bloom and fizz with proliferating resemblances and analogies. The painting's imagery has the layered quality of a rebus or encrypted joke in which the punch line might be "vulva." The secret subject is everywhere and nowhere, constituted of many parts, variously inflamed, soggy, or gushing. The female sex organ becomes a burning city, a pile of iridescent wild game, flowers, fruit, streams, volcanoes, and mountain gorges.

Heffernan's work conjures the past as a fictional place fabricated by means of a hands-on study of the historic archive and a practiced imagination relaxed about blurring the difference. The past becomes an effect of the present. Iconographic references to older works are happily unreliable as they paraphrase, mime, or burlesque familiar types. Her majestic interiors are filled with ersatz masterworks. These depicted paintings refer to types that we can't specifically identify but that possess a credible sense of pedigree. Her work flaunts a guilty delight in luxurious stuff and dazzling painting effects while mourning the loss of our ability to possess either that wealth or an innocently un-self-conscious exercise of those effects. The old-fashioned look of a Heffernan painting is both homage to the masters and an outrageous bid to conscript their schemas and effects—originally developed to serve religion or secular power––into her own psycho-poetic service. She employs the nuanced theatrics of European painting to make an allegory of contemporary consciousness.

Heffernan's treatment of female protagonists under conditions of mutation and transformation cause the mid-twentieth-century paintings of Leonor Fini, Remedios Varo, Leonora Carrington, and Dorothea Tanning to look like precursors. Heffernan's paintings can echo the lonely lyricism often found in their work, but hers are augmented by a robust engagement with the Old Masters and contemporary gender studies. Her spontaneous inventiveness and hyper-elaborated iconography cast her as the overachieving great-granddaughter to that first generation of female Surrealists.

In *Self-Portrait as Agnostic III*, 2003, the amount of time it must have taken to articulate the dense surface contrasts with the fleetingness of flying birds, licking flames, and swarming butterflies paradoxically frozen in the now-dry paint. The straight lines of the room's architecture become woozy when reflected in the antique mirror, just as the miniature city rising above a floor-length skirt in the center of the picture is distorted by a fire enveloping it. By means of an array of rhyming forms, *Self-Portrait as Agnostic III* reflects upon painting's character as a transformational aperture to other worlds: the mirror, the reflected doorway, the fireplace, curtains, and other paintings in the room bracket the whole image. One of those paintings, hung close to the room's ceiling, reflexively depicts a woman undergoing brain surgery, suggesting that the work's theme is mind and the uncertainty of knowledge. Heffernan conjures nature and history as slightly exotic, grand and vividly unreal. In her world, they are ambivalent forces that both threaten the subject's autonomy and give power. The conventions of pastoral, romance, historic fantasy, and magical realism are well suited to Heffernan's vision because they pass off demented artifice as something natural. Those idioms are discursive positions from which Heffernan can posit a hallucinatory past and assert the power of fiction to overwhelm perception; memory and imagination are like an unruly forest encroaching on a corporeal field. Perhaps Heffernan's work spells out an alternative theory of cancer, in which too much history causes uncontrolled, self-consuming growth. But in her case the terminus is not death but an ecstasy of frozen potential.

2006

Hannah Wilke

HANNAH WILKE'S FINAL SERIES OF WORKS, *Intra-Venus*, speaks from a time immediately prior to her death in 1993. With the help of her husband, Donald Goddard, Wilke created life-size photographs of herself during treatment for lymphoma. The works are documentary evidence of all the insults and deformations to her body wrought by illness and its treatment, as well as Wilke's complicated relationship to her own physical decay. *Brushstrokes* is wads of the artist's hair, lost during treatment, pressed under glass into picture frames. *March 18, 1992* presents four bandages from a "bone marrow harvest." The precise dating of the works chronicles and memorializes a grotesque medicalized dying augmented by Wilke's irrepressible vitality throughout the process. Her art-making became an intense form of living, an extension of the terms and preoccupations of her life's work. These images have a retroactive effect on her earlier body-performance photographs, functioning as an epilogue to what is now starting to acquire an almost narrative structure. The consistent depiction of her nakedness over the course of a career navigates through the dynamics of personal relationships, exhibitionism, narcissism, feminism, and sexual politics. The act of undressing becomes a kind of dressing-up even under extreme duress. Wilke invariably treated the public gaze as a medium in which she could playfully vacillate between deadly serious games of provocation and confession. Her camera and its surrogate—our attention—acquire a magical potential in Wilke's hands, bestowing on her the power to deform or pleasurably transform.

Wilke's last images express the voiceless unrepresentability of physical pain. She shows us the raw and bloody insides of her open mouth and plugged nose in a pair of photographs called *June 10, 1992 / May 5, 1992*; the dates show an unrelenting decline and recall what J. K. Huysmans referred to as the "useless, unjust, incomprehensible, inept, abomination that is physical pain." Pain doesn't just resist language, it actively seeks to destroy it. The mute indignity of suffering usually causes people to shrink from the public gaze and encourages the culture to quarantine the dying. Wilke's earlier documentation of the death of her mother sought to heighten the vividly living part of dying while her last work emphatically substantiates the universal certainties of pain and death.

1994

Don Ed Hardy

THE TATTOO WORK of Don Ed Hardy is characterized by its vivid articulation of detail and careful attention to the nuances of the "collector's" body. Skin is a semi-permeable envelope between our inside and the outside, an organ that breathes, filters, and registers the accumulated scars and imprints of a life. In Hardy's tattoo *Freeway Panther*, the snarling predator is pictured tearing its claws into the very flesh on which it was drawn, functioning as an allegory of the act of tattooing as well as an aggressive extension of the collector's ego. The traditional popularity of tattoos among prisoners, members of gangs, and the armed forces is understandable given the conspicuous nature of their constricted freedom; the tattoo can be a gesture of permanent nonconformity as well as a reinforcement of identity. It exercises a poignantly defiant and sometimes absurd claim over the body.

A tattoo can sketch a map of what Paul Eluard called "the solemn geographies of human limits." It covers, modifies and enhances nudity. With tattoos, private fantasies and cultural stereotypes are baptized in pain and displayed in defiance of biblical, social, and sometimes judicial taboo. Hardy's work in Trina Von Rosenvinge's photograph *Man o' War Rising* is a tour-de-force of whole-body tattooing; oceanic and plasmic turbulence envelop the arms and back of the tattooed. Articulated in the voluptuous space of flesh, this stylized image turns the figure inside-out in dissolving pulsions of flame, viscera, and surf. It is a reminder of Kafka's description in *The Penal Colony* of the prisoner's ordeal. "During the first six hours the condemned man lives almost as before, he only suffers pain." After the sixth hour "insight dawns upon the most stupid." The end, memorialized so frequently by tattooed skulls, is death.

1992

Alix Pearlstein

OUR SKIN FAILS TO PROTECT US. Modesty and comfort require that we dress up most of the time. When Alix Pearlstein dresses up in her video *Egg Yang*, 1995, we wonder how

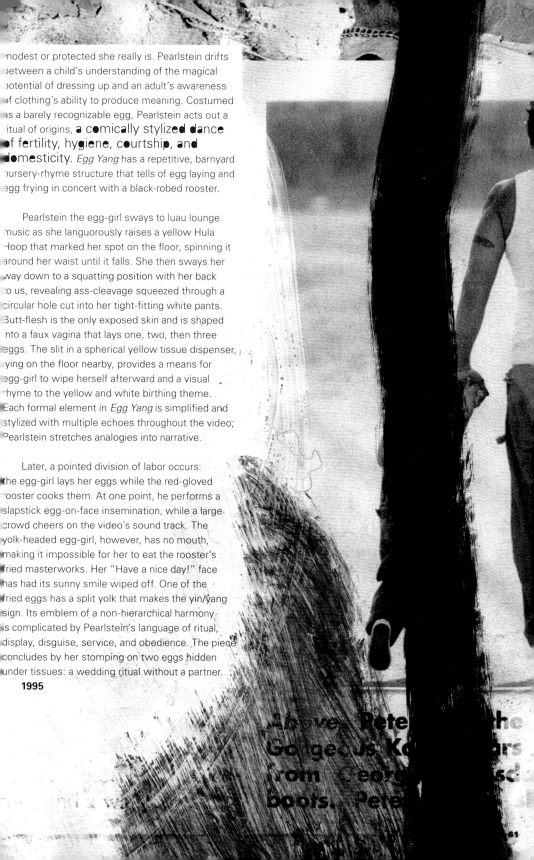

modest or protected she really is. Pearlstein drifts between a child's understanding of the magical potential of dressing up and an adult's awareness of clothing's ability to produce meaning. Costumed as a barely recognizable egg, Pearlstein acts out a ritual of origins, **a comically stylized dance of fertility, hygiene, courtship, and domesticity.** *Egg Yang* has a repetitive, barnyard nursery-rhyme structure that tells of egg laying and egg frying in concert with a black-robed rooster.

Pearlstein the egg-girl sways to luau lounge music as she languorously raises a yellow Hula Hoop that marked her spot on the floor, spinning it around her waist until it falls. She then sways her way down to a squatting position with her back to us, revealing ass-cleavage squeezed through a circular hole cut into her tight-fitting white pants. Butt-flesh is the only exposed skin and is shaped into a faux vagina that lays one, two, then three eggs. The slit in a spherical yellow tissue dispenser, lying on the floor nearby, provides a means for egg-girl to wipe herself afterward and a visual rhyme to the yellow and white birthing theme. Each formal element in *Egg Yang* is simplified and stylized with multiple echoes throughout the video; Pearlstein stretches analogies into narrative.

Later, a pointed division of labor occurs: the egg-girl lays her eggs while the red-gloved rooster cooks them. At one point, he performs a slapstick egg-on-face insemination, while a large crowd cheers on the video's sound track. The yolk-headed egg-girl, however, has no mouth, making it impossible for her to eat the rooster's fried masterworks. Her "Have a nice day!" face has had its sunny smile wiped off. One of the fried eggs has a split yolk that makes the yin/yang sign. Its emblem of a non-hierarchical harmony is complicated by Pearlstein's language of ritual, display, disguise, service, and obedience. The piece concludes by her stomping on two eggs hidden under tissues: a wedding ritual without a partner.

1995

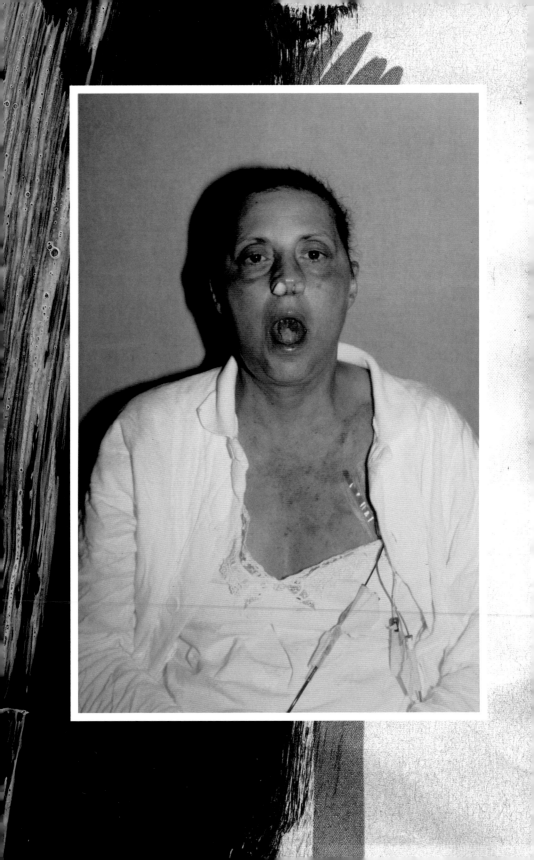

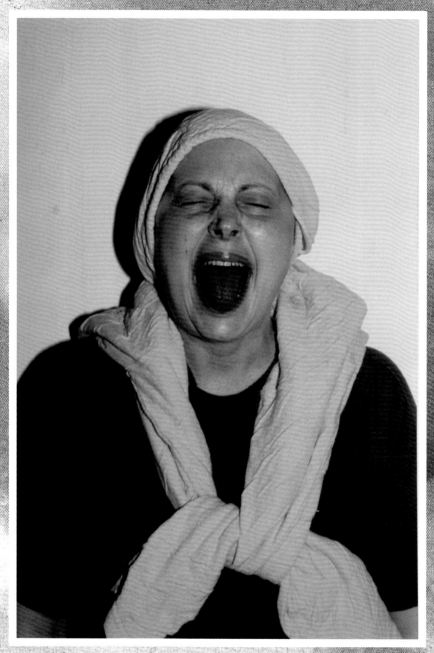

Hannah Wilke, *Intra-Venus #5, June 10, 1992 and May 5, 1992,* 1992-93

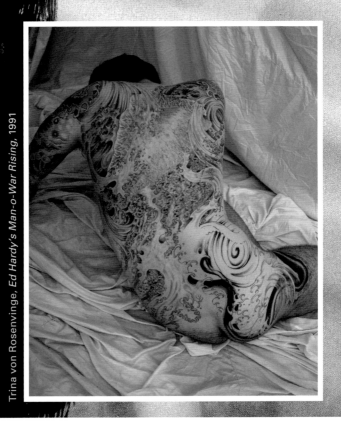

Trina von Rosenvinge, *Ed Hardy's Man-o-War Rising,* 1991

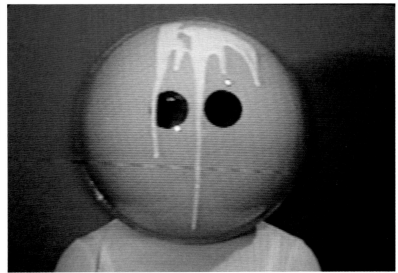

Alix Pearlstein, *Egg Yang,* 1995

Mary Heilmann and Elizabeth Cannon

WHEN PEOPLE DRESS UP, they entrust their image to the skills of a clothing designer. A good designer helps people to be more themselves, or who they might prefer to be. Mary Heilmann and Elizabeth Cannon in their collaborative painting-and-clothing installation *Crimson and Clover*, 1995, convert the notion of clothing as a protective masquerade into something more abstract and metaphysical. *Crimson and Clover* is about a disappearance of the artist into the work. Their installation consists of clothed tailor's dummies placed in proximity to loosely gestured abstract paintings with related geometric motifs and festive color schemes. The dresses and paintings relate to one another as variations of specific, patterned themes. While ostensibly addressing the creative exchange between two artists in different disciplines, this installation also narrates **a passage from the body through clothing to the disembodied image**: a romantic passage from the cosmetic to the cosmic.

1995

Tanya Marcuse

SOME OUTFITS—a wedding dress, for instance—have more signifying power than others. Tanya Marcuse's photographs in her *Bridal Suite*, 1995, memorialize the complicated expectations such objects inspire. These exquisite, intimately scaled, black-and-white platinum/palladium prints follow a dress from its plastic-sheathed promise on a tailor's dummy to its diaphanous translucence on a bride's barely seen body. Close-ups of bridal panties seem to catch an erotically saturated moment between dressing and undressing, as if **the wedding were a minor offstage event between the preparation room and the nuptial bed**. The bride's passage through these clothes is a magical one that leaves her nakedness transformed. The tight cropping of the photographs casts the clothes as fetish objects as a soft light washes the image with a haunting carnality.

1995

Mary Heilmann and Elizabeth Cannon,
Crimson and Clover, 1995

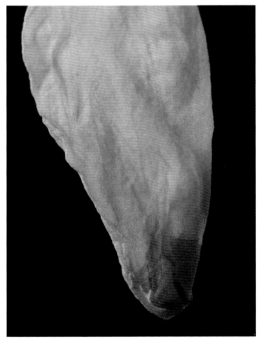

Tanya Marcuse, *Bridal Suite N°6,* 1995

Hair Piece

Civilized men today… are clearly embarrassed by anything that reminds them too much of their animal origin.

Sigmund Freud (from preface to J.G. Bourke's *Scatalogical Rites of All Nations*, 1913)

WHAT ABOUT HAIR? It seems to be a kind of evolutionary leftover one is compelled to address. Its continuous growth, its incontinence, requires regular attention in the form of cleaning, cutting, binding, or willful neglect. People articulate themselves on the social stage with a hair vernacular. Its uselessness and plasticity help it sustain complicated and highly evolved meanings asserting sexual identity, age, status, ethnicity, and role. These meanings are usually expressed by the way hair is cut or bound up: the ways in which its growth is repressed. Hair dramatically enacts, on the body's stage, relations of the public to the private and the irrepressible to the repressed.

We can find fruitful analogies between the production of art and the body's production of solid material, illuminating some of the links between people's drives to make, exhibit, and acquire art. Hair and feces, the two most obvious examples, sit on opposite sides of our bodies' public and private selves, and both sit at the limit of our ambivalent claims of authority over it. While defecating is periodic and inspired, hair growth is continuous and absolutely involuntary. Feces and hair acquire symbolic associations with power through our efforts to regulate them. Young children partially work out the limits of their emerging power over themselves and their parents during toilet training. Later, hair becomes an important signifier of one's conformity to or rejection of social norms. Art is a kind of speech that is used by individuals and institutions to articulate the nature of their power. Think of art as hair on the body politic.

Rona Pondick is known for her sculptures made of turd-like forms treated in a variety of ways. By drawing out in the public what is essentially private or internal, she caricatures traditional accounts of the expressive act and echoes the process by which hair becomes a social discourse. Pondick's work has proposed a kind of myth of origins for sculpture as articulated feces. The compressing and squeezing of the intestinal system is atavistically rendered onto her materials. Metaphors for hairdressing sculpture and cloaca coexist in *French Knot*, 1989, in which she celebrates hair and feces as the twin gods of the plastic impulse. This "hair piece" is emblematic of the psychological underpinnings of a body-oriented art practice that we find in the work of a variety of other artists. I explore, in this essay, the current resurgence of the use of hair as an important instrument in this practice.

All individuals live their lives within hair codes, in a fantastically complicated history of hair from early man onward. Brooks Adams has called the history of hairdressing a "ritual celebration of the durability and growth of a body substance [that reflects] the cosmetic and symbolic supremacy of the head." The relation of hair to sexuality, cemented by the appearance of new hair at puberty, compels cultures and individuals to address its strange power. Religions have evolved codes designed to regulate the unruly power of hair. Forbidding women to show their hair, requiring or forbidding men to cut theirs, seems to bear witness to the braiding of sexuality and power. The association of hair and power, and its relation to the cut, we see in the mythological stories of Samson and Delilah or Medusa, and historically during a period in Europe when women suspected of witchcraft were routinely shaved of all hair in order to weaken them.

The evolution of the hairdresser's art has always been associated with the uses of fashion by the privileged. Portraiture throughout the history of art—depicting bobs, wimples, tresses, zazzere, beehives, bouffants, pompadours, hedgehogs, flips—bears in its visualizations of hair the imprint of these elite. The dramatic feats of engineering periodically found in hairdressing stand as a perverse expression of a superiority over lower classes, by crippling the owner's ability to do little else but socialize. Some eighteenth-century European hairpieces rose many feet above the head, requiring elaborate support structures and occasional alterations to doorways and carriages. Men from the Mashukuluma group in East Africa are known to have tapering ornamented hairpieces a yard long. By severely circumscribing its field of discourse, and by commanding towering prices, much contemporary art similarly reduces itself to a badge of social prowess. Some current work concerned with the body, however, has tried to give this badge the embarrassment of unwanted hair. The seeming omnipotent capacity of the market to coopt an art practice has helped renew interest in the body as a subject that figures in that process. The increased potency of medical science and the legislative questions it raises turn the body into a battleground in which rival interests confuse the already tenuous claims people have over themselves. Recent drug-testing procedures, for example, use hair to discover chemical traces of substances that have passed through the bloodstream. Hair's rate of growth has its own cycle that is influenced by psychological states. The cylindrical filaments become an indexical diary of one's life with clear forensic uses.

Artists like Jeanne Dunning, using photographs of hair, or Liz Larner, with an object made of actual hair, have explored these relations of power to the body. By withholding an authorial voice and the facial identity of her subject, Dunning's photographs of hair become an occasion to examine the subtle exertions of power between artist, subject, and viewer within the conceptions of portraiture and advertising. Larner's Lash Mat, 1989, consists of a collection of short hairs attached in a row to a long, narrow support. The clinical detachment of the arrangement leaves a sinister void in our knowledge of the hairs' origins. Anonymous subjects each relinquished a part of their bodies for the piece—that part that both ornaments and protects the eye—who then look back at us as powerless ghosts.

It is easy to see how anxieties about our identity play themselves out in hair. Hair is often the focus for narcissistic fixation. People work out the terms of symbolic mastery through the freedom or obedience they effect in their hair. Just as wigs are used to disguise gender or identity, haircuts and hairdos are our medium for the creation of a willed identity. Sue Williams, in her painting See Price List, 1990, uses extreme and dated hairdos to twist a social context around the lascivious action on her characters' mouths. Sexual stereotypes are savagely mocked with lurid innuendo. The amateur directness of her style creates a fiction of the artist as naïf that skews the work's oddball sophistication. Mike Kelley's drawing Double Lapping Tongue Brunette, 1989, charts the relations between mouth and hair by substituting two oversize tongues for a woman's flip hairdo. After freeing the tongue from its tasting, articulating the erogenous cavity, he displaces onto the coiffure its drooling power of speech. In another piece, Male and Female Brain Halves,

1988, hair grows directly from the brain. Making one hemisphere male and the other female, he uses hair to lampoon the idea of simple gender dualities.

Kelley's disruptive, illogical, and erotically charged images owe much to the Surrealists. Hair iconography, especially in its relation to gender, recurs frequently in Surrealist art. Meret Oppenheim's fur-lined teacup and Man Ray's substitution of hair for cello strings on Emak Bakia, 1926, spring to mind. Framed by a full head of long hair, Magritte's The Rape, 1934, reconfigures a woman's torso onto her face with a bald pudendum articulating a terse mouth. In 1965, Marcel Duchamp's L.H.O.O.Q Rasé [Shaved], a reproduction of the Mona Lisa without his seminal graffitied moustache, audaciously claims the unaltered original to be a shaved version of his own masqueraded L.H.O.O.Q. Both Duchamp and Magritte use the image of a woman to give a strange, aggressive charge to the absence of hair. Frida Kahlo's Self Portrait with Cropped Hair, 1940, enacts a drama of power and loss through the use of hair. Under the cruel musical line, "Look if I loved you, it was for your hair. Now that you are bald, I don't love you anymore," Kahlo sits in drag, her cut hair appearing animated as it is spread on the chair and floor around her, with a pair of scissors opened near her crotch. The theme of castration is sent into a turbulence of cross-gendered images. She denies the lover's power over her by removing the loved part. Both Duchamp's L.H.O.O.Q Rasé and Kahlo's self-portrait, play with the power of their gendered object by removing hair.

Curtis Mitchell, a contemporary artist, has with classic Surrealist disjunction woven hair into a braided rug in Untitled, 1989. As in Kahlo's self-portrait, the hair appears strewn about recklessly. Mitchell transforms the vernacular handicraft rug into a sportsman's trophy rug-hide akin to the decorative ornaments fashioned from severed body parts in the cult movie The Texas Chainsaw Massacre. Mitchell performs "surgery" in his art, cutting hair and grafting it onto new dermas. Curiously, the jobs of surgeon and barber were also joined in the Middle Ages and persisted into the early nineteenth century. Both jobs required the same cutting tools for their exercise of hygiene and repair. Patty Martori joins the two again in her sculpture Untitled, 1989. Updating Lautréamont's oft-quoted fragment, "Chance encounter of a sewing-machine and an umbrella on a dissecting table," she ornaments an examining table with a set of bangs running around its perimeter. The missing body is invoked by the hair while the imaginary dissection

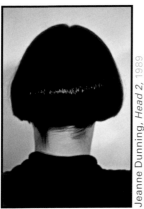

Jeanne Dunning, *Head 2,* 1989

David Humphrey, *Hair Piece,* 1995

would be performed with Surrealist tools. In Martori's piece, the activity of cutting is the invisible link between the two terms (hair and lab table), just as it was for surgeon-barber.

The taking of scalps, the use of hair in ritual, magic, or voodoo, the fetish, and the relic testify to the power of hair no longer attached to the body. The old tradition of lovers exchanging locks of hair can represent both a form of power over the other and a talismanic surrender to their power. Inverting the revulsion produced by material removed from the body, like feces or nail clippings, the lover's lock cues an imaginative reconstitution of the beloved's absent body. Like dreams, the meaning of the hair fetish is a condensation of memories, beliefs, and desires. By having part of a person become a sacramental stand-in for the whole, the process of representation aquires magical potential. Where a religious icon is considered by the believer to constrain some part of the divinity, fetishized hair likewise contains a powerful aspect of the beloved, but as a consequence of being extruded from his or her head.

Symbolist artists as diverse as Toorop, the MacDonald sisters, Beardlsey, and Klimt found in long, streaming, unbound hair a sensuous blurring of the distinctions between the figure and its environment. Their work reflected a nostalgia for a lost era of enchanted spirituality. Baudelaire, in his prose poem *A Hemisphere in a Woman's Hair*, recounts an intoxicated reverie of oceanic associations triggered by the smell of the beloved's hair: "Let me bite, a while, your ponderous black tresses; when I take your elastic, rebellious hair between my teeth, it's as though I were eating memories." Hair reminds us not only of the power our animal origins has over us but also of the strange and often perverse ways we conscript that power into the service of culture.

1990

Frida Kahlo, *Self-Portrait with Cropped Hair*, 1940

Curtis Mitchell, *Untitled (Hair)*, 1989

Mike Kelly, *Double Lapping Tongue Brunette*, 1989

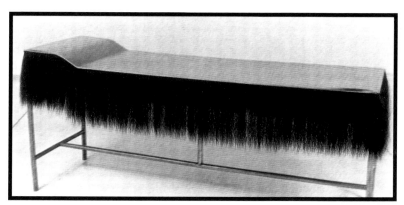

Patty Martori, *Untitled*, 1988

Naomi Fisher

work with living organisms in ways sometimes adapted by artists. Even when the artist's versions of those disciplines are skewed, their interventions with the living highlight themes of wildness and control, power and helplessness.

Naomi Fisher's exotic gardens are fecund and aggressive. The solitary protagonists in her photographs, bums in the air, are swallowed into tropical flora while thick jungle blossoms snuggle tightly between their blemished cheeks. How could these lively and unruly helonica or birds of paradise, seemingly rooted, have gotten between the subject and her panties without becoming damaged? In *Untitled (helonica)*, 2000, the figure's face is in the dirt while her ass smiles at the camera; bottom becomes top, verso/recto. Even though they are in classic postures of submission and humiliation, Fisher's blindfolded hams could also be greeting us with a "kiss my ass" rebuke. Her photographs encourage us to shift our identification between artist and subject, victim and witness, observer and observed.

Fisher's images play hide-and-seek with expectations. Leaves are where a face should be, underwear is neither on nor off, but the flowers printed on them seem right at home. Displacements and substitutions reappear like ritualized compulsions, always leading back to the primal seat of vulnerability and control. Fisher exercises an ambivalent exhibitionism. Georges Bataille noted that obscenity is "our name for the uneasiness which upsets the physical state associated with self-possession." Fisher's fashion-conscious character's self-possession is threatened from both within and without; the obscenity is nature. This is more explicit in her intimately surreal drawings, in which arms become branches, eyes sprout flowers, and plants exercise cruelty.

Topiary Man's intentions are unclear as he clutches a limply helpless girl in his leafy embrace. Fisher's spontaneous drawings are saturated with gothic longings and engulfment anxieties. An equivocal boundary between outside and inside is dramatized by the way she treats hair. In *Listening*, 2000, a half-naked woman in high heels puts an ear to the ground. Her long mane sweeps across the grass, which seems to creep back up her legs in the form of unshaved hair; grass and leg-hair are articulated with the same awkwardly groomed brushstroke. The listener's haunches, raised to the sky, seem to wait patiently for a spanking that never comes.

2000

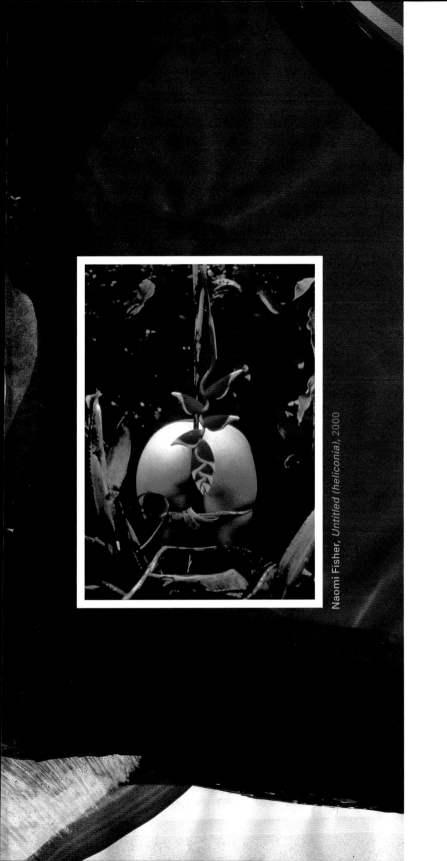

Naomi Fisher, *Untitled (heliconia)*, 2000

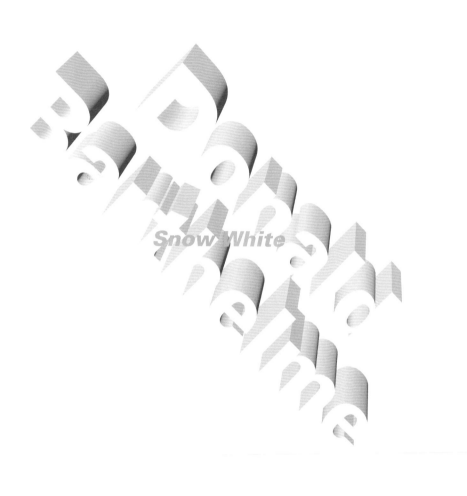

Snow White

Beaver College is where she got her education. She studied Modern Woman, Her Privileges and Responsibilities: the nature and nurture of women and what they stand for, in evolution and in history, including householding, upbringing, peacekeeping, healing and devotion, and how these contribute to the rehumanizing of today's world. Then she studied Classical Guitar I, utilizing the methods and techniques of Sor, Tarrega, Segovia, etc. Then she studied English Romantic Poets II: Shelley, Byron, Keats. Then she studied Theoretical Foundations of Psychology: mind, consciousness, unconscious mind, personality, the self, interpersonal relations, psychosexual norms, social games, groups, adjustment, conflict, authority, individuation, integration, and mental health. Then she studied Oil Painting I...

Catherine Howe, *The Spaniel*, 2000

Catherine Howe

IN SPITE OF THE SIGNATURE ON A PAINTING, we are never sure whose "voice" is displayed. When I asked Catherine Howe, "Are you making your paintings from within a role?" she answered, "If my paintings were books they would be written in the first person and that character would have some aspects of the author's personality, but not all, and the author might be of the opposite gender, but the true voice would always be there."

We should not take Howe's staged labors for granted. Her verve and spirited articulation of form spreads to every inch of each painting. The frisky dog in her painting *The Spaniel*, 2000, gives that work an unlikely animating motor; the dog stands for both the spectator, eager to participate, and the wily painter. The tail, an index of doggy spirit, initiates a corkscrewing line that runs through the spaniel's flexed body as it tries to tug a cloth from under the bare bottom of a seated girl. Wiggly marks rhyme the spaniel's tail with the girl's curly hair and out into the entire field of twisting brushstrokes that comprise the image. The sky's unraveling weather seems saturated with both the girl's and the painter's subjectivity. The naked sitter's upturned palms lazily gesture toward a world of blushing sympathies and fluid reciprocities. Her skin color gently echoes the turbulent sky with reddened elbow and forehead as other body parts drift faintly toward blue or green. Meanwhile, flesh-tones flush back into the sky. The naughty dog acts as semi-obedient surrogate for the painter's lively and attentive hand.

The girl is positioned like a classic artist's model, as much in front of the sky as before a painted studio backdrop. The mound on which she sits serves as a little habitat: It is a tiny deforested planet with a tree stump and picturesque patches of fuzzy grass. Like the painting itself, this model's whole purpose is to be looked at and, agreeably, to look back. She is uninflected by fashion or the ravages of a life. She is young and nameless, with moist, heavy-lidded eyes, juicy lips, and buoyant breasts presented for our delectation. She seems obedient and, perhaps, sexually available. Her grandeur is viewed from below, a dog's-eye view.

Howe sustains the vitality of cheesy painting conventions that convention-ally use high art to dress up lascivious interests. Her earthy painterliness is put in the service of stock aesthetic effects, as if to say, "The emotion is real, but these attempts to express it are dubious." The girl in *Spaniel* asks to be considered as if she were a person, while the painting itself asks us to consider the strangeness of this kind of painting.

Howe's paintings entangle desires, longings, and aversions with the imagination's plastic capacities. This is true of all figure painting, but Howe mixes these ingredients in special ratios; historic conventions are rendered idiosyncratic by her suave labors. By transcribing sight into touch, simple acts of depiction can bring faraway things to within arm's reach against the resistance of gooey paint. Howe builds compound relationships between historic styles, power clichés, and her own muscular touch. She causes the rhetoric of the image to argue out of both sides of its polymorphous mouth.

William Empson described a voice within the pastoral genre as saying, "I now abandon my specialized feelings because I am trying to find better ones, so I must balance myself for a moment by imagining the feelings of the simple person... I must imagine his way of feeling because the refined thing must be judged by the fundamental thing, because strength must be learnt in weakness."

2001

Robert Greene

ROBERT GREENE'S PAINTINGS SEEM UNEMBARRASSED BY THEIR SUPERFICIALITY— and why shouldn't they, when so much emotional resonance swells under their daubed surfaces? Greene renders nuances of a suburban yard with the aching languor of Antoine Watteau, and a flowerbed with the turgid density of Florine Stettheimer. Careless pleasures and leisure accompany the artist's excursions into the pastoral genre like the dogs that appear in almost every one of his works. Idyllic settings provide an encouraging sanctuary for his idiosyncratic play of raw and turbulent brushwork. Compressed accumulations and unbounded slurs of paint overflow the constraints of his ultra-civilized imagery to articulate lunatic qualities of feeling and light. Greene's hyper-conventional easel paintings seem both untimely and out of time; their calendar is stuck on the summer months while their detachment from the electronic velocity of mass culture highlights a tender aversion to useful activity.

A heightened distinction between tightly rendered people and their extravagantly smeared habitats characterizes Greene's episodic pictorial space; his protagonists are painted with a conscientious attention to specific detail and (we assume) likeness. These individuals are clearly part of Greene's private world, as if he were compelled to paint them because of how much he cares about them. The always-attractive men, women and dogs seem derived from photographs but each has a radiant aura in this secondhand life.

Together, 1997, for instance, pictures two people wrapped in robes on the lawn in front of their vacation cottages; a pair of dogs sniff each other in the foreground, their furtive contact contrasting with the human's poised separation. These beings, for all their iconographic importance, are dwarfed by a tangle of foliage draped across the top three quarters of the picture. **Different laws of nature are in effect here, as if vegetation has become responsive to the digressive swerves of the imagination.** Brushstrokes squiggle and knot into exotic flowers and occasionally break free to become colorful birds. Sometimes Greene's fecund rhapsodies renounce all representational responsibilities to become gay and bubbly abstractions.

1997

Sally Ross

SALLY ROSS'S IMAGINATION WORKS in the mode of Tinker Toys. In *Untitled*, 1998, she paints flowers seemingly constructed from prefabricated easy-to-assemble parts. She renders them with the attentive warmth of an artist before nature while casting them in a purely mental world far from anything perceivable. Turgid skies blend seamlessly into the ground under Ross's goofy flowers in their stylish bases. Sometimes the flowers are marshmallow-like cylinders, other times their comic thickness is shaped into crude petals. Ross employs a conventional method of painting that is namelessly old-masterish and without apparent irony. Her brushwork articulates the objects with nuanced and modest delicacy. Flower chunks and leaf shapes radiate color into the sympathetic cloudy backgrounds. Highlights swell into middle tones and shadows with a gestural lucidity at odds with her subject's cartoon clunkiness. **Ross's paintings reflect on the medium's traditionally serious capacity to describe appearances while exercising it as an elaborate form of play.** The posed formality of her subjects, bathed in oil paint's atmospheric devotions, projects a dignified seriousness. Her flowers will stay neat forever, always trimmed and immune from death.

Artists are gods over their fabricated worlds. They continue the child's activity of playing with blocks, toy figures, or dollhouses by other means. Control is comically exercised and helplessness is symbolically managed. They remind us that play can exercise the best part of our otherwise hardworking selves.

1998

Paul McDevitt

TWO BIRDS NESTLE in scruffy grass at the edge of town. They belong to a species of modern ceramics whose graphic abstraction renders any resemblance to living birds comic. Their natural habitat is on the shelves of people's homes, but Paul McDevitt, in his drawing *Flightless Birds*, 2004, has rendered them in a cartoon habitat out of doors. McDevitt relishes the way a picture can blur the distinction between things and images, the animate and inanimate, reality and imagination. His colored-pencil drawings often depict grand vistas wrapped in extravagant weather and populated by pop-ish chimeras, oversized toys, and authoritarian architecture. Much of McDevitt's labor appears long and manual: thousands of marks are carefully layered over the paper's entire surface to btain radiant effects nd carefully wrought etails. But McDevitt s as much an inspired ditor or mix-master as e is a diligent depictor. His compositing of ound imagery might e influenced by the echniques of digital rocessing, but a trippy ubjectivity holds it ll together. His work rganizes and recon-gures an archive, his ource-world, that we ssume grows daily and an potentially include ny image that serves is interest. Whether r not McDevitt is opying a Photoshop document or improvis-ng an unrehearsed mage on the page, we nterpret this work as naving come, in effect, rom his imagination during a long solo performance bent over a table with other pictures to guide him.

McDevitt's markmaking performs transformational tricks similar to those in a traditional drawing; the visual is translated nto the tactile; far is drawn near and big s made small by the hand-made marks. Inert matter becomes an intangible image on the page with a sense of space, light, air, and sometimes living presence. McDevitt's mages, though pro-duced by conventional depiction schemas like modeling and

chiaroscuro, stimulate our post-pop appetite for things both new and hyper-mediated. His markmaking, in effect, asks us to pause on these images for longer than we might because something astonishing is being pictured. His suave drawing style smoothes over the seams between images cut and pasted from different sources, as he quietly orchestrates discarded contexts and precipitates mutant turns. McDevitt harmonizes the lighting and color to lend the whole a sense of natural magic. He also uses genre, like the picturesque landscape, vanitas still-life or por-trait format, to provide an organization with subliminal themes. The unity sometimes feels like a joke. Everything is both laughable and beautiful, a crisscross of dreams and odd per-spectives, inventions and credible descrip-tions. The images are rendered as though they were in quotes, but we don't reason-ably expect any sources to be credited. The vernacular original-ity of McDevitt's images can seem both visionary and secondhand.

Sometimes locations are self-consuming. Place becomes an operation, dynamic, generative,

and destructive. *Flaming Moore* depicts a turbulent phoenix, revealed and concealed by the enveloping fire. Its groomed swirl of licking flames converts Sir Henry's modern-art personage into a metal-head tattoo or googly-eyed biker decal. In other pictures, like *Electric Night or Night in Motion*, we zoom out into effluvial atmospheres and animated nether-skies. These vistas have a flickering and chilly glamour that is paradoxically locked into position by McDevitt's implacable hatchings. His imagination digs up hallucinatory elsewheres buried around us.

McDevitt's drawings repay a debt to borrowed images while mourning a loss of contact with real things. But perhaps more importantly, they celebrate the possibility of an ecstatic synthetic vision in an era anxious about the possibility of originality and preoccupied with the overwhelming glut of images pouring in from countless sources.

2004

Robert Greene,
Together, 1992

Paul McDevitt, *Still Life – A Flightless Fall*, 2004

Untitled (yellow flowers)

Richard Phillips

FACES DRAW our attention right from birth. The history of art is crowded with faces soliciting our attention for all kinds of reasons. Richard Phillips's oversize portraits have the impermeable finish and absorbing allure of advertising images. They wear heavy make-up and come loaded with a cargo of pop glamour and recent historical style associations. Phillips renders a face as if it had no attachments in the world other than our projections onto it; a rhetorical face, impersonating mass-cultural products that seek to arrest our attention and mobilize desire.

Jacko (after Jeff Koons), 1998, portrays Jeff Koons's famous sculpture of Michael Jackson. The circuitous itinerary from Mr. Jackson's already perversely self-crafted face through Koons's highly polished gold-tipped ceramic portrait to Phillips's painting dramatically confuses the route back to a living Michael. Phillips's work studiously complicates any sense that there is a living person behind his rendered faces while promoting an appreciation of the lives of secondhand images. We customarily read a face under the assumption that it is a showcase of the self, but Phillips redirects our attention away from interpersonal cues and towards socio-cultural ones. It is hard to imagine getting to know the person in a Phillips painting. Our face-hungry attentions are treated prophylactically.

A face has equivocal absorbency because we are aware of its capacity to deceive. Sometimes a slippery, unreadable face—like certain paintings--holds our attention longer than those that are clear and easy to know. We become absorbed in the task of figuring out who is behind the mask and why we are interested. *Portrait of God (after Richard Bernstein)*, 1998, repaints the renowned illustrator's *Interview* magazine cover of Rob Lowe at the height of his soon-to-be-blemished stardom. A white outline around Lowe's head and little targets for his eyes cast this boy as an extraordinary being. As Lowe gazes dumbly outward to an abstract beyond, Phillips's devotional hand-rendering reignites the star's now-cooled celebrity.

1998

John Currin

JOHN CURRIN'S NEW PAINTINGS PROMOTE ANXIETIES about the connection between a face and an individual's psychology. Currin's previous work consisted of a highly conventionalized presentation of types, like those found in high-school yearbooks or commercial portraiture. His new, ostensibly more expressive works establish similar rhythms between the individual and the generic. He initiates a shifting set of uneasy relationships between the artist, his subjects, and the spectator, especially concerning themes of power and sexual coupling. What does Currin think about his subjects? It's as hard to know as the thoughts of his depicted characters.

The Never Ending Story, 1994, shows a ruddy, blond-bearded man with a younger female companion. He stares earnestly into space while she gazes up with nubile attentiveness. This dapper Mr. Important strikes a pose of self-possession while demonstrating his possession of the woman's affection. Nearly all of Currin's paintings of couples contrast the male's autonomy with the female's dependence. Even in those paintings where the couple's mutual gaze turns inward, the woman hangs on or leans into the man. The sitters' untroubled self-consciousness leaks into each painting's organization. It is as if Currin were acting as an obliging commission artist for these fictional subjects. The flattering accomplishment of Currin's facture casts Mr. Important's radiant charisma and expansive potency as a form of self-advertisement. The shrewd fellow acts like he has it all—except that he does not exist. He is a product of Currin's imagination. In this respect, Currin remains elusive, painting representations of representations of types. His deadpan urbanity allows these paintings to simultaneously operate as jokes, provocations, or tender cries of the heart.

Some critics have noted a quality of mockery or condescension in Currin's treatment of the people in his paintings. While the history of portraiture could generally be characterized as an honoring of its subjects, there is also a fine tradition of cruelty in the act of

representation. Realism and caricature both emphasize the imperfections of subjects and eschew idealizations—Currin makes caricatures of the idealizations his imperfect subjects attempt to project.
1994

Frank Holliday

THE SUBJECT OF A PORTRAIT CONVENTIONALLY RETURNS OUR GAZE and, by his or her disposition, suggests the distance at which they should be addressed. We momentarily respect this, as with a new acquaintance, but eventually get close enough to scrutinize the painting's marked surface. As the depiction unravels into brushstrokes we exchange our relationship with the sitter for one with the artist. Frank Holliday inverts this conventional drama. His congestions of mark-making disclose themselves from across the room while his vivid depictions of eyes come into sharp focus up-close. We look through the expressionist dramatics to approach each eye's compelling particularity and intimate address.

The personages in Holliday's paintings don't always look directly back at us but sometimes stare off with the detached narcissism of a martyred saint. In *Iris*, 1999, the subject's upward-turning eyes suggest an exquisite pain familiar from Christian art. The painting's surface is scarred with a history of revisions and adjustments in sympathy, perhaps, with Iris's inward-turning subjectivity. Holliday has bifurcated himself into the refined underpainter of eyes and the gestural over-painter of extravagant feelings. Both are roles within a drama of looking and touching, building and destroying, being whole and coming apart.
1999

Susanna Coffey

ARTISTS HAVE for some time aspired to make art out of their life. They aim to make something enduring out of the ephemeral flow of experience in order to redeem or transform it. Adam Phillips writes that we need art in order to recognize ourselves; that the individual can "only know his most private or recondite preoccupations in the public language of culture. His privacy, at least, is a public life in secret." The question being not "Who am I?" but "How do I appear to myself?"

A painted self-portrait is a familiar and deceptively simple way of staging this question. Susanna Coffey has, for years, been painting almost exclusively before the mirror. Her smaller-than-life-sized heads, cropped at the chin, consistently depict herself staring out of the picture in locked frontal address. A range of headgear, such as glasses and hats, as well as make-up and theatrical lighting, introduce semiotic variations to her undeviating self-regard. For all the evident time and effort spent looking at herself, each painting feels hard won, as if her own appearance was barely recognizable. The coherent solidity of the Coffey-head seems at constant risk of coming apart. Her facture is an accumulation of small and distinct marks applied with searching awkwardness, like the touches of a blind person attempting to recognize a barely familiar face. These embodied perceptions testify to an abiding mystery of consistency; they seem to ask, "Is this the same person I have been facing in the mirror all my life?" A room full of these heads is a theatrical multiplication of Coffey into a motley family of her.
1997

Chris Ofili 1

THE FIGURES in Chris Ofili's paintings present themselves as powerful beings. Small magazine cutouts and generous quantities of glitter are embedded in a resin-skin that covers the surface. Strings of paint-dots crisscross the image like festival lights. This multitude of detail, however, is subsumed by cartoonish single figures that boldly dominate the image. Brushstrokes, when they occur, function as decorative or devotional elements, suggesting a ritually repetitive labor that celebrates the figure's comic regality. *The Naked Soul of Captain Shit* and *The Legend of the Blackstars*, 1999 picture a muscular black man in action hero garb consisting of a cape, ornamented belt and trunks that put his penis on display. Captain Shit gives a two-fingered hand sign as over fifty festive brown stars, each with a pair of eyes embedded in its center, cover the surface. The only pair of closed eyes nests in Captain Shit's solar plexus.

Third Eye Vision, 1999, stares back, not from beneath the painting's skin like Captain Shit, but from one of Ofili's densely ornamented elephant turds attached to the surface. This whimsically psychedelic work declares its visionary consciousness with stylized extravagance. Multicolored lines radiate from the central shit-eye while eccentric geometries, embedded glitter and festive strings of cut-out faces mix into Ofili's polyrhythmic delirium. His works assert a presence in the room with the restrained ferocity of royalty, drawing voodoo strength from the accumulation of relics embedded within their layered surfaces.
1999

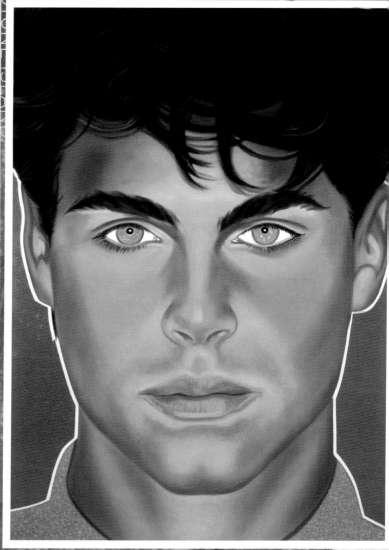
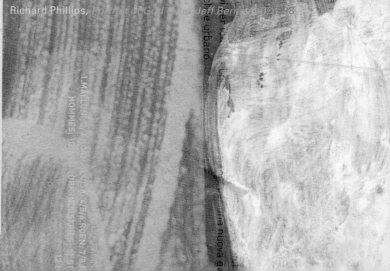

Richard Phillips, *Sons of God* ... and Jeff Berliner ... che urbano

John Currin, *The Never-Ending Story*, 1994

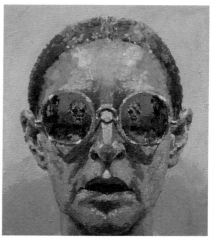

Frank Holliday, *As I Lay Dying*, 2006

Chris Ofili, *The Naked Soul of Captain Shit and the Legend of the Blackstars!*

Susanna Coffey, *Self-Portrait (Mirrored Glasses, Chrystie St.)*, 1997

Gillian Carnegie

artist Gillian Carnegie routinely includes a painting of her own naked bum in solo exhibitions. It's like a signature, even if we can't be sure if the bum is really hers, as she's cropped out any other way to ascertain its identity. *Belle*, 2006, is tightly packed with swift brushwork and a rotund derriere tipping onto one cheek to present a dusky suggestion of nether parts.

Carnegie's paintings are emphatically handmade testimonials to disciplined acts of looking. Her practiced depiction-labors mix bravura mark-making with analytic care. By executing each work differently, she stages this painting process as a primary subject. Her method balances a sense of obligation to the motif with an impulse to treat it as a pretext for aesthetic calisthenics. She employs the highly conventional idioms of landscape, still-life, and figure painting with some light-handed modernist stylizations like those of Andre Derain or early Piet Mondrian. Unlike those precursors, however, Carnegie's historically rehearsed gestures stage her work as "Painting" within the contemporary artworld's context of hyper-pluralism.

Cemetery Gate, 2006, like all painted representations, stands as both a barrier and an opening to the depicted space within. A checkered floor points in perspective to a vanishing point on the other side of the crenellated doors. It's impossible to know, however, if the dead are on this side or the other. Subtle varieties of gray within the barrier become a painting within the painting, a suggestively mournful auto-metaphor.

When Carnegie paints the branches of a leafless tree, as in *Section* or *Green and Silver*, her subtle geometricizing clarifies the particular branching pattern of each tree while articulating a taut painterly structure. *Green and Silver*, 2006, proposes an analogy between Carnegie's rendering of the tree and a bold pattern of thick intersecting lines, looking like patched cracks on a cement wall of the building behind. She equates her construction of the tree-image with the wall's cracking and repair; contingency addressed by craft. The crack-lines seem to grow from the tree while branches jostle with the sky in a figure/ground struggle. *Green and Silver* coheres like an animated, inscrutable, hieroglyph.

Carnegie's paintings convey an odd sense of loneliness; no one is around, and the season is cold. But the works surely anticipate, with their confidence, a life among others in the crowded world of Turner Prizes and gallery openings. Her bum, especially, anticipates spending time in public.

2006

Lucien Freud

In *Blond Girl on a Bed*, 1987, for example, he laboriously builds and revises the mass of the woman's body. The girl's bent position and flushed extremities highlight her awkward nakedness while the seamless continuity of the painting's surface is interrupted by accumulated bumps of painterly crust. Freud turns the act of observation into an austere power that constrains as it seeks to represent the human body; his paintings persecute his subjects into existence. The overbearing force of his gaze and its labored translation into impastoed paint conjures the sitters onto the canvas as brute matter. The metaphoric equivalence Freud constructs between flesh and paint, rather than illuminating the feelings of the other, speaks of their detachment from any social context other than the oddly imprisoned one before him within the unadorned studio. The paintings eloquently articulate an unbridgeable space between the artist and his subjects. Each sitter's enforced immobility and intensified specificity, their de-animated status as a still life, anticipates what will eventually be true—that they each *will* be dead.

1994

Matisse and Magritte

...the interrogation of painting in any case looks towards this secret and feverish genesis of things in our body.
Maurice Merleau-Ponty

THE DIFFERENCE BETWEEN Matisse and Magritte is the difference between being given a set of paints by your mother to help recover from a serious illness and having your mother throw herself from a bridge to a watery death in the middle of the night. The sense of health, wholeness, and bodily consciousness in Matisse's work would issue from that maternal gift as Magritte's dissociations and enigmas would issue from his unthinkable loss. Both stories constitute myths of origins for two bodies of work operating in an expanded self-consciousness of the conditions of sight.

Seeing, in Matisse's painting, is an embodied act of imagination. Across the long and continuously engaged career laid out in John Elderfield's thoughtful retrospective at MoMA, we can follow the painter's elaborated reorganization of things in the world through the subjective language of paint. Objects are rendered both internal and external by his rough-hewn representational schemas. The reductive and inventive tendency of these schemas, from the early divisionist pastorals to the later pattern-oriented work, approaches a heightened sense of connection between seeing, thinking, and making. Merleau-Ponty has Matisse partly in mind when he writes, "Painting awakens and carries to its highest pitch a delirium which is vision itself, for to see is to have at a distance."

This distance is signified by Matisse's lifelong attachment to subject matter removed from the world of utility, such as the still-life, artist's studio, pastoral landscape, or ornamental figure. His blunt marks override detail and construct a world in which objects, patterns and representations can interact on the same level. Color, as a result, becomes an important instrument made to serve a variety of pictorial purposes while retaining its status as an emblem of the artist's subjectivity. These detached subjects also argue for a consideration of the painting as a microcosm. Fishbowls, windows, doors, paintings within the painting, and the presence of figurines iconographically develop this theme. The artwork's organization and internal hierarchy aspire to the condition of an organism born into paint. Matisse's images of women are curious in this regard: they are often treated as little more than figurines or flowers, a hackneyed metaphor Matisse seems to

ave intended. Their image,
however, does not seem to
be a target of his carnal desire
but is figured within a more
diffuse carnality of looking.

Where Matisse is
embodied looking, Magritte is
dissociated signifying. He perversely writes, "I always try
to make sure that the actual
painting isn't noticed, that it
is as little visible as possible."
If he shares with Matisse a
preoccupation with the act
of representation, it is to
render it problematic and paradoxical. Where Matisse's
practice is an image of
health, Magritte's is a
kind of neurotic hygiene,
a paranoid cleanliness
that conceals more
than it protects. His
representational means are
a form of copying borrowed
from illustration vernaculars.
This anonymous, generic style
delivers the images into an
environment of enigmas. A
space is activated between
words, images, and things
that allows notions of desire
and love to circulate but
remains blind and incomplete.
Is it possible for an image of
the lost Mother to haunt his
use of signifying processes?
His attempts to establish
solid connections tend toward
helpless dissociation or
betrayal. Magritte often had
others compose titles for
him, such as *The Treachery
of Images* or *A Taste for the
Invisible*, that embodied his
fascinated alienation from
representation. "Indifference"
was the word he preferred—
the source of his work's
hyper-normal peculiarity and
dry, melancholic humor.
1992

John Wesley

of flat shapes and
constrained black
outlines keeps sub-
jectivity and sentiment
below the surface.
His art speaks in an
uninflected language bor-
rowed from period comics
and illustration, which
makes their idiosyncrasy
all the more startling. Slight
displacements or subtle
shifts of form confound
expectations initiated by the
image's strange familiarity.
In *Sofa*, 1982, the image
of a reclining nude woman
is painted with the same
awkward flatness as the
couch she lies on, but the
couch claims a greater reality when we notice that the
woman's face, knees, and feet
are cropped when they hit the
couch's edge. She is like an
image printed on the fur-
niture. Her hand disappears
between her legs to suggest
that solitary gestures (other
than the ones used to make
this painting) are within arm's
reach. The Magrittean paradox
of a picture within a picture is
given a kinky pop twist by the
work's brazen artificiality.

Fruit Tree, 1996, presents
itself with the cut-off dumb-
ness of a cartoon background.
One tree, two clouds, three
birds, and six pieces of fruit sit
as if waiting for a punchline that
never arrives. We count them,
but they don't add up. *Fruit Tree*
stares back with a blankness

that belies its subtle formality;
odd breaks of symmetry, eccentric drifts of hatching lines,
and skewed blobs of foliage
give the painting an unlikely
pulse. Wesley's nether-region
between quotation and invention is inhabited by the contrasting virtues of cool detachment
and psychological charge.
1996

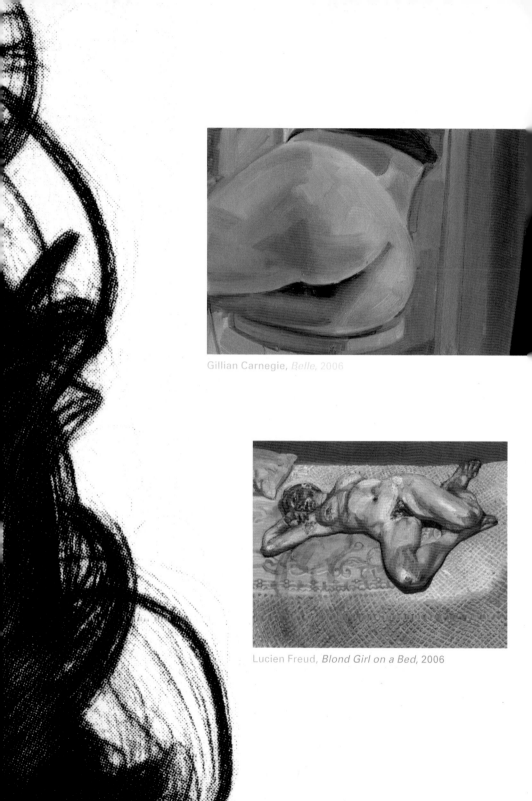

Gillian Carnegie, *Belle*, 2006

Lucien Freud, *Blond Girl on a Bed*, 2006

Rene Magritte, *The Key of Dreams*, 1930

Henri Mattise, *Odalisque in Grey Culottes*, 1926 – 27

Chris Ofili, *The Naked Soul of Captain Shit and the Legend of the Blackstars!*, 1999

When I Think About You I Touch Myself

I search myself
I want you to find me
I forget myself
I want you to remind me

The Divinyls, 1991

PAINTERS CONVEY A SENSE OF TOUCH in their work by vividly depicting the texture of objects or by the compelling vivacity of their markmaking. Some eras care more about tactility and the material qualities of things than others who prefer more symbolic or expressive virtues. The Dutch golden age, with its acutely observed imagery, stands out as a high point in the celebration of rough, smooth, dry, and moist. Artists have pictured flesh for the entire history of visualized tactility. Skin, in this history, moves through cycles of sensuousness, ascetic astringency, and subversion. Modern artists showed less interest in the rendering of surfaces than in radical acts of embodied vision. Their work came to the marketplace more dependent on the merits of its first-person singularity than on nuanced description.

An art object can be understood as a surrogate for the artist. The signature grants ambassadorial status to a work before it joins the great world of objects and people outside the studio. Artworks gesture out to a limitless future of passing strangers in frozen attempts to make contact. The privacy of the studio and the solitude of making art expose artists to accusations of being cut off or worse: masturbatory. Artists sometimes confirm this with self-protective justifications like "I do this for myself" or "I don't care what anyone thinks." Handmade art objects, in a sense, perform a displaced self-touching. Lynda Benglis' video *Now*, 1973, is a caricature of the artist's imaginary autonomy. She slowly guides herself into position for an open-mouthed electronic kiss with her electronically doubled self. *Now*'s self-sufficiency, though, is a momentary feint; Benglis is performing for us and is in love with the medium.

Artworks are crowded with solitudes. The *lack* of contact between artist and viewer must be part of the artwork's enduring and distinct appeal. The paradox of detached connection might have fetish-like powers that could help explain the persistence of such an inefficient form of pleasure. Pictures engage us partly because we are able to occupy their spaces with our thoughts. Artist and viewer are, in a sense, having solitary conversations enabled by the forever off-frame other. Both interlocutors fluidly oscillate between the fictionalized subject positions "I" and "you." Artworks, like novels, encourage us to travel and identify with invented others.

We view an easel painting from roughly the same position as the artist when he or she stopped work; the space between then and now collapses. Easel paintings conventionally face us at eye level on the wall in the approximate disposition of another person. They greet us and request our acquaintance while showing how different and special they are. The gaze and body language of the painted subject reaches out according to practiced and usually familiar social codes. Depicted subjects might still be alive or may never have existed, but the conjured person is here before us and will be for others long after we're gone.

We can't touch the figures within a painting. Its surface can be felt, with permission, but the rendered body is for our eyes only. We are eternally separated from pictured people by the same marked surface that constitutes them. A gateway is stroked into existence by the artist's practiced hand so that near and far coexist on the work's skin as adjacent daubs, the visible world squeezed within arm's reach.

Some paintings shamelessly seek to arouse while others promote a critical detachment that examines sexiness from a distance. Does self-conscious criticality neutralize the depicted figure's sexual charge? Is our instinctual way of looking at bodies and negotiating their allure disabled if an image forces us to zoom out?

The person in the picture may seem to address us, but the artwork constitutes the artist's address. The work's "voice" alternates between first and third person as our attention slips between looking into the image and looking at the object. Raw material and the impression of space coexist dynamically and subliminally. The circulating viewer walks through a room of figurative paintings as an animating other. He or she is asked by each image to participate by means of coaxing, imploring,

seducing, or exhorting.

Sometimes the rhetoric makes assumptions about us. (Theory would call this the enunciated spectator position.) We become entangled in the work's persuasive operations while the pictured figures present themselves as though they were aware of being looked at. The artist is invisible matchmaker, as significantly absent as we spectators were at the moment he or she made the work.

Spectators are infinitely replaceable, but consequently have the freedom to ignore both the person in the picture and the demands of the work itself. Figures in pictures don't necessarily want the same thing as the artist; their independence is crafted but can sometimes seem to have autonomous agency. But what if we don't want what the work seems to expect us to want? We can enjoy or misread however we choose: the choreography of marks, the idiosyncratic details or the odd way the work holds together or seems to fall apart. We can pleasurably resist the work's designs on our desires.

George Quaintance's portrait of Glen Bishop, made in 1956 for reproduction in a physique magazine, assumes a shared interest in the male body. His work negotiates the period's legal restrictions on homoerotic depictions with restrained panache. Quaintance winks in acknowledgement that we know how the censorship game works while serving up a desirable guy. The law has less to say these days about what body parts can be shown but propriety and erotophobia continue to inflect the presentation of bodies. The man in Dana Schutz's vigorously painted *Reclining Nude*, 2002, is aglow with awareness of being looked at. He stretches from edge to edge without shyness about his erection and seems proudly aware that his odd appearance might be pleasing to someone. Vivacity can be transmitted to depicted figures through brushwork. Moise Kisling's stylized *Portrait*, 1943, tries to flatter his subject with hedonism, dancing marks and Mediterranean light while affecting Modern Art's radical indifference to popular taste.

2002

David Humphrey, *Sierra Love Team*, 1997

Kurt Kauper, *Cary Grant #2*, 2003

David Humphrey, *Bathers*, 1996

GB Jones, *Prison Breakout #2*, 2003

Moise Kisling, *Large Red Nude*, 1949

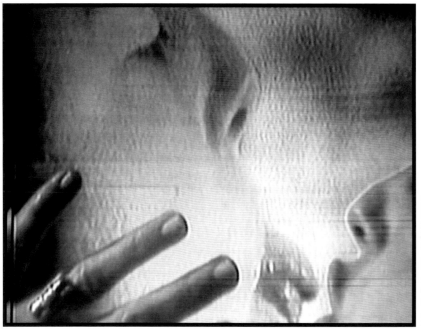

Dana Schutz, *Reclining Nude*, 2002

Jo Hormuth

"ONE TOUCH AFTER THE OTHER, ONE TOUCH AFTER THE OTHER," was how Cézanne narrated his way of making a painting. It could also describe how Jo Hormuth's work is made. While Cézanne's method reconstituted vision in tactile terms, Hormuth's method is blind to pictures. She instructed massage professionals to execute various strokes into wet clay, which she subsequently cast and painted in shiny monochrome enamel. Each *Untitled*, 1999, piece hangs on the wall as an empty frame and registers one type of stroke repeated around the perimeter like an ornamental pattern. The works are variously pock-marked, squeezed, smeared, fingered, or pinched into their form according to each specialized massage gesture. Pincer compression, basic myofacial, or scooping are strokes originally directed to passively reclined bodies with closed eyes but now exercise themselves for our passing scrutiny. They ask us to pay attention rather than instructing us to relax.

Hormuth disengages the connection a painting habitually affirms between touch and expression. We wonder what the strokes in a Hormuth would feel like if they were applied to our body rather than understanding them as expressive of the artist's special singularity. Both interpretations depend on our sense that the mark is an index of direct contact. This evidence prompts all kinds of imagined stories, ranging from the testimonials of conventional painting to the ingenious conundrums generated by minimalist/conceptual practices. The hole at the center of a Hormuth, the blank wall, stands for all artworks in their role as a place to project our imaginings.

1999

Medardo Rosso

FOR ALL THE EVIDENCE of being hand wrought, Medardo Rosso's sculptures seem shaped by the force of light. Their smeared dissolution paradoxically catches both the fleeting quality of a light-drenched glance and the durable heaviness of raw matter. In 1906 Rosso stopped making new sculpture and devoted the last twenty-two years of his life to editing, recasting, and documenting earlier work. He stopped the clock as a river of new and increasingly radical art was spilling onto the cultural stage and twentieth-century Europe was streaming toward its catastrophic future. In a sense he did with his career what his artworks do; arrest the flow of time and extend an invitation to linger over the pause.

Rosso's explicit and innovative aim was to render in sculpture the quality of a frozen impression. Rosso used photography to focus and extend this aim. The word "impression" describes his spontaneous modeling in clay of an observed subject as well as his subsequent castings and recastings of the object into different materials. Eccentrically cropped or drawn-over photographs of the sculptures, like *Aetas Aurea*, 1886, extend the impression onto paper, oddly restoring to it a sense of dematerialized perception or memory. The photos obscure the particular material of the object, emphasizing its image; they are impressions of impressions. Some seem as much images of living people as they are sculptures. A washed-out photograph of a sculpted laughing face, for instance, seems to catch that passing gesture more naturally than the labored density of a bronze cast. The sculpture's unnatural beauty flows from this congealed incongruity.

Rosso's objects emphasize a distinct point of view, as opposed to the multiple views built into traditional in-the-round statuary. Seen from the back or side, his depictions often yield to an undifferentiated pile of stuff. Wax, one of Rosso's preferred mediums, catches this sense of contingency through ts supple translucence and liquid mobility. *Aetas Aurea*, 1884-5, renders the figures as if they were caught between creation and dissolution. The work is marked by a fluent turbulence of caresses and jabs that make and unmake it. Their meltedness reminds us what they are made of and their vulnerability to heat. Rosso uses sculptural cropping, through the recasting of fragments, as a photographer might. He creates, through these exerpts, what André Breton in a later description of the uncanny would call "a sign of the reality it no longer possesses."

1999

Julian Trigo

JULIAN TRIGO'S PAINTINGS ARE WAYWARD allegories of the encounter between an object's materiality and a viewer's interpretative projections. A rectangle of unmodulated color is presented as an *elementary* point of origin onto which Trigo applies charcoal drawings of children. The purity of the single-color painting is besmirched by images of equivocal innocence. Children of undetermined gender, dressed in shirts and naked below, are shown engaging in ambiguous sexual probing. The background colors initiate associations of tainted juvenilia: dingy baby blue, aging baby-doll pink, and urine-stained yellow.

The repetitive touch and smudge of Trigo's charcoal mark-making dirties the ground and also echoes the rooting and rubbing carried out by the pictured children. Their closed eyes suggest that, for this moment, they live in a sightless world of touch, guided by their tiny schematic hands. Our sight, which penetrates into this fictional space, sees a world fashioned by the taut and frequently revised touch of Trigo's probing hand. In the largest work, *Untitled*, 1994, a group of children is seen engaged in similar playful intimacies. Each point of contact between them, no matter how casually innocuous, is covered with a small black square, both censoring and forever taping together the furtive connection. The curious uniformity of these children suggests that their interactions are in a narcissistic utopia of non-hierarchical reciprocity. The kids could be either perfectly mirrored peers or a single, multiplied individual. The sense of the works as dirtied monochromes is augmented in this painting by liquid stains; a drawing effect that doubles as an effect of the children's play; an involuntary leakage. Trigo's charcoal line, in contrast to the stains, is dry and dusty, and despite its rigorous architectural structuring, seems fragile; it would be easy to wash these canvases clean again. The traversed boundaries between artist and his object have left a trace that sustains our interpreting and presumably *unclean* attention.

1994

Jo Hormuth, *Massage Therapist Frame
(Scooping Technique),* 1999-2000

Medardo Rosso, *Portrait of Henri Rouart*, 1889-90

Julian Trigo, *Untitled*, 1994

Squeezy

I PURCHASED
A GROUP OF
STUFFED ANIMALS
at a church flea market
recently and relished their
sense of having a past;
they were either loved
and abandoned or gifts
finally discarded after a
guilt-diminishing waiting
period. When I was
working on the plaster
bunny in *Squeezy*, 2000, I
decided to stuff some of
those furry creatures into
the object's interior. By
attaching a video monitor
to *Squeezy* that plays a
long, looping, close-up
of other stuffed animals,
I could elaborate the
connections between
looking, making, and
a desire to project life
into inanimate things.
Squeezy encourages a
conversation between
its flickering and paint-
smeared video monitor
and the brightly colored
lumps, fur, and goo of
its animal forms. The
work hopefully performs
a mixed-up love act
in the intimate space
between hands and face.
2000

David Humphrey, *Squeezy*,
2000

David Humphrey, *Bunnies*, 2006

Wet Clay

AS FAR AS CLAY IS CONCERNED I'm *unclean*. My hands never touch the stuff, but its primordial slime haunts my work in caricatured form. The limits of clay's fecal plasticity, though, have yet to be determined. Armies of ceramicists and clay sculptors, I'm sure, are pushing those limits at this moment with or without the benefits of artworld patronage.

Many ceramic artists I have spoken to have anxieties about the status of clay as a medium in contemporary art. I think their questions are founded not so much on any property of ceramics as they are about its status within the mainstream discourse of contemporary art. Different mediums, in themselves, are not promoted or ignored there; what thrives are contents or activities that elaborate a historically evolving set of stories: so-and-so's work upends a certain tradition, this or that new practice rehabilitates, interrogates, simulates, or critiques some aspect of culture. There is a paradox, though, in the wish to promote and sustain ceramic art's unique properties while lamenting its isolation, in cherishing the comforts of likeminded artisan communities while wishing to be included in the club of international art grooviness. Curators, writers, collectors, and artists have preoccupations that cycle, converge, and digress in unpredictable ways. I see no reason why somebody's clay can't squeeze into the game.

My work seeks the unexpectedly expressive within the ultra-conventional. I conscript the mass-produced sentimentality of cute ceramic figurines for service in my pop-surrealist idiom. I acquire these kitties, booties, lambs, dogs, and children at flea markets or yard sales and appreciate their sense of having a past. Their other past as soft and wet clay is faintly alluded to in the goo-like biomorphic paperpulp forms I model to hold the ceramic pieces together. Discreetly placed holes and openings in the original figurines (to make sure they don't explode when being fired) are given a thematic prominence as the pieces are rotated and joined with others. Unlikely connections are established between parts while identities are buried in the pulp-form. My pulp-work performs ambivalent love acts by joining, covering, and augmenting tactile contact with the ceramic originals. I hope each piece crafts a dynamic equilibrium between the hybridized elements while honoring their modest dignity. If the figurines turn out to be more coveted than my artworks, the pulp can be dissolved and the ceramics recovered.

I love the hollowness of a ceramic object. It can seem as full as a pair of lungs, breathing in the feelings people project. We are shattered when a cherished object breaks, but patience and glue can restore a wounded wholeness. "Clay history" speaks only if we care to listen and have the imagination to speak back.

2001

David Humphrey,
Kitties, 1997

David Humphrey,
Dogpack, 1997

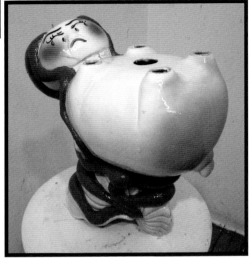

David Humphrey, *Crypig*, 2001

David Humphrey,
Hunter and Quarry,
1999

David Humphrey,
Booty Bank, 1998

David Humphrey,
Dogstack, 1997

Mike Ballou

MIKE BALLOU PERFORMS his aesthetic operations on plastic figurines. He toys with their intended purposes by cutting them up, patching them together, and painting them in startling configurations. If miniature plastic figures are ciphers onto which children project fantasy scenarios, the toys, at play's end, remain physically unchanged. Ballou's play, on the other hand, leaves these cowboys, Indians, soldiers, and animals permanently altered. Sometimes they become composite multiple figures, other times they are patched together into one. Siamese twins, mismatched grafts, disordered mutants, and blossoming hybrids populate Ballou's tabletop sculptures. The parts are glued together, but a deeper unity is achieved by means of a thick coat of glossy enamel paint. Sometimes Ballou paints like an earnest hobbyist, making sure that horses are brown with white underbellies and foliage is green. At other times his painting obeys subjective principles analogous to the way the pieces are assembled. Psychedelic patterning adorns a deer that sprouts bushes while a decorative red spot on a horse leaks paint down its tail into a congealed puddle on the ground. Ballou's fluid and unpredictable painting liberates the toys from their brand-name identities while redefining them as artworks.

1998

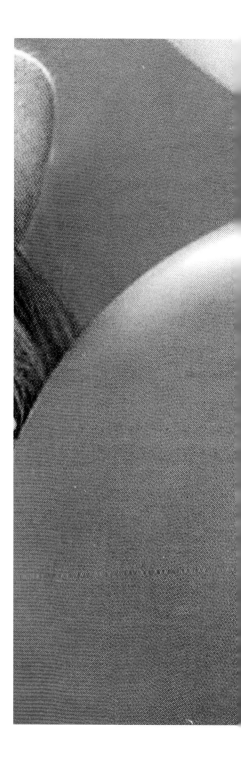

Mike Ballou, *orange cave (audience member)*, 1999

George Stoll

SPONGES ARE MARVELS of absorbency, efficiently drinking in moisture to become soft and heavy versions of their formerly stiff selves. George Stoll honors these modest cleaning tools with a series of burned balsa wood and alkyd sculptures. By carefully rendering the sponge's perforated surface and genial brightness, he celebrates its peculiar beauty.

Absorbency is a negative virtue; its purpose is to hold as much as possible in the slightest container (its structural ideal is to be all cavity). Absorbency is a model for artworks that seek to soak up attention with minimal self-presence, to absorb us while expunging themselves. Stoll's painted wood objects embrace this model paradoxically. His work's ability to function as an actual sponge is an illusion. Its delicacy and keen articulation of surface ask instead to be saturated with our sensitized attentions, to become a counter-Bounty, as it were, a slower-picker-upper. But his art's hypermodesty is a ruse as the works swell with pride in their accomplished craft and chirpy, extroverted color.

Single blocks, two-color diptychs, or monochromatic triptychs are all covered in perforations of varying size, density, and angle. Each work is shaped as much by the logic of Stoll's hole-making process as by the mimetic logic of sponge simulation. What at first appears to be a careful depiction is also the result of an obsessive/repetitive behavior. These sponges are, moreover, resolutely clean and display themselves with retail abundance along the gallery walls. They stare back with the blank alacrity of a product waiting to be of service.
1997

James Hyde

PILLOWS OFFER COMFORT and decor opportunities. They ask to be touched and supply conforming support for our body at rest. James Hyde's new oversize pillows have been touched plenty, leaving a caked residue of filth. A pillow's gentle invitation for contact is terrifying coming from Hyde's eight-foot *Massive Pillow*, 1999; it would dominate most living rooms and threaten our sense of repose. *Massive Pillow* is really a stuffed painting, executed with the Cezannian "one touch after the other"

method. Even the grubby color is suggestive of landscape in the manner of romantic postwar abstraction. The possibility of seeing into a fictional picture space, however, is destroyed by the pillow's striating folds and bloated form. The space within the painting becomes literal stuffing; its contents are crumpled newspapers.

Hyde's upholstery is a trope that reflects on painting's activity of coating, covering, and marking. It provides a way to rethink the materials of canvas, understructure, and wall in terms of dysfunctional furniture. His operations force the paintings to fail at picturing but succeed as sculpture. Each work is a caricature of a ruin.

If *Massive Pillow* is besmirched, Hyde's *Pool*, 2000, provides what could have kept it clean: a vinyl slipcover. It is empty and clear except for the fabric edging that holds its vinyl faces together. It could protect but, as an artwork, has come to need protection itself. The slack form acquires unexpected grace through Hyde's multiple color divisions along the fabric edges. Its emptiness attains a fragile delicacy as it safely encloses a volume of air from our unclean contact.
2000

Mamma Andersson

LOOKING INTO SOMEONE'S FACE can be like looking into their bedroom: We feel an intimate uniqueness that conceals as much as it reveals. Mamma Andersson's paintings, like faces and bedrooms, bear traces of a subjectivity under the influence of a past we can only intuit. In her first American exhibition, titled "Rooms Under the Influence," this Swedish artist conjures a sense of history with paintings of interiors and landscapes suffused with evocative details and moody atmospheres. In spite of the blank-seeming conventional formats of her paintings, Andersson is a suave depictor. She complicates point-of-view by blending the distressed and watery hand-madeness of the work with evidence of photographic sources. Andersson dramatizes the uneven transformation of paint into image as a metaphor for a person's fragile hold on reality.

All these works from 2006 are painted on long unframed wood panels attached directly to the wall, except one snowy landscape on canvas. *Title* might be considered a different sort of object, a rop coming from one of Andersson's depicted rooms. Some paintings include people: A child walks a few paces ahead of an adult on a dirt road in *Coming Home*; in *Leftovers* five women are bathing, dressing and sleeping in a disheveled room; in *About a Girl* eight women, variously aware of being observed, hang out around a table with pictures of geishas and Disney's Snow White on the wall behind them. Like Pierre Bonnard and Edouard Vuillard, Andersson diminishes the distinction between people and things, but unlike those Nabis masters, she renders the relation between objects with all the nuanced psychological density appropriate to people.

In *Backbiter I* and *Backbiter II*, nearly identical variations of a decorated wall and ornamental mantle, Andersson exercises both a curatorial and anthropological imagination by weaving the histories of these objects into new stories based on their arrangement: In one framed image, a hooded swordsman threatens a girl, while a yellow-shirted ceramic black person on the mantle gestures over them with a fan. The large mirror in *Backbiter I* reflects a tidy bedroom while its twin above the mantle in *Backbiter II* is an expressively painted symbolist landscape; both are pastoral images of places promising detachment and repose.

Andersson highlights the way people reveal themselves in their decorating decisions. At the same time she reflects on picture-making itself by making analogies between mirrors, photographs and her own handmade transcriptions of other images. Andersson's muted color and puddling paint create humid atmospheres of bruised and rumpled humanity.

2006

Elizabeth Campbell

IN *In House (A Standardized Affectation for Telepresence)*, 2000, Elizabeth Campbell has constructed an interior at once banal and uncanny. A two-room windowless white building bisected by a hallway precisely duplicates an unkempt bedroom on either end of the passage, down to the wrinkles on the bed-sheets, trash in the wastebaskets, tossed laundry, and inexpensive personal junk covering every surface. Each object radiates a forensic significance after we discover and start checking the accuracy of her doubling. The replication renders precise what seemed sloppy, intentional what seemed inadvertent. Campbell disguises work as carelessness and transforms carelessness into eloquence.

It is astonishing what happens when the singularity of a person's living habits, made up of constellations of purchasing choices, is reproduced. Campbell highlights this mass-produced replaceability while helping us to notice every detail as if we'd seen it before.

We become snoopers, looking into the trash, slightly opened drawers and purses, checking out underthings and other private material. If we touch anything, though, the twin-world's fragile order is destroyed. The entrances to the two rooms are at opposite ends of the hall, so we must carry a mental snapshot from one room to the other to compare their matching details. The fictional inhabitant seems to be sexually active, a Prince fan, and a smoker who is thinking about quitting. She worries about worrying about herself and believes that her acute sensitivities don't have to be a liability. *In House* has the attributes of a diorama, a museum period room, and a crime scene.

Pinned above the bed is a word-drawing called *Diagram of Me*, which charts various roles Campbell has assumed in her life, including daughter, student, girlfriend, artist, citizen; each role spawns a branching set of associations consequent to it. The drawing is an anachronism, a telepresence, within the fiction of the younger self established by the rooms. It is consistent with the image of a self-preoccupied person suggested by the many self-help books, cosmetics, personal hygiene products, and a handwritten list that begins "How I look hiking through the Grand Canyon / How I feel when I buy yeast infection medication at Walmart / How I feel at Planned Parenthood / How an older woman looks at me when I walk into Planned Parenthood." A partially opened notebook reveals a continuation of the list that suggests that this activity could be endless. Repetition operates as both symptom and possible cure for Campbell's theatricalyzed compulsions. Her list is retrojected evidence that ambitious contemporary art can have roots in seemingly pointless youth behavior.

2000

George Stoll, *Untitled (polyurethane painting)*, 1993

James Hyde, *Massive Pillow*, 1999

Mamma Andersson, *Leftovers*, 2006

Elizabeth Campbell, *House (A Standardized Affectation of Telepresence)*, 2000

Tal R

TAL R APPLIES PAINT with a sloppy authority. He smears, trowels, and squeezes massive quantities of thick oil color straight out of the tube to depict places associated with the life of an artist. *Art School, Drawing Room*, and *Model Alone in the Studio* are decoratively organized large paintings schematically representing the architecture of artmaking and a few objects, like bottles or tables, belonging in those spaces. Tal R is an Israeli-born Dane who shares with many modern artists, from Picasso to Pollock, an enthusiasm for the simplicity, directness, and innocent vitality of children's art. But in contrast to those unschooled qualities, the title of this series of paintings suggests a more detached French-style death-of-the-author conceit: *"Le peintre n'est pas là."* The painter isn't there. Is "Tal R" a role he has made for himself to question authenticity, or is he just saying that he didn't depict himself? Each work includes a bold signature that strenuously exercises Tal R's time-honored claim of authority and dominion over his work even as that claim is questioned by the exhibition's title.

The Model is a hailstorm of variously sized and colored spots intended to be an extreme close-up of *Model Alone in the Studio*. Zooming in on the *The Model* reveals a very dense paint crust embedded with blob shapes cut out of paper. These clunky and oversized pixel-dots make a joke on reproduction-based painting while appearing to be a jaunty and intuitive abstract painting. *Model Alone in the Studio* features a nude woman crudely drawn in charcoal directly onto the white ground, augmented by gooey paint-lines squeezed from the tube. A dark green cow-pie of a blob describes the model's left nipple while a smaller cadmium one describes her right. She's a snout-nosed muse that takes her role seriously even if we wonder how seriously Tal R takes her.

Tal R's tone is exuberant and festive. He paints a wide and elaborately ornamented frame around each picture to celebrate its contents. Elements from the interior of *Drawing Room* are ingeniously lined up to parade around its perimeter. Frame and picture coexist in an amplified world of spontaneous make-believe; Tal R's pictures are hyperbolic, like children's theater. In some paintings the frame takes over the whole picture to become an uncomplicated pattern of marks. *Inn* and *Innn* are made entirely of red, orange, and green triangles, circles, and dots arranged symmetrically and concentrically.

Tal R doesn't want us to forget that his artworks come here from elsewhere. He might be hiding out in his studio, but other artists are probably with him. His paintings celebrate the artist as a member of a utopian tribe in which the worthless is valuable, the ridiculous is taken seriously, jokes are the only imperative, and drinking will happen, *n'est-ce pas?* **2007**

Thomas Trosch

THOMAS TROSCH'S PAINTINGS OF FANCY LADIES with their art collections affect a paradoxical lightness, simultaneously pretty and rugged. He blends allusions to other artists, most notably Florine Stettheimer, the queen of deceptive frivolity, and Philip Guston, the muck-master of comic threat, and sustains their reductive stylizations and fierce commitment to a muscular application of thick paint. His conspicuous handmade laboring relates incongruously to the genteel leisure exercised by the idealized social types in his pictures, liberated from having to work. Fine ladies of breeding like these know a meringue from a madeleine and how to construct a sophisticated decorating scheme but would be disconcerted by the clean-up and messy labor required to make a Trosch. His confectionery touch boldly purveys large quantities of paint in excess of its depictive function. The surfaces are dramatic topographies that swell from the raw canvas into mountainous peaks and viscous glacial slabs.

The figures in Trosch's interiors are surrounded by their collections of highly simplified abstract paintings. Like Guston, Trosch favors the squarish blob as a basic unit of pictorial organization. It is a container that holds large quantities of paint and the potential for transforming into other things, like furniture, clothing, eyeballs, or dogs. The blob's blunt versatility alternately builds analogies and resemblances or collapses back into dumb matter. Trosch disperses these forms across the canvas into a subjectively coherent patchwork. Dresses and other patterned apparel skew the gener-

frontal organizations
n irregular shapes and
ts of scale to give
 work a sense of life
 ependent of depiction.

 Trosch's paintings
 cipate a place among
 things in upscale
 nes, in spite of the
 that the collectors
 is pictures don't own
 thing that looks like a
 sch. Perhaps he wants
 void confusing these
 noisseurs with the
 s he anticipates for
 self. Trosch's people
 e huge unblinking
 s, as if to express their

ndrew
Masullo

NDREW
ASULLO'S
MALL PAINT-
GS CAN LOOK like
autifully wrapped gifts
ned to the wall. Their
ght color suggests
 heerfully decorative
 nitude, but as our
 perience of the work
 folds, differences
 tween them become
 creasingly important and
 eir patterned surface
 ens into expansive
 pths. Most of his work
 s a densely painted skin
 at sometimes continues
 ound the canvas's
 des or blossoms into a
 ck, lumpy crust. The
 ecise execution of the
 pmost layer covers
 evident history of
 vision and other images
 neath; its cosmetic
 pacity suggests
 nknowable sub-

very large appetites for
seeing. They are idealized
viewers whose whole life
consists of doing what
we do in passing while
looking at this work. We
are free to identify
with any number of
roles articulated in
the work: spectator
delector, collector,
or confector. The
stylized eccentricity and
period overtones of these
paintings cast them in
the mode of storybook
arcadias where everything
has always been and
will continue to be gay.
2000

strata. If Masullo's
paintings are like wrapped
gifts, they teasingly
resist being opened.

Sometimes Masullo's
resolutely abstract images
seem symbolic or narra-
tive. In *3042*, 1994, variously sized and colored
dots touch at their edge
while adhering to a curva-
ceous yellow shape slung
from the left. In *3037*,
1994, two white dots drift
from a loopy red frame
that continues to contain
the other nine. Five mul-
ticolored teardrop shapes
radiate from a large letter
"J" in *3022*, 1994. The
generic imagery tamps
down the sense of an
encrypted personal
content while seeming
to diagram something
specific and important.
1994

Gabriel Orozco

GIFT WRAPPING, as opposed to the packaging
of a new consumer product, is designed to obscure
what it envelops. It places ornamental obstacles
before unforeseen pleasures, while a commodity's
disposable and festive packaging promises, with
information and image, all that could be fulfilled by
ownership; both coverings declare their contents to
be special. Artworks often conform to one or the
other of these models by treating the relation of a
package to its contents as the work's subject matter.

Gabriel Orozco's *Yogurt Caps*, 1994, comprises
four blue-rimmed, clear plastic lids symmetrically
positioned on the gallery's four walls. The extravagant
slightness of his presentation grants details of the caps,
like their stick-on labels, a heightened importance. A
different sell-by date is stamped on each lid. Orozco's
fragments of would-be garbage allude to the discarded
container and its nutritious contents, as well as to the
body of work from which this particular piece issues.
The yogurt is replaced by the milky expanse of white
gallery and perhaps a joke on the word "culture." The
transparent lids function as lenses focused on the
gallery wall and on the phenomenon of Orozco's career.
Yogurt Caps's casual reference to sales and a freshness
envelope suggests a playful self-criticality--but one
that only makes sense given his success. The work
presents itself as an ephemeral utterance
at the limits of commerce and intelligibil-
ity, but *Yogurt Caps* has the subtlety of a
stage whisper enshrined within Marian
Goodman's impressive midtown space.

Orozco's *Soft Blue*, 1993, sits unobtrusively on
a bookshelf. A small star and the letters "CCCP"
are printed on a sphere made of soft blue plasticine.
Since the freshness date has expired on the Soviet
Union, *Soft Blue*'s reference has the surrealist charm
of a Magritte word painting. Orozco's works function like an archaeological fragment awaiting the
challenge of interpretation; so much depends on
figuring out what's missing. Critic Benjamin Buchloh,
a little worried about the muteness of Orozco's
work, writes, "[His] objects exude a silence that is
always aware of its inflicted and transitory status; it
is neither ostentatiously displayed as an aesthetic
privilege nor internalized as an inescapable condition."
I thought the "inflicted and transitory" character of
his work heightened the ostentation of its claims to
aesthetic privilege when packaged in a fancy gallery.
1994

Tal R, *Drawing Room*, 2006

Thomas Trosch, *The Pink Lady*, 1999

Andrew Masullo, *3003*, 1994

Jill Giegerich, *Untitled*, 1991

Soma Zone

A BUILDING, according to the poet Paul Valery, is a "durable, decorated, defended mass, limpid with glass, made for our use, which will contain our worlds, from which our smoke will escape." I'm picturing Valery's building as a cartoon head spewing cloud-like thought-bubbles. Jill Giegerich's artworks are often made with building materials and are like heads in the way they appear to be having thoughts. Many of her works are pictures of things expressing other things, the way a teakettle expresses a cloud of steam or a hot air balloon lifts off from a wooden platform. The things in her work produce thoughts in the shape of other things: things begetting things begetting things. Sometimes the things are just thinking of themselves, generating duplications and multiplications, such as *JG-1991-10*, in which thirteen burning and dripping candles gather unceremoniously on a sandpaper shelf below, as if to collectively imagine the larger sculpted one above.

A rope-limned silhouette of a man's limbless torso, *JG-1990-15*, is positioned below three gnarled wreaths of twisted rope. The wreaths rise up the wall like expanding smoke rings. Who is this faceless strongman, so flexed and downcast, appearing more than once in Giegerich's work? Perhaps he's a worker laboring at some cropped-off task; maybe he's working on himself. He is cousin to the silhouette in a MEN AT WORK sign. But perhaps Giegerich is more concerned to alert us to work already completed, the work itself here before us. The same guy in *JG-1983-18* looks like he's been sheathed in an armor that both constrains and protects him, as if the viewer's projections were a threat. But Mr. Strongman is as unconcerned with our passing attentions as he is absorbed by his off-frame labors.

When we make a picture of an object in our heads we perform an effortless and nearly involuntary act of craftsmanship. Giegerich's artworks are like mental images made in a carpentry shop. They are cobbled together, perhaps repaired and modified, but without the gravity-bound solidity of furniture on the one hand or the ephemerality of imagined things on the other. Her objects often exist in a netherworld of geometric diagrams, shadows, and reproductions. For all their heavy lumber, her depicted furniture and buildings are abstract. They don't claim a presence as things but are like physically embodied possibilities. Their skewed angles relate to a particular point of view, as if they were seen from an exaggerated angle, a perplexed perspective not ours. *JG-1991-10* tips emphatically into our space and off the wall anamorphically, as if its off-plumb disposition is making fun of architectural rationality.

Giegerich's constructions, like *JG-1991-4*, reflect on the subject of ornament while inventing new forms of ornamentation. She celebrates the way decoration can covertly produce dreamy analogies and unlikely allusions within a soberly functional object. *JG-1991-4* mixes a fragment of ornamental carving with a photocopy of a similar leafy pattern. The serpentine curves of photocopy and found object echo and rhyme each other to become one organic system. The script-fonted word "Soma" is written on the right to mirror the carved wood on the left, containing two halves of this new body between them. "Soma" means body but also refers to an intoxicating plant juice used in Vedic rituals. Giegerich's imagined anatomy pulses with a hallucinatory reverie of circulating analogies and analogies of circulation.

Sometimes Giegerich adheres photocopied images to her objects. Photocopies are already something of a ruin of an original photo; their loss of resolution and characteristic degradation is romantically picturesque. Her treatments amplify the sense that time has passed, both at the level of an aged-looking image and as evidence of a labored process. The photocopies provide both a trompe-l'oeil surface texture and a collaged-in reference to other subjects. Meanwhile, the brassy presence of actual candlesticks, french horns, and kitchenware collage their way into Giegerich's angled spaces from the world of real things. The readymade elements have more authority and less hand-inflected subjectivity than the photocopied or depicted elements and highlight the differences of voice between them. Sandpaper, rubber, wood, wax, copper, paper, and plywood conjure a sense that there are secret affinities between the elements. Giegerich nudges the substance of these materials in the direction of metaphor by playing hard against soft, smooth against rough, and things against absences. Valéry said that analogy is "the faculty of varying images, of combining them, of making part of one coexist with part of another and perceiving, voluntarily or otherwise, the similarities in their construction." He says, "Here words lose their virtue." Giegerich's analogies connect seeing to making.

Horns, megaphones, and amplifiers recur frequently in Giegerich's work. They say, like pedestals and drum rolls, "Behold! Here is something special!" We might think of the artwork as a PA system that paradoxically amplifies the artist's "voice" out of the object's fundamental silence. The cone that frequently sticks out of a Giegerich object could also, conversely, be understood as a receiver, like a dish antenna or an old fashioned hearing aid; her work is trying to listen,

Giegerich uses symbols with a light hand. She employs meaning fragments to promote a reticent but emphatically materialized content. She also uses strategic blanks, symbols in reverse, to solicit our projections. Does Giegerich risk

obscurity by cultivating a semi-private language? Perhaps some intangible judgements, praises, longings, or dreads need protective insulation to develop. These unverifiable contents also need the viewer's participation to gain strength. Perhaps our intuitions need a measure of security before they can rummage freely through subtle preferences, inclinations, memories and feelings. Giegerich's work shows ideas developing independently of language. Her practice even seems to be having an argument with words. Pictures, to James Elkins, are always to some degree "confusing, daunting, unexpectedly obdurate objects that possess formidable defenses against quick readings." Giegerich's work turns those defenses into invitations. She has constructed a sanctuary for interpretive play.

Giegerich has spoken of her desire for an image that is "empty enough." And how empty is that? Her work sometimes projects an alert lassitude, a reserved poise, neither needy nor pushy, occasionally jaunty but steadfastly private. She uses reticence as critical distance, a distance filled with the psychological charge of thwarted romanticism.

Valery said "Architecture is not, as a rule, comprehended." Not because people are stupid but because there is too much for anyone to absorb, too much to ever be described. That's good for art because there is freedom and musical sense in the fact that a structure's context and our point of view are in perpetual flux. Jill Giegerich's objects stimulate this flux into a harmonized plenitude.

2002

Dumbstruck

The word or words that make what I looked at to be itself were always words that to me very exactly related themselves to that thing the thing at which I was looking, but as often as not had as I say nothing whatever to do with what any words would do that described that thing.

Gertrude Stein, *Tender Buttons*

WE FOLLOW STEIN'S SENTENCES word by word looking for her sense. Painting followed by painting is how curatorial sense is more loosely built, but often, like Stein, the project is to tease at the limit of what can be named. The "things," in this exhibition authored by the artist Clint Jukkala, are paradoxically called "unnameable." His name (and idea) holds together a heterogeneous array of paintings by artists who each conjure unrecognizable objects. Connors, Ferris, Martin, Moyer, Overstreet, Blank-Rosenblum and Webster are names that adhere to their artworks in tenacious counterpoint to Jukkala's theme but also trace the outlines of a living aspiration in contemporary art: to test the limits of language with abstract paintings after the acknowledged collapse of the anti-language aspirations of modern art into a collection of conventionalized idioms. These new paintings explore the possibilities of invention within the unexpectedly eccentric contemporary language of annexation, plunder, and citation.

My favorite unnamable object in recent art history is the notched egg/portal in Henri Matisse's painting *The Moroccans* at MoMA. Its enigmatic sense of necessity and poised isolation within the painting is a byproduct of Matisse's peculiar will-to-form. He seems to be trying, with workman-like earnestness, to get it right, to distill his relation to the observed subject into an essence but, instead, has hatched an image appropriate for this show.

What we thought was profundity is made of surfaces like a stack of dirty plates.

William H. Gass, *Habitations of the Word*

THE NAMELESSNESS of the images in this exhibition extends an invitation for us to project. The paintings present de-semiotized objects that nonetheless promote allusions and analogies to familiar things. Suggestive likenesses emerge thanks to the visual cues provided by these artists and by our irrepressible habits of navigating the visual field. Keltie Ferris's atomized dots and line fragments hover between conjuring an image and anarchic collapse; their disheveled exuberance masks a keen formality. Palma Blank-Rosenblum's futuristic architectural images test disorder from the other side; they are built as if for rational purpose but without identifiable function.

Swifter than light the world converts itself into that thing you name, and all things find their right place under this new and capricious classification… call it a blossom, a rod, a wreath of parsley, a tamarisk-crown, a cock, a sparrow, the ear instantly hears and the spirit leaps to the trope…

Ralph Waldo Emerson, *Journals*

EMERSON WANTS US to feel our thoughts more directly than when we craft them into phrases. Does naming drain perceived objects of their intractable otherness by converting them into language? Giving something a name might be an exercise of power but these painters promote the object's resistant otherness. The protagonists in Carrie Moyer's paintings are congestions of spilled paint and delineated shapes that confront us with our tendency to anthropomorphically project agency into objects. The close-at-hand intimacy of things is evoked, disassembled and reordered according to deceptively straightforward logics in Matt Connors's constructed paintings. The works in *Unnameable Things* raise questions about the effects of language on perception in the context of contemporary culture.

The sacred was grounded in a pictorial practice of nonverisimilitude, in opposition to every poetics or rhetoric of verisimilitude… a pictorial practice of dissemblance.

Georges Didi-Huberman, *Fra Angelico, Dissemblance and Figuration*

FOR DIDI-HUBERMAN, DISSEMBLANCE, as exemplified in the faux-marble sections of Fra Angelico's paintings, was a way to theologically enact unrepresentable mysteries; the automatism of spattered paint could perform as if it was a supernatural otherness infused into the visibly familiar aspect of things. Pictorial conventions are employed by these painters to stage non-figurative picture-events. As a consequence the opacity of the medium is intensely contrasted with the transparency of the picture fiction and process becomes thematic. The iconic and diagrammatically abstract figures in Chris Martin and Chuck Webster's paintings promote a devotional relationship to their images. Clearly delineated elements are laid out as if counting them could matter (the syncopated five against six layers of Webster's blob-tree; six, two, then five fuzzy Martin dots punctuating his woozy biomorphs) but the math is hard to reckon because the axioms are occult. Baker Overstreet's symmetrical images share Martin and Webster's iconic geometry but with a heightened sense of comic menace.

I imagine a version of pictures in which a miscellany of ill-matched and ill-behaved marks congregate into assemblages that sometimes look as if they possess linguistic sense and then dissipate into rudimentary "meaningless" elements.
James Elkins, *On Pictures and the Words that Fail Them*

I IMAGINE A VERSION OF CATALOGUE ESSAYS in which a miscellany of ill-matched and ill-behaved quotes and paintings congregate into assemblages that sometimes look as if they possess linguistic sense then dissipate into rudimentary "meaningless" elements. The stubborn muteness of painting dramatically contrasts with the easy loquacity of advertising's instrumental picture-rhetorics.
2007

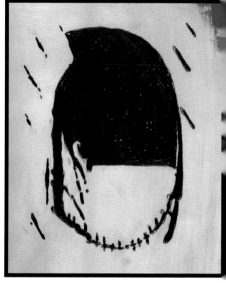

David Humphrey, *Detail from Matisse's Morrocans*, 2007

Carrie Moyer, *Rope Dancer*, 2007

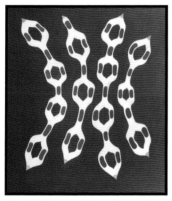

Chuck Webster, *Deep Beneath My Fingers*, 2007

Chris Martin, *Untitled*, 2002-4

Martin Ramirez

HE REFUSED TO SPEAK, but with the aid of tongue depressors to draw straight lines and glue made of spit and oatmeal, Martin Ramirez made some of the most articulate images of modern times. Torqued landscapes undulate around a religiously infused repertory company of trains, zoomorphic cars, and armed people on horseback. He would surely be surprised to find his work a model for much that is produced within the asylum/studios of contemporary MFA programs.

2008

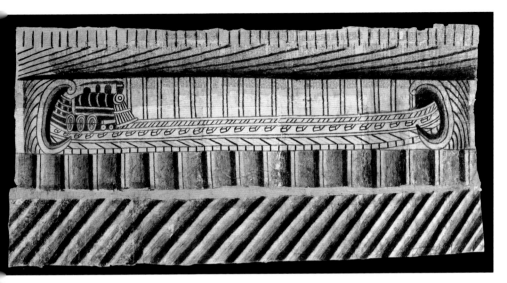

Martin Ramirez,
38 UNTITLED,
1948 - 1963

Tarmo Paso and Martin
Ramirez, at DeWitt
State Hospital in Auburn
California c. 1950s.

Carl Ostendarp

CARL OSTENDARP'S WORK MAKES a virtue of dopey muteness. His irreverent tone and the second-handedness of his imagery resist attempts critics have made to intellectualize his practice as a meta-commentary on the utopian history of abstract painting. Ostendarp's use of reductivist graphic elements encourages the idea that painting is a language-like signifying practice while limiting the amount of content it is capable of purveying. In *A Kick in Time*, 1994, the horizon intersects the hook of a large periwinkle question mark silhouetted against the sky. The image is a caricature of hermeneutic solicitation. It asks us, with smiley innocence, to consider the content to be a question. The meandering edge between pink sky and washy off-white ground assumes the position of a blank sentence punctuated by the oversized question mark. Likewise, *Untitled*, 1994 presents the stem of an exclamation mark sitting on the horizon, divided from its anchoring dot below.

Ostendarp's *Untitled* is a flat, cartoon splatter. The paradoxical wetness of its carefully delineated turquoise splash, like the exclamation mark, sits with mock exuberance on the washy violet ground. The off-pitch sweetness of Ostendarp's pastel colors locates his neo-formalist project somewhere near the nursery. His work encourages us to wonder if abstraction's traditional aspiration to inhabit a space outside language has become a point of ridicule. Is a burlesqued form of that aspiration the new way of sustaining it?

1994

Fiona Banner

CAN A PERIOD EXCISED FROM THE END OF A SENTENCE still function as a stop? Without words a period has no meaning, except in the eccentric production of Fiona Banner. She makes oversize graphite depictions on paper of periods in various fonts in order to execute a hyperliteral form of close reading. While the period is a humble punctuation mark that operates with near invisibility at the terminus of sentences, it swells to insistent proportions in Banner's work, a blind spot. She has loaded its bodiless functionality with a cargo of association and matter. Her periods become ridiculous ends to sentences never uttered. They shout "STOP!" in the face of the paper's blank whiteness.

Artworks, too, in the way they solicit a pause, can be understood as punctuating the flow of consciousness. The evidence of labor and accumulation of substance in *Bodoni*, 1999, for example, arrests attention in the manner of abstract images. The circuitous route Banner's period has traversed—from its origins as an undistinguished text navigator to its bloated destination in a gallery—forms a narrative, however, that deviates from abstraction's anti-narrative tendencies.

Bodoni's repetitive mark-making accumulates illegibly, like writing on top of itself. Her period acquires a mute density that, while no longer articulating the pause or breath between utterances, speaks of an unrepresentable excess of language embodied without content. Banner traffics in words, even when they are physically absent. When her work includes actual writing, such as the narration from memory of Michael Cimino's film *Deer Hunter* in *This is it*, 1999, the words feel abandoned. Their life as utterances seems used up, adrift in an anamorphic nether-space between projected shadow and dumb stuff. Banner sends writing into a restlessly dynamic world of things and images to collide with our ever-moving expectations and desires.

1999

Rémy Zaugg

ONE WAY to describe a monochrome painting is as a canvas washed clean. Whatever image one might expect to see has been scrubbed away, and new interpretations are to be projected onto the antiseptic blank. Rémy Zaugg silkscreens some descriptions of that blank directly onto white monochrome paintings. In a work from the series entitled *From the Past*, 1990–94, the words ELAPSED, MUFFLED, DELETED, FINISHED, EXTINCT and EFFACED are printed in off-white directly onto the painting's pristine surface. The words articulate the belatedness of certain Minimalist aspirations, while their pale contrast to the ground embodies the meaning of the words (and perhaps also his interpretation of Minimalism's ongoing significance). The reductive specificity of a non-metaphorical, nonrepresentational, and emptied-out Minimalist object has become conventional and familiar. Zaugg filled it with what the originators labored to exclude—associations. When he prints the words FADED, CHOKED, EMPTY, ERASED, ENDED, and BLANK onto a painting, it's hard to know whether he intends to lament, sneer, or simply describe. We see words in the past tense, constituting a paradoxical leftover; emptiness has been effaced, a blank wiped out. Other works suggest that Zaugg intends to be neutral, preoccupied with reflexive rhetorical conundrums. JUST IMAGINE YOU ARE/ STANDING HERE/IN FRONT OF ME is written on a large canvas, asking us to imagine what is perhaps already the case, depending on how we understand "me." What at first seemed an epistle of longing cools off when the adjacent painting asks to JUST IMAGINE/THE PAINTING SEES YOU/ BUT YOU DO NOT SEE IT. The reciprocity seems pedagogical: theoretical, programmatic, or banal.

1994

Marcus Raetz

MARCUS RAETZ dedicates his work to the vicissitudes of looking. He elaborates the conditions of sight into metaphors, images, and allegories. Casting the immobile act of reading into a motile world of objects in space, his word pieces literally can't be read from a single position. Art is always encountered in passing, but a Raetz needs our motion to disclose the work's text or reveal its image. In pieces such as *TODO-NADA*, 1998, a second word is hidden behind the face of the first. As we move around the object, TODO emerges to eclipse NADA after a transition in which they are both illegible: "All" replaces "Nothing." *TODO-NADA* has the marvelous ingenuity of an anamorphic palindrome. *SAME*, 1996-99, is similarly ingenious. Wire letters spelling the word "same" sit before a mirror that uncannily reflects them without reversing the text. A stroll to the other side of the piece shows the word still unreversed in the mirror. Each view has eclipsed the natural inversion of the other. It's a trick that mocks expectations and coaches an attentiveness to perceptual habits.

Raetz renders mobility conspicuous and necessary. His works highlight the way seeing is not a static or passive operation but involves cognitive anticipations and a synthesis of dynamically shifting perceptions. Sight lines and light directions are structured as physical forces. *Nichtpfeife*, 1991-92, is a senseless ribbon of cast iron until we are positioned to recognize the careful depiction of a pipe and a sly reference to Magritte's painting *The Betrayal of Images*, whose famous legend "This is not a pipe" *Nichtpfeife* wordlessly refigures. We tread carefully through a Raetz exhibition aware that our point of view is structurally integral. His work warps the centrality of vision by toying with our processes of recognition and misrecognition.

1998

Carl Ostendarp, *A Kick in Time*, 1994

Fiona Banner, *Bodoni*, 1999

A SELFPORTRAIT
THE TOWN
A WINDOW

Remy Zaugg, *A Selfportrait The Town A Window*, 1990

N A D A

...us Raetz, *Todo-Nada*, 1998

Gulliver's Travels

Since Words are only Names for Things, it would be more convenient for all Men to carry about them, such Things as were necessary to express the particular Business they are to discourse on.

Chuck Close

CHUCK CLOSE'S NEW PAINTINGS look good from about seventeen feet, where his depiction methods seem to extrude a lunatic potential from the features of his portrait subjects. One step closer and the mark-making becomes uninspired; step further back and the paintings become familiar brand-name heads.

2007

Ricci Albenda

RICCI ALBENDA ASKS US TO LOOK VERY CAREFULLY at what our body is programmed to ignore: minutiae within the sense of sight. Our brain thankfully fuses the different information sent by our right and left eyes into a single three-dimensional vision of the world. It conveniently overlooks each eye's subtle irregularities of strength and character. Albenda has constructed a project called *Do You See What I See*, 1996, to draw those deviations into consciousness. Seven apparently indistinguishable paintings of the word "people" are variations and copies designed to reflect the conditions under which they were rendered; painted with only the left eye, the right eye, or the mind's eye, at 12.5 or 25 feet. With a hypochondriac's attention to detail, Albenda scrutinizes what he calls "the individual experiences of my left and right eyes." Using a customized generic font he attempts to depict the idiosyncratic warp each eye applies to this word.

For all its narrowly focused attention to detail, however, there is another warp to Albenda's project. As we compare images, noticing small deviating curvatures in serif details or off-degree drifts to each letter's axis and alignment, our confidence begins to erode in disorienting ways. How can we judge these precise measurements with our eyes alone? The word "people" becomes lost in the seven repetitions; the spelling seems wrong and its meaning diffuses. The word "people" is completely irrelevant to our task of trying to see the differences between paintings. Albenda sends the meaning on vacation so it can return later, perhaps after we have considered the relation between language and perception. Albenda has performed a solitary self-administered test in which we others are anticipated by what the word signifies. An oversize period sits to the right of the word in each painting as if it were the snipped-off end of a sentence whose beginning we can only imagine—an example could be "Perhaps there is a relationship between Albenda's preoccupation with his eyes and his connection to other people."

The careful hand-paintedness of these works amplifies their first-person point-of-view while also casting a shadow of uncertainty on the evidence being presented; Albenda can say, or paint, whatever he wants. He shows great skill working the edges between white background and black word as he adjusts the details of the image. His revisions "tell," in almost narrative fashion, of his desire to get it right. We can't see, however, what he sees without factoring out our own idiosyncratic warps. The paintings seem to reflect the bend of Albenda's ocular experience but our own eyes skew the images again. We are spun into a little maelstrom of dissonant perceptual minutiae. Vision, we have been taught, is entangled with sensory-motor behavior. When Albenda focuses on micro-ocular phenomena he indirectly illuminates his own complicated behavior as an artist. The intensity of his mimetic labors seems guided by a hope for sympathetic magic; that the act of copying could possibly bring about changes in the source.

1996

people.

Willem de Kooning

WILLEM DE KOONING IGNORED the insulting bafflement of old age as he plunged into a last decade of explosive productivity; between 1983 and 1985 he painted more than fifty paintings a year. The airborne radiance, muscular inventiveness and comic lyricism of these last works continued their forceful evolution until illness finally shut the artist down.

De Kooning's late paintings established interpictorial dialogues with his earlier work through the use of tracing, projectors, and copying. His vocabulary of forms, found in *Fire Island*, 1946, *Orestes*, 1947 and *Woman*, 1953, was later enlarged and simplified in cartoon-like ways. Sometimes de Kooning would look at a drawing or reproduction held in one hand while painting with the other in order to inject the earlier forms into a new picture. Toward the end assistants would often project a drawing onto a blank canvas to get him started.

Untitled XIX, 1985, features a swerving tangle of red and blue lines buttressed by antic yellow shapes. A stylized yellow teardrop is limned by red, white, and blue as it pulls toward the painting's right edge. A pastoral whiteness both floats between and buoys the colored elements. De Kooning used a spackling knife to give the ground a power to exert pressure on the line's cursive itinerary. These late paintings groom his earlier collisions of paint into a torqued choreography of mutually defining forms.

A skeptical grace inflects de Kooning's sense of purpose. He was always proud of his workman-like intimacy with materials and techniques, but his gestures serve a sly pictorial wit in which expectations are systematically derailed. De Kooning's work, from the beginning, made unequivocal assertions about contingent states of presence; his marks dynamically build and unravel the forms in ways that are surprisingly sexy. The biomorphic parts relate to each other as an erotics of adjacency in which boundaries are nudged and jostled with slippery urgency. The visual puns of his *Women* series, in which a torso could become a face or slur into a landscape, relaxes in his late works to register the internal pressures and imperatives of his process.

De Kooning pursued a lifelong investigation into pictorial coherence. He famously referred to himself as a slipping glimpser, indicating both his preoccupation with small perceptual moments and his embrace of the accidental. The athleticism of his glimpsing, though, and the comic timing of his slips, in the late work, changes the sense of that original self-characterization. He became a practiced master in control of a big vision. Meanwhile these last works have none of the weight and death-awareness sometimes associated with Late Style. De Kooning collapses Kierkegaard's notion that we live forward but understand backward; it appears that dementia lightened his burden of memory without impairing his historically informed forward drive.

2007

Milton Resnick

MILTON RESNICK'S PAINTINGS CLAIM A KIND OF EXISTENTIAL IRREDUCIBILITY, a "pure" presence. In recent work, Resnick has introduced crude figures into his signature habitat of atmospheric muck. While painted mostly in gouache, which is less viscous than oil paint, they continue to project a sense of dense privacy. Stripped of individual characteristics, the painted figures seem to be rag doll ciphers of the artist's desiring will. If his earlier paintings attempted a transcendence of the self by diffusing it into an allover field, these newer paintings attempt to distill a self out of that that field. The figure is only slightly differentiated from its ground. Titles such as *The Judgment of Paris*, *Sphinx*, and *A Serpent on the Scene* invoke a narrative context without much help from brushstrokes unconcerned with the demands of making a representation. Indeed, it is often unclear whether we are presented with the figure's front or back. These figures are both coming into and evacuating the picture.

1997

Jorg Immendorff

IT IS HARD TO LOOK AT a new work by Jorg Immendorff without thinking about his robust forty-year career or his challenge of making very large paintings with advanced Lou Gehrig's disease, amyotrhic lateral sclerosis. Gone are the mid '80s lighting effects, exaggerated perspectives, and politically charged German narratives. Immendorff's last work embraced a more individualistic symbolic content. The five oversize *Untitled*, 2006 paintings are compositions derived from sources ranging from the master etchings of Dürer, Hogarth, and de Gheyn, to photographs from magazines and newspapers. Immendorff continued, however, to make Big Paintings redolent with Big Ideas: ideology, culture, the self, death, and the body. **But his old jaunty tone became elegiac while the politics turned inward.**

Bigness, for Immendorff, was always complicated by crappiness, which, in the vernacular of '80s German painting, indicated critical distance combined with a refined anarchist connoisseurship; the artist must not show too much interest in the painting's quality or risk betraying its radicality. That attitude seems to have diminished, but not vanished, as Immendorff began painting with the help of projectors and assistants.

In a few of the paintings, trees spread across silvery twilight atmospheres with depictions of windblown newspaper, magazine, and book reproductions getting caught in their branches. The various modes of representation from Immendorff's source-images (prints, photos, etc.) are also suggested in these paintings as he layers them into composite worlds. In another *Untitled*, the biomorphic silhouette of a painter's palette encloses an etching caricature of a group of eighteenth-century men singing in the background while a woman in Renaissance-modeled biblical robes strolls across a landscape in the foreground. The painting is bisected by an anamorphically stretched photo-image of a man raising his hand, perhaps taking an oath, inside a transparent beaker. The repetition of alchemical images in many of these paintings suggests a desire for their various parts to combine into transformational wholes. *Untitled*'s oversize palette contains the chattering of many different pasts now orchestrated into Immendorff's enigmatic song of himself.

Another *Untitled* painting features a Vesalius flayed man presenting his own unraveling musculature beside a vascular red plant with an image of a Siamese-twin hermaphrodite tangled in its leaves. Immendorff's last paintings promote analogies between inside and outside, individuals and the cosmos. The melodramatic picture-theater and agitational aspirations of his earlier work are sustained with a melancholic brittleness. A rusting cast-iron sculpture from 1999 of a dead tree trunk with a palette and painter's maulstick is like a nineteenth-century-style cemetery memorial to the Artist.

Immendorff's image pile-ups declare a resistance to legibility underwritten by political outrage and aggressive narcissism. He creates a politics of space in which his role is both performer and audience.
2007

Willem de Kooning, Untitled XX, 1977

Milton Resnick, *Judgement of Paris*, 1991

Jörg Immendorff, *Untitled*, 2006

Ike and Me

DWIGHT EISENHOWER WAS THE BLAND GRANDFATHERLY PRESENCE ON THE TV of my earliest childhood. The 1960s slowly pushed his memory into a prehistory fossilized somewhere deep in my father's soldierly sense of responsibility and my aversion to that sense. Art school fortified my aversion even as my application portfolio was filled with stone carvings I had done with Dad's tools and hobbyist coaching. Dwight Eisenhower, like my father, made art in his spare time.

Even as contemporary art has perennially defined itself against the unconsidered appetites of popular taste, artists, myself included, have mined the vernacular for unexpected insight. Many of my paintings are variations or interpretations of works I find online or in flea markets. Dwight Eisenhower's paintings presented an irresistible adventure. His work exemplifies what Christopher Bollas would call normotic, the pathologically normal. There are no displays of fancy brushwork, no compositional or iconographic ingenuities, no indication of art-historical knowledge or ambition. Ike's work has just the right mix, for my purposes, of rhetorical modesty, hyper-conventionality, and subtle idiosyncrasy borne through awkwardness and error, but underwritten by our knowledge of his life as the victorious Supreme Allied Commander and post-war President of the United States. Ike was the author of a successful memoir and, consequently, very aware of the earning power of his signature. In 1968 he published a suite of "limited edition" reproductions of his paintings with the name of each owner printed below the image alongside its title, size, medium, and copyright.

Ike copied greeting cards and family snapshots, but his preferred idiom was the pastoral landscape, images of simpler times with variations on covered bridges, water mills, and family farms. He painted, at Winston Churchill's suggestion, to relax. But the unrelaxed spectator happily looks for the buried cargo of ideologies and unintended associations, links between the work's banal operations and dominating social structures, repressed themes and off-beat formalities.

The Deserted Barn, 1958 is Ike's depiction of a derelict building surrounded by signs of a life now over. Its compositional (normotic) straightforwardness seems to mask an elaborately encrypted code-language. Every pictorial element lines up as if it were part of a glyph-sentence. The hatching lines that depict the barn's deteriorating roof tiles march horizontally with casual cuneiformic regularity until an uncanny hole appears in the shape of a Greek cruciform. Doors and windows, trees and fences all seem to be arrayed in hieroglyphic code sentences. The barn's dark interior suggests a longing to speak a language it has failed to learn, while, outside, the abandoned red wagon and water pump, with lowered handles, echo the aging Ike's self-reflective theme of a now-passed usefulness.

I begin my treatments of Ike's compositions by doing a loose copy, which often becomes the location for characters inserted from my image repertoire. I make one-way collaborations in which the long transcription of Ike's image builds an emotionally inflected connection between us. The effort draws me to marvel at the labored specificity of his choices: this cone-shaped tree here, that oddly rendered rock placed so deliberately there. My attentions constitute a form of contact, intimacy within a context of extreme detachment. I'm spending at least as much time making these images as he did. My feelings about his spaces inflect the progress of my work. Ike's semi-skilled efforts promise accessibility to the powerful man through the back door of his conformist solitary passion. Politics and the military are team sports; painting is for tyrants.

Within mainstream art discourse, especially in 1968, Ike's work was considered ludicrous, reactionary, and sentimental. Today his work can more easily be seen as a charming relic whose rhetorical simplicity no longer threatens. Since Dad's death I have come to cherish his carvings, while, in some parallel softening, contemporary art is less inclined to insist upon its radicality. Do we automatically assume, given our knowledge of Eisenhower's politics and country club patrons, that his paintings are consistent and coherent reinforcers of the status quo? His escapist intentions have become happily complicated for us partly because of his art-historical blindness and also because we have come to enjoy, perhaps even to be moved by, dated clichés and earnest mistakes.

Eisenhower was instrumental in developing the American highway system and an early form of the Internet, but his paintings are mute on those subjects. My paintings treat Eisenhower's blankness as though it were pathological. I, perhaps also pathologically, introduce sexual overtones and semiotic horseplay to his material, playing fast and loose with the historical record. Like an amateur, I fuck things up in my own way. Perhaps becoming President could help me relax.

2006

Dwight D. Eisenhower, *The Deserted Barn*, 1958

Dwight D. Eisenhower, *The Covered Bridge*, 1958

David Humphrey, *Ike's Woods*, 2006

Eisenhower at his easel.

Jeffrey Vallance

COMBINING THE DEVOTED THOR-
OUGHNESS OF AN OBSESSIVE WITH
THE IRREVERENCE of an art-world prankster,
Jeffrey Vallance has assembled "The Richard
Nixon Museum." One of the small galleries at
Rosamund Felsen was converted into a full institu-
tion of Nixon artifacts, complete with a library,
gift shop, and tape tour. Vallance caricatures the
recently opened Nixon Library and Birthplace as
a curio hound's collection of personal treasures.

Some titles from Vallance's library, consisting
of a shelf-sized selection from the vast Nixon bibli-
ography, help to guide us: *In Search of Nixon, The
Facts About Nixon, The Nixon Nobody Knows, The
Nixon Theology*. Nixon's image here is multiplied
beyond the bounds of coherence. It expands the
contours of his familiar historical persona to diffuse
into a mythically comic atmosphere. *The Nixon
Museum Cabinet*, at the center of the exhibition, contains an impressive inventory of Nixon
memorabilia and commemorative objects—nail-
clippers, golf balls, watches, roach clips, thimbles,
paperweights, matchbooks, pins, coins, toys,
glasses, silverware, masks, clothing, and more, all
augmented with Nixon iconography, and the much
sought-after campaign button "They Can't Lick Our
Dick." The incantatory monotony of his repeated
and mutating image cycles us back to the ominous
campaign slogan/mantra "Nixon's the One."

These Nixons, however, are Vallances. Nixon
is absorbed into the rhetorical voice of Vallance's
art. By including original works among mass-
produced portraits and bric-a-brac, Vallance divides
himself as both the overarching collector and the
collected. The fact that Nixon's career
spans the period of Vallance's childhood and adolescence suggests that
what is being collected are memories.
An *Autographed Drawing of Richard Nixon* was
made by Vallance in 1971, when he was 16.
The artist forged living links between Nixon, his
own teen past, and the present by copying the
ex-president's signature onto the portrait. Each
article is evidence of a lost past and an attempt
to recollect order from it. Vallance shamelessly
blends his personal Nixon fiction with the ones
on public record, amplifying the slow process by
which facts are organized into a fictional collective
"self" by institutions, politicians, and individuals.

This is consistent
with Vallance's earlier
projects, which also ad-
dressed the intersect-
ing terms of religion,
folklore, and national
symbols. The work
that grew out of his
visits to the kingdom of
Tonga and Iceland were
likewise testaments
to the impossibility of
ethnographic objectivity
and celebrations of the
impure hybrids those
interactions tend to
produce. His radically
un-ironic method and
Boy Scout thorough-
ness give the work a
deadpan hilarity while

earning access to keep-
ers of the faith. Vallance
has also done work
based on written corre-
spondence with various
institutions and public
figures, such as the
Vatican, U.S. senators,
and foreign heads of
state. Such letters both
highlight the extreme
power asymmetry
between Vallance and
his subject, and also
create a document in
which they are joined.
Identity is confirmed,
even if abjectly, by of-
ficial correspondence.
1991

Jeffrey Vallance, *The Traveling Nixon Museum*, 1989

Hildred Goodwine and the Desert Caballeros Museum

I WOULD HAVE TRAVELED VERY FAR out of my way to see Hildred Goodwine's paintings of "Happy Horses," but I saw them while visiting my grandmother in Arizona. Goodwine's "believable scenes of barnyard behavior" threw off my seen-everything sense of aesthetic balance. She executed her paintings in the '60s for "Western and regional interest greeting cards." Like most greeting cards, her work is disconcertingly eager to please, but I felt their saccharine atmospheres as almost too innocent, as though her depictions of interspecies frolicking would break into depraved mayhem as soon as I turned my back. I would like to make paintings that do that.

This is also what I love about Wickenburg's Desert Caballeros Museum, where I saw Goodwine's paintings. I enjoy the awkward earnestness of the place, especially its period rooms stuffed with pop objects culled from people's homes, local thrift stores, and antique dealers. The rooms are inhabited by mannequins from a recent past acting out that era's fantasy about a more distant past. There are also sections of the museum for history, geology, and Native American objects as well as the museum's collection of Western art. The arrangement tells a story of eccentric cultural compass; the constellation of stuff is a caricature of the encyclopedic museums of the east.

My late grandfather put a lot of time and effort into the Desert Caballeros Museum after he retired; raising money, renovating the building, and expanding the collection. He spent his life in the East, so cowboys, Indians, and desert life were exotic to him. I think, like Goodwine, my grandfather's labors sometimes produced effects satisfyingly divergent from their wholesome aims.

2000

Hildred Goodwine, *Cup O' Sugar,* 1973

Douglas Blau

THERE DOESN'T SEEM TO BE A FIT-
TING WORD for picture literacy; like picturacy.
Everybody is "picturate" in their own way, depending on what pictures they've seen and how they've
learned to look at them.

Douglas Blau's *Genre: The Conversation Piece*,
1993 is divided into three salon style installations
of hundreds of photographs and reproductions.
Like his earlier piece *The Naturalist Gathers*, 1992,
Genre: The Conversation Piece is a dense clustering
of related imagery framed identically to diminish
the differences between painting, commercial
illustration, photojournalism and film stills while
amplifying characteristics of the figurative genre.
The imagined, the staged, the historical and the
contemporary are coaxed into easy coexistence
while image rhetorics are highlighted. Where Blau's
The Naturalist Gathers was auto-figurative in the
way it allegorized the process of cataloging, *Genre:
The Conversation Piece* is autofigurative of its
relation to the spectator; it proposes various versions of the viewer as a silent auditor. To converse
with a picture is partially to suspend disbelief and
step into its fiction; boundaries soften. Blau's
arrangement of closely related fictions encourages
us to slip from one picture to another without
completely recovering those lapsed boundaries.
Images of people talking with each other range
from large governmental assemblies to smaller
conferences, gaming situations, committees,
parties, intimate domestic settings and one solitary
person talking on the phone. We see conversation as a flexible medium of social bonds.

Except in the case of a Whistler self-portrait,
nestled within a cluster of hazy landscapes, there
are almost no figures that look out toward the
viewer. Our spectatorial role develops
as a trans-historic eavesdropper. By
not providing any background material about the
images Blau encourages us to invent narrative
possibilities within and between them. He uses the
collection as an instrument for meta-storytelling.
Cataloging, cross-referencing and comparing don't
result in clear taxonomies so much as a shifting
cloud of differential relationships and unfolding
poetic sense. Blau examines the ways genre, myth,
and ideology are rhetorically interrelated in the
picturing of social groups. *Genre: The Conversation

Piece* is itself, of course, a conversation piece.
Like the work of a nineteenth century gentle-
man naturalist, we are presented with gathered
specimens, seemingly detached from their original
context and the imperatives of commerce. The
special and intimate character of ownership for
this collector is rendered paradoxical in a gallery
exhibition space. Like a conversation, though, the
particular history of each image and the story of
how it came into Blau's possession is something
no person can own. The grandiose and obsessive
eloquence of *Genre: The Conversation Piece*
scrambles the interpersonal and the interpictorial.

1993

Rachel Harrison

ELIZABETH TAYLOR would probably not be
happy about the unflattering pictures of her that
Rachel Harrison has embedded in the stuccoed
wall of *Bustle in Your Hedgerow*, 1999. The black
wall is an emblem of the privacy dividing Liz
from the prying paparazzi who took these tabloid
photographs. Liz, in a pink nightgown, is pictured
here in two shots taken just moments apart. The
two photos are embedded into different faces
of Bustle's L shaped wall so that they cannot be
seen at the same time. Harrison dilates the short
passage of time between those moments as
well as the meaning of the wall. The blurred and
touched-up images were produced to embarrass
the tired and overweight Ms. Taylor by proving
to us that she is all-too-human. But in Harrison's
treatment Liz is not just like us but becomes a
star in a new system of unhinged references.

Untitled, 1999, is a framed photograph
pinned to a lumpy green blob; a fat middle-aged
white man is pictured sitting with a young Asian
woman. What joins the man and woman in
Untitled seems as incongruent as the connection
of the picture to the bright green lump, both are
now permanently but precariously attached. The
woman looks back over the man's oversized
gut with a dissociated awareness of their asym-
metrical and probably sordid bond. He is doubled
in a mirror behind them that strangely doesn't
reflect her, his gut occluding her body. *Untitled*
is a cyclops asteroid whose orbit catches a
glimpse of this young woman's eclipsed life.

Harrison's photos are attention-magnets that
reorient all the other attributes of the sculpture.

The photographs are details with a disproportionate power to signify, hot spots that refuse to explain their role. In *Reno*, 1999 a photo of a man in a control booth is embedded like a television screen into the surface of the craggy dark object. The work is a caricature of a sculpture sitting askew on its pedestal; it playfully mocks the conventional hierarchy of object and base, image and frame. The geometry of the base blossoms into a more gnarled and disorganized form on top while the surface and color suggests a material of great density. Our gaze, as we stare down at Reno, is echoed by the technician's attentive relation to his consol. We assess the work's illusory weight without the advantage of the worker's electronic equipment or the burden of being chained to a job. He's interpreting data according to a standardized criteria while we apply the unregulated standards of art spectators. The photo, which we don't notice until circling to the back of Reno, refigures and rewards our role as ambulatory browsers.

1999

Douglas Blau, *The Conversation Piece*, 1993 (detail)

Rachel Harrison, *Reno*, 1999

Kate Kuharic

KATE KUHARIC'S PAINTINGS ARE
FILLED with objects. Here's a list: one can of
Campbell's mushroom soup, one jar of Ragú spa-
ghetti sauce, Susie from the St. Louis Knights of
Columbus, the Radio City Music Hall Rockettes in
white pantless tuxedo drag, a Dirt Devil MO912000
vacuum cleaner. The list is long but very specific.
Everything in a Kuharic painting is emphatically
specific, described in detail by her high-resolution
mark making. Kuharic's depiction-labors are
devotional; they declare, by the evidence of time
and effort, that each object matters. She invites
us to have feelings for the hyper-specificity of her
objects while also demonstrating that they are not
isolated singularities. Kuharic's objects are deeply
embedded in a system of meaning, placed into
image-sentences with socially charged content.

Bill Brown, in his book *A Sense of Things*,
writes, "Thingness is precipitated as a kind of
misuse value." He points out that we have a
heightened sense of things when they are momentarily out of context. He uses the example of a
knife used as a screwdriver, but one could equally
refer to the symbolically retooled objects from the
painting *Backwards Flag*, 1999: two cushioned
chairs with floral upholstery, a young smiling
lesbian of a recent type, a dolphin sticker and a
Snoopy sticker stuck to a female miner's hardhat.

Kuharic's amped-up pictures derive from
photographs. Collage is used as a source and
method of organization, but her renderings produce
a heightened sense of presence. They aren't
just pictures of pictures; the paintings
prefer to elbow past the intermediary
photograph to conjure the presence of
original objects. Nuanced inflections of light
and edge secure each object into its functional
place within the compositional machine. Kuharic's
images radiate a sense of urgency in a style that
could be called Hyperbolic Realism. Objective
description is performed with intense subjectivity.
Her eccentricity thrives at both the level of tiny
marks and macro image selection. Severe cropping
gives some pictures a contingent snapshot quality
that tips the densely packed, highly constructed
compositions off balance. Conventionally unrelated
images and discontinuities of scale are dispersed
into promiscuously suggestive allegories. Human
subjects and inanimate objects are rendered

equivalent within the
densely colored and
built-up paint-skin.
Kuharic's ambitious
paintings sustain in con-
temporary terms what
T. E. Hulme praised
in historical modern
art, a "poetics of
sensual immediacy and
fragmentary vision."

*Super Bowl
Sunday*, 2003 takes
place in a world
brought low by disaster.
The corner of a tiled
bathroom stands alone
in the center of a chaos
of twisted pipes and
shattered houses. Six
product-flowers made
of spanking new con-
sumer products float
over the detritus like
alien spacecraft. One
of them, for example,
is made of fourteen
bottles of Gatorade
that fan out from a ring
of personal hygiene
products encircling
a ready-to-eat meat
sandwich. Kuharic's
tone is celebratory;
newness and desirabil-
ity blossom ecstatically
over the ruins. The
painting exempli-
fies what Brown
calls "the labor of
infusing manufac-
tured goods with
a metaphysical
dimension." It
reroutes a mass
cultural narrative of
objects, from a story of
production-distribution-
consumption to one of
deviant transformation.
Kuharic takes products
out of circulation

to recycle them
before they are used.
Freshness is preserved
by reinvigorated narra-
tive potential. Kuharic
saves consumer goods
from becoming waste
at the same time as
she saves them from
being used at all.

Kuharic's paintings
bear their secrets in
plain sight. Jokes are
hidden in a jaunty
picture-puzzle manner,
like a rebus. The tone
of her references and
associations range from
intimate to alienated.
Desire and aversion
are solicited according
to personal interest.
Kuharic's objects
are conscripted into
a regime of open-
ended narrative and
gendered symbolism.
All elements of the
painting are ceremoni-
ally locked into position.
Everything is where it
ought to be, but Kuharic
is both controller and
resister. Her imagina-
tion collides with the
congealed facts of
contemporary culture
to shake out ideas and
ideologies that might
be impacted there.
A Queer Populist
Hallucinatory Realism
celebrates the pos-
sibility of an alternative
to the existing order;
Kuharic shows that
the world is perhaps
already different from
what it seems.
2004

Kate Kuharic, *Super Bowl Sunday*, 2003

A Brighter Urge

A performative utterance is an offer of participation in the order of the law. And perhaps we can say a passionate utterance is an invitation to improvisation in the disorder of desire.
Stanley Cavell

THE WORDS

engraved on Jenny Holzer's marble bench ask "What urge/will save us/now that sex won't?" Maybe we hadn't thought that urges *could* save, but Holzer's "us" conjures a humankind in trouble. Before now, it suggests, things were different, brighter and sexier perhaps, but surely in the dark about what has come to pass. How about violent urges? McDermott and McGough's painting *The Vilest Way* sings with words painted in a variety of ingeniously fancy fonts "violate me/in violent times/the vilest way/that you know/ruin me ravage me/utterly savage me/on me no mercy/bestow."

Making art, of course, comes from an urge, mostly to bring new things into existence, but also to make a difference with them. Negativity, disorderliness, doubt, or misgivings can agitate the status quo. McDermott and McGough invite us to exercise aggressive urges that hold little promise of saving anything except the intensity between us and *The Vilest Way*. But like all good artworks, *The Vilest Way* performs its aesthetic operations with a faith that transformations will occur, even if only at the scale of one consciousness at a time.

Does the utopian urge always issue from an unhappy present? Negative artworks can both reveal conditions we weren't paying attention to and provoke us to imagine changes. Art is optimistic about loss; because artworks are relatively permanent (designed, mostly, to outlast us) they resist change and transience even if change and transience are their subjects.

Sometimes matter is tired and surrenders to entropy, rot, or decay, but metaphor, like mushrooms and compost, thrives on the weary forms. David Altmejd's *The Settler*, 2005 is a visionary celebration of debilitated and prodigal matter; it is a ruined chimera of interpenetrating animal, vegetable, and mineral substance. Mirrored crystalline forms, fur and clothing set in a theatrical display-case future tell a Gothic story that includes the ambient spectator's shattered reflection. Roxy Paine's *Vertical Mushroom* is like a woodsy cousin to Altmejd's settler. A stack of successively smaller species of mushroom grows from the cap of the one below to buoyantly demonstrate an uncanny poise and supra-naturally cooperative hybridity. *Vertical Mushroom* balances its bright ingenuity with a nervous sense that something is terribly wrong with the "natural" world. Artworks help us adapt to being unsettled and perhaps embrace unsettled as a positive value. Art encourages us, with impressions and feelings, to imagine the present as a fragile contingency that could be radically otherwise.

The future has arrived and its name is the present.
Terry Eagleton

Many contemporary artists work in the anticipatory mode of science fiction, paradoxically articulated in traditionally crafted materials. Alison Elizabeth Taylor's *Desert Forest*, 2006 depicts, with wood inlay, images of young adults hanging out around a campfire. Her *Russell Road*, 2006 pictures two women with a sports car parked in front of a geodesic home in the desert. Taylor's crafted marquetry exemplifies a pre-digital mode of representation while her imagery subtly and simultaneously suggests a post-apocalyptic survivalist utopia. The well-being of her small, quasi-tribal groups seems troubled by unseen, off-frame threats. Their simplified existence seems irradiated by the undulating wood-grain patterns of the marquetry.

Caspar David Friedrich's painting *The Sea of Ice*, 1823-24 ponders the cruel and magnificent implacability of nature, the catastrophic sublime. Karl Haendel ponders Friedrich's now-destroyed painting, sometimes known as *The Wreck of the Hope*, by copying it in pencil, tearing the drawing in half and then recontextualizing it with framed renderings of a family snapshot, a *New Yorker* cartoon, and a super-8 film canister. Haendel performs multi-

alent acts of devotion
and vandalism within
a self-curated context
of second-handedness.
His handmade repro-
ductions are extrava-
gantly inefficient but
obtain a slow-motion
grip on our culture's
ever-increasing surge
of visual material.
Haendel's strenuous
efforts highlight the
inherent ambiguity of
images, so routinely
pressed into com-
mercial or ideological
service, even as he
conscripts them for
his more subjective or
deviously critical aims.

These artists tell
elaborate stories about
the way urges bump
into obstacles, about
the way making an
art object can be an
act of salvation. They
convert limitations
and thwarted desire
into elaborate tales of

good-humored triumph
in an oppressive
environment of con-
formity and injustice.

The brilliance of the earth is the brilliance of every paradise.
Wallace Stevens
2006

Roxy Paine, *Vertical Sequence 4*, 2006

David Alltmejd, *The Settler*, 2005

WHAT URGE WILL
SAVE US NOW
THAT SEX WON'T?

Jenny Holzer, *Selections from Survival:*
What Urge Will Save Us…I,

Alison Elizabeth Taylor, *Desert Forest,* 2006

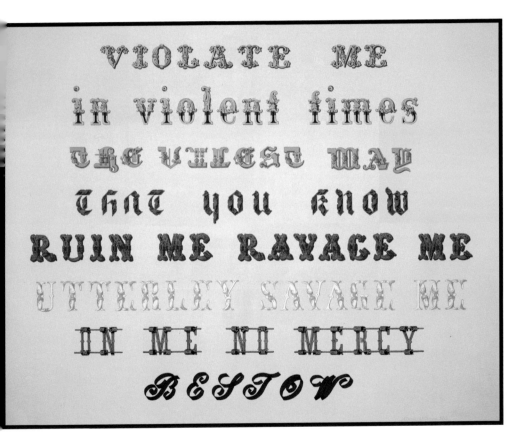

McDermott & McGough, *The Vilest Way*, 2005

Barnaby Furnas

BARNABY FURNAS'S NEW PAINT-INGS TOY with volatile forces that burn, punc-ture, explode, and flood. Three jumbo paintings are called *Red Sea* (Parting I, II, and IV), 2006 and invoke the Hebrew God's protective wrath with twenty-foot pours of brilliant red paint split-ting open against a clear blue sky. It's impossible to know whether we are viewing this deluge from the point of view of pursuer or pursued, but *Red Sea*'s depopulated grandeur suggests dead-ly force. Smaller paintings in the 2005-06 series depict single figures spurting blood from ritually applied wounds. Furnas uses the wetness of paint as both a theme and medium to perform incendiary acts of cruelty and celebration.

Furnas, for all the speed of his painterly execution, spends a lot of time torturing Jesus. Almost half of the fourteen paintings of single figures in this series depict the crucified one at various gory stages of his martyrdom. In *Before the Cross* I and II, Furnas's man of sorrows is seen through an atmosphere of bloody slashes that seem to both emanate from him and rain upon him. Two paintings called *Resurrection* evoke the Shroud of Turin with their puddling paint and spooky x-ray inner light. Two other Furnas paintings depict the abolitionist John Brown, who, like Jesus, was a reviled and murdered political criminal.

Furnas slyly toys with principles of the icon, fetish, or effigy by means of devotional paintings that victimize his subjects. Icons, fetishes, and effigies, for believers, possess a living, or indivis-ible, connection to what is depicted; behavior toward the representation is understood as behavior toward the person. Iconoclasts and iconophiles share this assumption about the power of images with Furnas who acts as both maker and destroyer. *Heart Fucker* presents a florid man in a gray pinstripe suit with a tie suggesting the confederate flag. The medium, listed as urethane, dye, and crayon on burned and cut stillborn calf skin, tells a story of innocence and ritual sacrifice even before we see the heavily vandal-ized image. Holes cut and burned into *Heart Fucker*'s surface seem to bleed while irreverent graffiti defaces it. The immobile bodies of Furnas's subjects passively endure their wounding trials while the artwork's ecstatic splatters and spills celebrate painting as a powerful force of creation and destruction.

But Furnas's depicted bodies have no interiors; they are, like paintings, all flat radiance and dramatic effect, easily punctured. His spasmodic ruptures of fragile boundar-ies could also function as a metaphor for art's weakness. His paintings possess a feeling of ethical panic at a time when art's charmed irresponsibility, in the face of ominous circumstances, is regularly being questioned.

2007

Inka Essenhigh

A SHINY BROWN LIQUID stretches across the top of Inka Essenhigh's painting *Large Fire*, 1998, like flames of chocolate. Upholstered with mint-cream cushions and restraining straps, the brown form seems to sink and rise at the same time. Below, two guys in padded uniforms attend to an apparent casualty of the viscous conflagration. The victim's hand drips with brown goo while a stretched filament of the stuff is stuck into his headless trunk. Is the brown coming out of him or does it come into him from above? Either way, it's a nasty business.

Large Fire's chocolate flames, rendered with high-gloss enamel, are an exaggerated dramatiza-tion of the slippery and aggressive power of wet paint. In Essenhigh's world, liquid is not only leaked or expressed from within the figures, but also threatens from without. Paintings like *Deluge* or *Virgin and Volcano* (all 1998) likewise allegorize paint as a comically mutant force of nature.

Essenhigh's images are made from flat shapes of slightly muted color conscripted into their various identities, such as rain clouds or palm trees, by tightly cinched black lines. Reflective monochrome backgrounds provide color-coordinated stages for these board-game disasters. Essenhigh's world is similar to prefabricated toy systems, such as Lego or Playmobil, with their interchangeable parts, cast plastic gear, uniformed action figures, and easy application to aggressive or paranoid scenarios. Shiny surfaces and flat shapes reinforce a sense that everything is made out of the same malleable material, with Essenhigh acting as both manufacturer and consumer. The highly wrought stylization of her depictions redouble a sense of control over subjects already disciplined by their role as playthings.

End of the World features a herd of fleeing and self-entangled horses. Parts are missing while the legless animals are propelled by obscure means. An unsaddled pistol-wielding cowboy stirs up anxiety as the cracking ground anticipates the end of everything. *Public Spirit* shows Marines having trouble undressing while they cavort on a floating cornfield pad. A cadet with braided hair lounges alone nearby. The faceless corps of figures in Essenhigh's paintings are sometimes hard to recognize; gender is pliable; limbs are cauterized; uniforms stretch into prosthetic gear for faceless muscle-bound amputees. Essenhigh perversely crafts a regulated and disaster-prone universe. In her orthopedic imagination of corrected flesh, everyone is trussed or unraveled—plugged, pinched, and bound into a cramped restlessness.

1998

Jane Fine

GOOEY paint runs downward to gravity's unceasing command. Its drippy legs elongate submissively until they've run out of juice. Paint-drips conventionally signify a relaxation of the artist's control; they look like accidents. But semi-autonomous paint-blobs are compelled by Jane Fine to co-operate with other blobs. She causes viscous goo to congeal into throbbing organs. Marker lines are then deftly drawn over these paint-piles to bind, suture, or corral them into entities capable of fighting against each other and launching onto antic adventures. The forms connect to each other with a clammy and sometimes hostile embrace that produces a psychological charge. They are imbued with personality without having a face. Camouflage greens lunge at candied reds and oranges. Martial exoskeletons face-off against confectionery invertebrates. Endomorphs and biomorphs cavort spasmodically.

The entities are arrayed across fields of unpainted woodgrain partially carpeted by colored rectangles. These organs do their squirting, drooling, and shooting on a smoothly Arcadian tabletop battlefield, a turbulent cartoon paradise. Fine's congested blobs seem slow moving but perform their actions with lively animation. They are self-entangled and perhaps can be understood as one complex subdivided self. The painting is in conflict with itself, jauntily mixing metaphors and ways of painting. Fine's protagonist-self is at play here, symbolically managing conflicts like a child with toys. The blobs, in effect, hand off energy from one to another, as in a Renaissance or Baroque battle painting, to build the composition's interconnected dynamic. Combat links the various parts of the painting into a paradoxically cooperative fight-dance. Now that the paint is dry, however, Fine's combatants are eternally stuck in her exquisite quagmire.

2004

Barnaby Furnas, *Red Sea*, 2006

Inka Essenhigh, *Virgin and Volcano I*, 1998

Jane Fine, *Battlefield III*, 2003

Alexis Harding

GRAVITY HAS a lot to say in Alexis Harding's gooey process paintings. His truth to materials testifies to much warping and straining of wetness as it attempts to dry.

2007

Eva Lundsager

EVA LUNDSAGER EXERCISES DRIP MANAGEMENT. She meticulously ornaments the fact that dry paint is a stilled image of its original sticky viscosity. When paint runs, its many little legs obey gravity according to the thickness or thinness of the dilution. The downward flow can be disoriented when the support is skewed. Lundsager renders paint's wetness festively weightless. Paint-drips conventionally signify a relaxation of the artist's control because a spill can wash away traces of the hand that made it, even when that loss has been rehearsed a zillion times. Her small paintings, however, are insistently constructed to highlight the drip's iconographic character.

Lundsager's arrested drips are embedded like jewels into her densely organized pictures. The work's diminutive scale and lapidary radiance invite us to notice the small details. Lundsager both slows the drip's pace and stretches its reach. Carefully placed dots, flat shapes, and smudges restore evidence of her mark-making while the spills are trimmed, pruned, and cultivated like unruly garden plants.

1997

John Pfahl and Elliott Puckette

JOHN PFAHL, IN his newest photographs, freezes the unrelenting surge of Niagara Falls into an unnatural stasis. His close-cropped images eliminate the human accumulation around the falls, its factories and tourist industry, to restore some of Niagara's celebrated sublimity. The photographs contain the majestic spill while emphasizing its interminable overflowing; we marvel at how the plunging torrent slurs into cloud and sky. Pfahl employs historically honed pictorial conventions to capture these dissolving effects of light and vapor: The mighty St. Lawrence pouring itself over the horseshoe precipice is pictured with calendar-art luxury. Nevertheless, one senses a desire to return to the oft-pictured cataract free of honeymooners, souvenirs, and commerce—free of its history as a symbol and official nature spectacle. A photo like *white-plumed billows*, 1996, encourages a vertiginous or euphoric loss of orientation. No wonder Niagara is a popular location for suicides.

Pfahl's photo-chemical rendering of water in transformation performs other transformations. The stilled force of the falls in photographs, like a *jagged verge* or *the fatal brink*, both 1996, acquires a waxy, metallic sheen. One senses a different form of matter captured by the camera's technological eye. The familiar Niagara is rendered strange. Nathaniel Hawthorne writes in *My Visit to Niagara* that "the vapor and the foam are as everlasting as the rocks which produce them, all this turmoil assumes a sort of calmness,"

LIKE A PHOTOGRAPH OR HANDWRITING, the basic character of a painting is also one of arrested flow; each painting is frozen at the moment the painter ceased work. Wet paint sluices and responds to forces applied to it, especially the artist's touch. Elliott Puckette toys with this condition with an ultra-civilized flourish. She incises calligraphic inventions onto dripping monochrome grounds. The filigree image that presents itself in each painting is a continuous, cursive line without beginning or end. Its loopy formality both mocks the casually stained ground and dresses up its undisciplined liquidity. Puckette's images recycle and enlarge a nearly lost art of ornamental penmanship. The dynamism of the flowing stroke, however, is carefully rendered by an accumulation of small razor scrapes into the flowing ground while Puckette's polished allusions avoid writing's signifying function and idiosyncratic expressivity. Instead they celebrate a potential for absurd decorative refinement. Her groomed curlicue is a virtuosic and illegible nonsense.

Puckette's images reflect the free flow of imaginative invention pushing against the regulating constraints of convention. Lines must thin and thicken, loop and curl according to historically evolved cursive logics. They slyly pronounce the ancient truism of ballet and music instructors, that freedom is attained through discipline.

If Pfahl has amusingly echoed his name in the Niagara Falls photographs, Puckette has rendered giant undecipherable monograms of hers. Their encrypted signatures, like Medardo Rosso's impressions and arrested career, inscribe a desire to stabilize life's inexorable course. They memorialize anticipated lost things. Their works ask us to marvel at the transient when distilled into an immobile object. They hit time's pause button to delay our dizzying rush to the falls' fatal brink.

1996

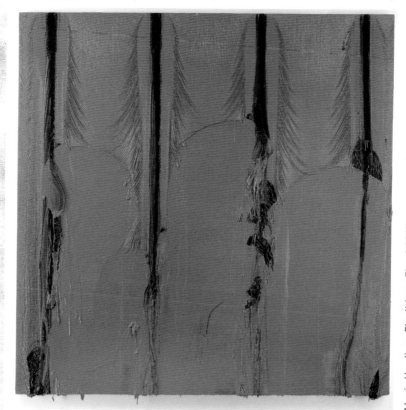

Alexis Harding, *Flexible or Fixed*, 2007

Eva Lundsager, *Old Wound Aches*, 1994

John Pfahl, *The Fatal Brink*, 1996

Elliott Puckette, *Wake*, 2003

Kenneth Goldsmith

IN THE SPAN OF ONE week in 1997, Kenneth Goldsmith, if we trust his accuracy, uttered 183,685 words. Wearing a tape recorder and later transcribing every word into the seven "acts" of *Soliloquy*, Goldsmith produced a 281-page document that he used to wallpaper the interior of Bravin Post Lee gallery. The transcription of these words and the editing-out of everything his interlocutors had to say surely took longer than speaking them. *Soliloquy* presents itself as a precise rendering of part of the artist's life in which the ease of speech rubs against the tedium of secretarial labor. The simplicity of Goldsmith's concept contrasts dramatically with the complexity and irregular idiosyncrasies of his unedited transcription. **The work's conceptual purity provides a pristine background for the messy content of ungrammatical and inefficient daily spew:** from the routine labors of life to news-breaking gossip, domestic intimacies, and banalities.

Goldsmith is a connoisseur of the unedited, part of a tradition that includes John Cage, Andy Warhol, Fluxus, and Minimalism. He writes/speaks, "I'm always talking about the volume of language that's around… What would your language look like… if you collected every piece-of-shit word… that you said for an entire week." *Soliloquy*'s wallpaper enacts an incarnation of speech while it solicits an audience for private experience. Goldsmith converts the back and forth of social life into a one-way address. Isolated from the world, the artist's words are redirected at us. We are free to wonder how *Soliloquy*'s monologue differs from literature and how this indiscrete material might get him into trouble. **Although its reserve is playful, *Soliloquy* is as literary as a wiretap.** The work quietly mocks the idea of writing as a careful arrangement of words or as the agonized construction of an authentic voice, but it rewards our casually prying glance with unexpected interest. *Soliloquy* asks us to pay special attention to spoken words while suggesting that they are also as meaningful as snowflakes in a blizzard.

Goldsmith propels his private life into the public but remains masked like a squid in its own ink. His gesture blurs the boundaries between self and world, and functions as an exaggeration or caricature of narcissism, which Christopher Lasch defined as a "dependence on the vicarious warmth of others combined with a fear of dependence, a sense of inner emptiness, boundless repressed rage, unsatisfied oral cravings, …pseudo self-insight, calculated seductiveness, nervous, self-deprecatory humor." Here, the sense of self depends on the consumption of *images* of the self. Much of today's art strives to attain this status of a symptom. Understood in this way, art is caused by the world as much as by the artist—like a runny nose.

1998

Charles Long

CHARLES LONG'S NEW multicolored sculptures are like playthings, but ones that play mostly with themselves. Long effaces himself through the autonomy he has built into his new sculptures. His art acts out a drama of self-enclosure while playing tricks on the relation between form and function. This series of sculptures runs loopy variations on the basic situation of an elongated blob sitting on a shelf. Each element—shelf, blob, and shelf-leg—at some point stretches to become one of the other elements; a blob elongates into a shelf or a leg grows into a

blob, which in turn rests on another shelf that might sprout its own distended blob.

My Colorful Family, 1998, for instance, is a caricature of a Donald Judd sculpture. Its bright colors and cartoon softness suggest a plaything without hard edges or swallowable parts. Long's recombinant system has an absurd self-sufficiency; it always plugs back into itself. These are self-shelving forms without openings, their insides sealed off. If Judd's shelves were a critique of earlier distinctions between a sculpture and its pedestal, Long's are a burlesque. His forms droop and sag with exaggerated obedience to gravity and converse with each other in tones of tender banality.

Long's biomorphism confers qualities of life to inanimate objects while his retrostylizations add a layer of cultural commentary. Each sculpture's groovy intraconnectivity is modular, built from repetitions and doublings. Long punningly suggests that these artworks are psychological diagrams, naming one piece Robert's Shelflessness, 1998, for example. The sculpture's elongated and pretzeled formality stands as the self's comic emblem.
1998

Richard Prince

THEIR EYES ARE SCREWY; one eye looks toward us while the other drifts. They neither return our gaze nor focus on anything in particular. The life-size guys in Richard Prince's Untitled, 1998 paintings don't express themselves, but the paintings in which they appear articulate sensitivities more emphatically than anything we have seen before from this slippery artist. Prince has created artworks over the last two decades that distinctly shade our interpretation of these new ones. His characteristic indexical cool urges us to see these imaginatively layered figure paintings as pastiches, as something whose originality we should doubt. He seems to be making things up, but handwritten notes often turn out to be silkscreened quotes from other works, while the stylized pen drawings of human heads look naggingly familiar, like the people in paintings by John Graham or George Tooker. Shopping lists, jokes, and song lyrics reappear in various works. "So if a couple from Kentucky get divorced are they still brother and sister?" reads one that may be a comment on the cross-eyed guy in the painting.

I imagine Prince amused at overhearing someone's comment that he "knows how to draw." It seems that he does, but perhaps the apparent earnestness of this work obeys what he has called, in an earlier context, an "undesired fidelity." These works might represent what he has wanted, but could never allow himself, to do and now can, but only in this highly qualified way. The guys in the pictures, anyway, can't do much. Their oversized and agitated hands are frozen in the vicinity of their schematically hand-wrought genitals. They don't see straight and are immersed in an elaborately symbol-strewn environment. They have no ears. How are we to interact with them?

Prince consistently highlights the gap between an image's original purpose and its reception as an artwork with his signature. His jokes, objects, and photographs emphasize the unacknowledged potential in his source material to produce wonder and skewed beauty. But what happens when the source is the artist's own doodling? We now mistrust the facts, partly because the paintings are handmade, but marvel at the suave inaccessibility of his motives. Chattering content saturates milky atmospheres of paint as Prince transforms his role from detached spectator into an engaged and playful performer, something almost pure.
1998

Drew Beattie & Daniel Davidson

DREW BEATTIE & DANIEL DAVIDSON, in their series 100 Drawings, 1998, use the technical operations of mimicry, masking and erasure to dramatize their condition as collaborative artists. They present work as both evidence of interactive behavior and a representation of fictional worlds inhabited by people and animals. Beattie & Davidson make drawings that seem built out of the intimate

byproducts of lived lives. The casual stains and blots that cover their work conjure a history of fluctuating attention, of momentary use and reuse, of touching and retouching. Doodles made while on the phone, self-reminders, and corrected lists on reused papers constitute a well-employed sub-genre of contemporary drawing: automatist readymades. In a gallery, objects of this type look like a cross between a relic and an illuminated manuscript.

A peculiarity of the Beattie & Davidson collaboration is that their works seem to speak with many voices but none recognizable as Beattie's or Davidson's. Indeed, their drawings contain an inventory of contemporary drawing practices established by other artists: Twombly, Polke, and Schnabel, among others. The works provide no fixed positions for its two players; it's a theater of multiple selves in which the artists' identities are staged, concealed, and merged rather than revealed. In one set of drawings, the collaborative effort is figured as a Rorschach blot in which left and right are bilaterally symmetrical. **Beattie & Davidson's work occurs within the infinitely variable social unit of the**

couple. We see only the surface effects of private interactions, like a couple exchanging personal tics, finishing each other's sentences and amending whatever the other says.

Beattie & Davidson's collaboration share the historic Surrealist desire for an unexpected encounter with one's self outside the self: the uncanny, Breton's *L'Amour Fou*. Beattie & Davidson's games produce both the accidentally profound and the hilariously impossible. One series of drawings was produced by playing the game Hangman, in which each wrongly guessed letter of a secret word requires the drawing of another part of the hung man, a comic reminder of the Surrealist collaborative game Exquisite Corpse. Each completed word rings out as a cryptic evocation: bicoastal, styrofoam, angelfish, wilderness... Drawing as a rule-bound group activity produces and lampoons coherence. Beattie & Davidson are connoisseurs of chance encounters and masters of the off-handed **1998**

Kenneth Goldsmith, *Soliloquy*, 1996

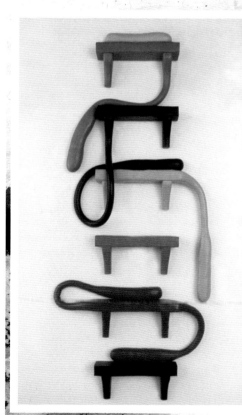

Charles Long, *My Colorful Family*, 1998

Drew Beattie & Daniel Davidson (detail) *There's Summer and Fall*

Between You and There, 1999, 1997

Bijou Karman

The Essential Solitude

In the rare instances when
a living person shows simili-
tude with himself, he only
seems to us more remote,
closer to a dangerous neutral
region, astray in himself and
like his own ghost already:
he seems to return no longer
having any but an echo life.

John Coplans

JOHN COPLANS HAS FOUND an engaging way to turn his back on the spectator and himself. His preoccupation is with the psychologically linked material of photography and flesh. His turned back functions not so much as a refusal as an invitation to enter an environment of skin. Pictured in large, closely cropped, black-and-white photographs, these backs are framed and squeezed by the undulating inner edge of his arms and echoed geometrically by a curious division, in which slightly unmatched images of the upper and lower torso are separated by a small white border. The artwork's front is the artist's back. Distortions caused by the way his arms squeeze into his back from the sides and by the slightly mismatched top and bottom halves of the works, render the image slightly strange. Coplans seems to be both stimulating and protecting himself. By these auto-sceptic self-manipulations, he becomes another to himself in ways very different from the role-playing found in much contemporary photographic self-portraiture. Because of the back's blankness, its general lack of incidence, small details become an inscrutable text written on the soft, white page of his aging flesh. The moles, hair and wrinkles of his skin are disorientingly intimate. In *Self Portrait (Back no. 16)*, 1996 his hairy stalk of a torso plays phallic; in *Self Portrait (Back no. 10)*, Coplans' arms crop the top of his ass crack so that it resembles a female pubic cleft. By omitting his face, the photographs offset this exhibitionist display of private acts with formal reticence.

The back is probably the least expressive and unresponsive part of the body. Yet, through his subtly denaturalizing surrealist conventions of enlargement and close cropping, Coplans renders this zone unfamiliar and eloquent. His manipulations both cut the flesh from its normal context and civilize its formless expanse as art. Perception easily glides through the seamless skin of the photographic surface to the pored, blemished and wrinkled texture of his body's enveloping membrane. Coplans' flesh has a sense of irreducible presence and blunt mortality.

1996

John Mandel

PAINTING, LIKE THE CLASSIC NEUROTIC, is afflicted with memories. The practice's long history inflects every gesture, image and the materials themselves. For some this is a source of comfort and reassurance while for others it represents signs of morbidity and moral taint. Painting is peculiarly equipped, though, to make evident the ways the past is woven into the present. John Mandel's recent work engages this eloquent pathology to build commemorative allegories of history, knowledge, and the self. Mandel's arcana come with a symbolist fin-de-siècle pedigree; his work, like theirs, aspires to the redemptive capacity of a fevered imagination.

Each of his paintings is organized around a tightly rendered central image—a book, a dog, an anvil, a fish. The pictures are composed not so much to render these objects as recognizable things but instead as enigmatic glyphs in a foreign tongue. His images are fragments pulled from their natural context and inserted into a more language-like syntax. The carefully painted words, however, are never in the artist's mother tongue but range between extinct languages, Spanish, and German. Books are rendered without titles or, when open, without writing on the exposed page. Monochrome panels, an unfolded cloth, and a dead fish speak with resonant blankness. The ostensible muteness of these images is complicated by tantalizing clues about their refusal to speak. The intensity of realistic detail and the reverential somberness of the presentation give Mandel's objects a sacramental tone. A whippet stands with the erect posture and dumb nobility of a show dog in a painting dedicated to the existential theist Martin Buber. The vivid particularity of the dog, however, is undermined by the words *Ich Und Du* (I And Thou) floating on either side of it. A hermetic rebus is constructed with the dog as a grammatical crux.

Mandel's paintings submerge narrative but animate analogies. *Mein Hertz, Mi Corazon*, 1991, superimposes a sharply focused image of an anvil over a loosely painted torso without limbs or head. Its gastrointestinal system is visible below while the anvil covers the chest and the heart floats outside the body as a spectral sketch. The digestive convolutions of the intestines echo the themes that circulate around *Mein Hertz, Mi Corazon*.

Much of Mandel's work is animated by the opposing impulses to reveal and disguise. In another piece

Xiriguana, 1991, a title derived from an extinct South American language, a grandiose doorway is ornamented with the faces of two Incans and the word "sangre." Octavio Paz, speaking of the ancient Mexicans, said, "The link between ourselves and the other depends not on resemblance but on difference. We are united not by a bridge but by an abyss." Mandel's work is haunted by a sense of mourning that issues from this abyss.

1991

David Diao

Kafka remarks with surprise, with enchantment, that he has entered into literature as soon as he can substitute He for I."

Maurice Blanchot

EFFORTS TO RENOUNCE AUTHO-RIAL CLAIMS over the artwork are inevitably undermined by a world that needs to blame, praise, or own something with a name. Curated exhibitions can be a case of using others to speak in the organizer's voice while some contemporary solo exhibitions present themselves as curated evidence of a multiplied self. David Diao does both with his series of paintings "...a real allegory" that graphs a variety of data from his twenty-two year career that conceals the lived life with vital statistics.

Diao's work gleefully enshrines the so-called death of the artist... *a real allegory*, 1991 continues his project of making paintings after the last painting. *Sales 2*, for instance, plots the dates and number of paintings sold between 1968 and 1991 radiating around a flat red circle (the conventional indication of a work that's been sold). The works are graphs that would conventionally be used to measure a production that is finished, by an artist who is dead but not forgotten. While the unexplained disparity in sales (twenty-two in 1973; zero for 1981 through 1985) is of anecdotal interest, the terminal closure of information around the circle suggests that this cryptic emblem hides a secret. The artist's name or signature is visibly absent, except as it appears in old art magazine reviews silkscreened onto the painting *Plus and Minus*, suggesting that Diao's address is constantly shifting between first and third person. The "Diao" presented in "...a real allegory" is one only seen by others. The painting *Studio*

Visits represents the eternally closed cover of a journal presumably containing accounts of what others said him about his work, just as *Mean Things* promiscuously refers to what was said by and about him to others

Much of Diao's recent work is a commentary on the idea that painting is regulated by its own specificity, that its power in modernism was derived from preoccupations with the material conditions of support and surface. These Diao paintings toy with the ontology of abstract art by asking, "Does the representation of an abstraction continue to be an abstraction the way a representation of a graph is still a graph?" With his high standards of painterly craft and elaborated references, Diao slyly substitutes his own name for that of "painting," while suggesting that its material condition is what others say about it.

1991

Richard Pettibone

A STRIKING CHARACTERISTIC of the cultural moment is the abundance of quotations, reproductions, and simulations in art. A thousand flowers have bloomed in a rich compost of copies—from Andy Warhol to Elaine Sturtevant, Philip Taafe to Mike Bidlo, Sherrie Levine to Richard Pettibone. The view that all cultural production is a variation of the already made has become folk wisdom among artists. Pettibone differs from his orthodox copyist cousins in the reverence and scholarly wit with which he treats his models. His work has the finely tuned attention to detail of a miniaturist whose objects we can scan and manipulate like dollhouse gods. In Pettibone's world, a variety of textual quotations and copied artworks are folded into each other in a continuous process of rereading and remaking.

One series from 1990 resulted from a cross-fertilization of Ezra Pound, Shaker furniture, and Constantine Brancusi, a hybrid of the written, plastic, and applied arts. These sources share a vigorous moral character in the pursuit of abstract form. Honesty, clarity, unity, and discipline are absolute principles in their intersecting worlds. Pound writes that "inaccurate art" is not only bad but also immoral, and while Pettibone's precision is evident in his craft, his copies introduce odd deviations that undermine their trustworthiness. Subtle moral puzzles appear in a wall piece inscribed with the Pound quote "The temple is holy because it is not for sale." The suggestion that these are votive objects in a temple of culture is compromised by the fact that Pettibone's object *is* for sale.

Pound, through his participation in the Vorticist movement, was a champion of the abstract tendency in sculpture. But where Pound championed sculpture as a poetics of form liberated from representation, Pettibone celebrates those values within a naked representational mode: the quotation. A favorite Shaker song anticipates the moral imperative of international modernism by declaring, "'Tis the gift to be simple." The image of the authentic artist or author diffused into other voices is rooted in Pound's modernism, while Pettibone's vision is confounded by a rigorous anti-originality.

As in Confucius (quoted by Pettibone in a Pound translation inscribed on a modified Shaker table), the authority of ancestors is understood as the basis for social and cultural strength. But by selecting only part of a Brancusi and omitting the rest, the artist plays both the slavish devotee and the impudent vandal. His quotes exercise a parallel ambivalence by alternating between careful inscription and crude graffiti. The celibate Shakers are graced with an ambiguously humble progeny; their strict functionalist objects have spawned useless artworks. Pettibone disengages the anxiety accompanying influence by allowing quotations to sharply define the difference between him and his models.

Pettibone's highly crafted objects are a deconstructive folk art. The complexity of his rereadings convincingly brings scholarship into the studio without diminishing the importance of the physical object. His skewed copies have the effect of refreshing subsequent experiences of the originals by undermining the way we habitually recognize cultural icons disseminated through reproduction. He creates a doubt about their exact shape. Pettibone's inaccuracies enhance the original's power to stimulate meaning.

1990

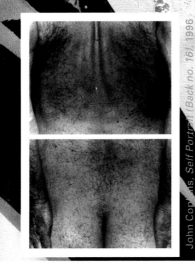

John Coplans, *Self Portrait (Back no. 16)*, 1996

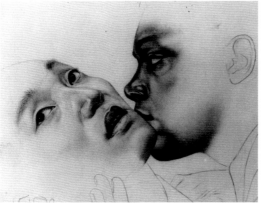
John Mandel, *Untitled*, 1990

JOURNAL
*Studio
Visits*

David Diao, *Studio Visits*,
1991

Richard Pettibone, installation view,
1990

Steve McQueen

STEVE MCQUEEN, IN his silent video piece
Deadpan, 1997, stays implacably and unrespon-
sively vertical in a remake of a Buster Keaton gag.
McQueen arranged for the façade of a house to
fall on him, leaving him untouched thanks to a
perfectly placed and open second story window.
The piece begins in total darkness; the gallery
walls and floor are painted black. The first time
the facade falls, we view it from inside the small
building, as though the gallery's projection wall
falls away to reveal a light-filled landscape outside.
The work is a drama of repetition; the
facade falls again and again, viewed each time
from another angle. The sequence has a detached
formality, focused first on the architecture then
expanding to a full frame engagement with the
complexity of McQueen's unresponsive face.

What starts out as a sight-gag quoted from
movie history evolves into a work that is not so
funny. Surprise diminishes after each drop of
the wall. The black-and-white images have a rich
and melancholic quality that slowly builds to an
emotional pitch by the time McQueen's face
commands the frame. It seems like he is going to
cry. The opened house reveals two empty rooms;
the downstairs has no window or door and the
upstairs has only a mysterious door at the back.
Each time the wall hits the ground it stirs up an
anxious turbulence of leaves and dust. A gust of
air in one profile shot ruffles the artist's shirt. The
piece concludes with the heroic McQueen seen
from an absurdly low angle in his casual jeans
and t-shirt surviving yet another staged disaster.
1998

Jonathan Borofsky

WITH UPRAISED ARMS and oversized
white gloves, Jonathan Borofsky's *Ballerina
Clown*, 1990 is as conspicuous as the most brazen
piece of giantist roadside advertising without the
purpose of getting you to stop. America's roads
are message corridors that stimulate and punctuate the consciousness of drivers. Advertising
conventions have evolved to momentarily arrest a
passing driver's attention without compromising
their driving skills. Borofsy's thirty-foot *Ballerina
Clown*, on the corner of Rose and Main streets in
Venice, California, proposes a mental detour
down a winding associative road.

Ballerina Clown reveals and undercuts the twin
characteristics of public art as crypto-advertising
and inflated ego display. It was commissioned by
the builders as "the final compliment" to Venice
Renaissance, a huge mixed-use block-size project.
Wearing the mask of an unshaven hobo drunkard,
Ballerina Clown's address has the quality of a
lunatic's public raving or an obvious joke told too
loudly. Something very private has fallen into
public. Francis Picabia writes in a 1948 letter to
Gabrielle Buffet, "If one wishes to stir up the
masses should one not be the actor of oneself?"
1990

Dennis Oppenheim

THE NOTE OF VIOLENCE in slapstick
comedy often hinges on the actors being less
than fully conscious. When they act half dead their
unresponsiveness delivers hilariously catastrophic
results. Dennis Oppenheim's objects often perform
in this broad and sometimes menacingly comic
mode. In *Circle Puppets*, 1993, two oversized
robotic marionettes swing violently at each other
with metal pipes on a video monitor with the
now inanimate performers strewn chaotically
on the floor nearby. A second monitor displays a
close-up of hands mechanically playing a piano
with little bobbing heads attached to each knuckle.
Oppenheim's method is to take things apart and
to give those parts narrative independence. He
often uses images of hands to project a quality of
animation into his objects, as in *Finger, Churches*,
1994, where they hold the stumps of their own
dismembered fingers. Hands wear boxing gloves
in *Battered Tears*, 1994, and in the video *Stutter
Piece*, 1994, they appear reflected in water, presenting a toy to the viewer. Oppenheim's hands act
as agents in the world, frequently detached from
the rest of the body in their ambassadorial task of
negotiating analogies and navigating challenges.

Oppenheim's humor is ham-fisted, outrageous, and intensely physical. In the giant
testicular *Battered Tears*, 1994, twin foam and
fiberglass objects hang from the ceiling like oversized punching bags or teardrops. A pair of video
monitors squeezed between them shows a clown-
ish boxer walking backwards on a treadmill. The
boxer's face, however, is a mask on the back of the
walker's head; two fake forearms, attached at the
elbows, make his rhythmic stride appear backward.
Oppenheim ridiculously equates the consequences

of being hit (tears), self-improvement exercises, male stereotypes and speed bags. Oppenheim prefers a gag with multiple punch lines.
1994

Daniela Steinfeld

DANIELA STEINFELD IS IN A Krups appliance box with her legs hanging out. The rest of her is hidden, except for the part in her blonde hair. In another piece she hides in an overturned Bosch appliance box with her legs opened wide enough to stick out from the top and bottom. But what's wrong with her feet? In the Krups photograph she is relaxed, alert and undisturbed; her left foot is bare while the right swells to monstrously lumpy proportions inside its oversized sock. In *Affengeil*, 1999, her feet stick out of the stove-sized Bosch box wearing hairy animal costume gloves, converting her toes into clawed fingers. Legs spread again in *Wave*, this time into the air from under a Persian carpet. Steinfeld has a comic eye for lumps and subhuman characteristics. She has reduced herself to limbs, emphasizing the way our extremities can sometimes become strangers. Bodies seem to alter themselves from within; Steinfeld perversely joins the different associations men and women have with these changes.

Steinfeld hides herself in the manner of toddlers playing hide-and-seek who think that because they can't see us we must not be able to see them. Like them, Steinfeld asks us to look at her while she hides. She dresses up by paring down: no arms, no face. She is disguised as a dumb but emotionally charged object. Her disheveled actions perform substitutions, exaggerations, and metamorphoses with casual simplicity. It is clear that in the moment after the photo Steinfeld can easily return to her whole self. The works are like puppet shows in which objects and bodies slur distinctions between each other and between the imagination and the world. Steinfeld caricatures every photograph's twin character as a moment and as an object. Living flesh and inert matter enact dramas between an unruly inside and constraining outside.
1999

Rodney Graham

VIDEO INSTALLATIONS IN ART galleries navigate an awkward social protocol. Do we want to watch the whole thing? The spectator's freedom to come and go is much greater than in a theater but sometimes a cue to move on never comes. Does it matter when or how to walk through Rodney Graham's video loop *Vexation Island*, 1997, for instance?

The video cycles round and round with images projected on a single gallery wall. A parrot squawks as a wave washes across a sun-drenched beach with ravishing vacation-ad brilliance. Spectators decide whether to sit, stand or exit. Perhaps the first image seen is a falling coconut hitting the period-costumed artist on the head, knocking him unconscious for most of the video's duration.

Vexation Island tells, in nuanced cinematic terms, a loopy Sisyphusian story of a beached castaway who awakens long enough to be knocked out again by a coconut he has shaken from a palm tree. The video cycles again and again past an establishing shot of the small uninhabited island, asleep in turquoise tropical waters, to various tracking shots, pans and close-ups that move the video toward its denouement. Deft edits propel the loop's accumulating narrative while quietly introducing layered references to *Treasure Island*, *Robinson Crusoe* and *Mutiny on the Bounty*. Only the parrot, with its gestures, squawks and a single almost-intelligible two-syllable utterance, evidences signs of consciousness. Graham is playing the roles of actor and filmmaker, imitating Hollywood nature films, and television advertising.

Striped shadows from the palm tree overhead sway across the castaway's sleeping eyes in a playful imitation of REM sleep. Our hero is like an artwork: unseeing, mute, inert, and generously productive of meaning. A tightly framed shot of a large circular wound on the castaway's forehead is echoed by a similarly framed image of the blazing sun and again by the parrot's blank eye. The wound becomes like an eye, a portal into his head; the sun becomes a wound in the sky; the camera illuminates with a parroting eye while the surf reflects a foam-shattered sun. After our hero wakes up, we see the palm tree upside down, as if we too were lying beneath it. The camera's point-of-view ranges liberally, accumulat-

Tony Oursler

"I DO NOT TRY TO CORRECT PEOPLE WHO EXPRESS AN IGNORANT BELIEF," states the woman whose face is video-projected onto Tony Oursler's hand-sized cloth doll *MMPI #7 (Female)*, 1994. "I often go out of my way to win a point over someone who is opposed to me," she continues. But she is immobile—without hands or feet—and attached helplessly to a light-stand that holds her up at face level. The projected woman's distorted face (performed by Tracy Leipold) stretches across the front of the doll's blank head

ing associations and building expectations, until we finally see from the point of view of the coconut as it plunges in slow motion toward Graham's unresponsive and impenetrable head. Knocked out, he returns in a slapstick fall to the ground, to his sleep, and to the beginning of the film loop. This interminable cycle of waking, working, and sleeping burlesques our daily experience and wins an absurd victory over closure and death.
1998

as she tells us about herself. Her stern one-way address beseeches whoever will listen and doesn't register our presence or that we've drifted away. She commands, however absurdly, one corner of Oursler's installation with self-confident intensity.

Other works speak into the darkened space to raise a chattering din. Whenever someone enters from the outside, light floods in with them to temporarily erase all the projections. For an instant, Oursler's works appear as junk sculptures with faceless dolls. The small video projectors on tripods gain importance as the works lose their animation, only to snap back to life once

the door shuts and the room dims. This alternating emphasis between projector and screen heightens the images' fragility. Oursler's work fulfills a traditional romantic aspiration: to project life into inanimate matter. Like scarecrows brought to life by the wind, these disconcertingly crippled objects are animated by the uncanny breath of video.

Unlike robots, Oursler's techno-dolls have an exaggerated sense of personal history. The performances, usually close-up faces, emphasize the idiosyncratic individuality and tic-ridden fleshiness of his performers. They are alienated talking heads trapped within inert objects. *Getaway #2*, 1994, is an arresting life-sized head stuck between a bare, flower-patterned, mattress and the floor. Pinned near the gallery entrance, the woman's head barks, "Hey you! Leave me alone!" We are caught in an unwanted intimacy, unable to help someone who clearly needs it. The man in *(Telling)*

Vision delivers a speech in which he identifies himself with images he is watching: "I'm giving birth in a movie theater. Now I'm a construction site. I'm a helicopter shot." Oursler toys with our habits of empathy, projection, and identification.

In *Organ Play #2*, 1994, Oursler triggers anxieties about bodily wholeness in the manner of Samuel Beckett. Unlabeled jars arrayed on a table hold animal organs in formaldehyde. A man's and a woman's lips projected onto the meat speak with offhanded discomfort about the presence or absence of their insides. Background tape noise paradoxically renders them both here in the gallery and in some private setting elsewhere, while the connection between them is equally unsettled. They keep repeating, "I can't hear you." and "What was the original question?" We eavesdrop as her lipsticked mouth asks, "So, how ya feeling?" and in the background he answers, "Half dead."
1994

Anne Chu

WHY DO WE KEEP LOOKING for vitality in objects? Inert matter is over there, we're here;

we're alive, it's not. But collisions happen and sparks fly. Think of Pygmalion, who chiseled a lover from a block of marble to fulfill a fantasy latent in the vast history of figurative sculpture. Anne Chu is different: she hacks blocks of wood into figures that await animation by an imaginary puppeteer that will never arrive. Ropes connect her frozen puppets' arms and heads to an out-of-reach puppeteer's frame on the ceiling. The performance ended in Chu's studio when she finished the work of sewing, sawing, and assembling. Now these characters emphatically tell a story of their own making. Wire frames are ingeniously clothed to become torsos. Heads and hands are chopped from wood with a rough vigor that could be called violent if their storybookish dispositions weren't so benign. *Bestial*, 2003, is a ghoulish she-devil whose threats are rendered comic by cartoonish bear paws and a Humpty-Dumpty body. *Tracollo*, 2003, in dapper pajamas, has his face completely wrapped in bandages as though he was wounded by the act of having been carved. *Charming Girl*, 2003, holds her own little puppet-guy on a stick; but how developed can her performance skills be when the hand is a fingerless blob?

Chu's characters have limited agency. Their hands are without grasp. Their gaze is compromised by eyes that are sometimes closed, sometimes only partially articulated and occasionally left simply as a pair of gouged holes. These puppets seem constrained by forces larger than themselves. Even their incompleteness emphasizes a confinement to the world of material objects: wires spring out, seams show, and wood splinters or splits. On the one hand, Chu's sculptures argue for a secret life as a materials-oriented abstraction, their formalism disguised as vernacular figuration. Her ad hoc use of wood, wire, and cloth is, in this argument, only pretending to serve the theatrical content. On the other hand, the sculptures are expressive self-portraits that describe the artist as an ambivalent self-presenter, an incomplete dressed-up husk, endlessly deferring performances and social entanglements.

But Chu's big toys are suavely cosmopolitan with ranging allusions and shifting identifications. Syncopated construction methods of cutting, stitching, carving, and modeling mix high artifice with problem-solving practicality. Her work recruits historic precursors from China and Europe with a fluid anthropological imagination. We are invited to eavesdrop on lively conversations between Chu and the art of museums; their talk is affably intimate, mischievous, and expansive. Chu's robust sculptures neither depict other depictions nor are they pure products of the imagination; they are hybrid singularities ardently performing both possibilities.

2003

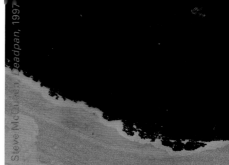
Steve McQueen, Deadpan, 1997

Jonathan Borofsky, Ballerina Clown

Daniela Steinfld, *Affengeil*, 1999

Dennis Oppenheim, 1994

Rodney Graham, *Vexation Island*, 1997

Tony Oursler, *Getaway #2*, 1994

Anne Chu, *Charming Girl*, 2003

Guillermo Kuitca

"theatrical," it is usually understood to mean they are showy—that they possess an exaggerated sense of drama. But it can also mean they make use of analogies with other aspects of the theater. Guillermo Kuitca's large-scale paintings are images of the seating plans used to help ticket-holders know where they belong. Other paintings in the series are smudged images schematically representing theater interiors drawn in perspective from the point of view of the stage. Each seat, though, is numbered and located with architectural accuracy. In most of these works the carefully ruled lines are enveloped in soft tinted clouds of smeared or spilled paint. These casual disruptions of the diagram's clarity give Kuitca's images a touched and handled quality; the chart's cool accuracy is warmed up with subjective heat and diverted from its original diagrammatic purpose. The marks speak in both institutional and subjective voices: the ruled and the unruled. Kuitca's worked surfaces can also be understood as stand-ins for what is known as the fourth wall: a fictional architectural skin separating the world on stage from the audience. The fourth wall is both a barrier and a portal that functions for both actor and painter as a field of address. In Kuitca's pictures the fourth wall is figured as a screen distressed by the colliding expectations of the artist and his imagined spectators.

The point of view represented in paintings like *Ein Deutsches Requiem*, 1995, though, is as much a proprietor's as it is an actor's. Performers have no use for seating diagrams; they use the fourth wall to shield themselves from considerations of theater as a business. Uta Hagen said that actors need their fourth wall "in order not to lose the sense of privacy and reality." Kuitca slyly suggests that the spectators of his paintings are anonymous ticket-holders or place-holding customers. All sight lines converge on the stage within the concentric architecture of spectacle, but our imagined role can alternate between performer and spectator in Kuitca's theater of facelessly collective solitudes.

1995

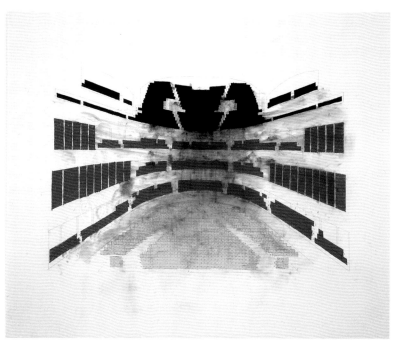

Guillermo Kuitca, *Ein Deutsches Requeim*, 1995

Laurence Hegarty, *Low Dishonest Times*, 2006

Laurence Hegarty

assume their positions. Bert, the sad thug, is paying unkind attention to the thoughtful William. Sigmund, the little king, watches nearby while Francis, preoccupied and aloof, gazes upward. Laurence Hegarty is playing with dolls. He arranges interactions between these men and sometimes performs unspeakable acts upon them. We can play too, because some of these mixed-media doll-like objects work like marionettes; we pull the string and Bertold Brecht kicks his prisoner William Butler Yeats. Sigmund Freud, played by Mongomery Clift, watches with his famous non-responsive attentiveness. But, like a toy, he's on wheels and could easily be rolled away, perhaps closer to Francis of Assisi, as depicted by Zurbaran.

Hegarty's installations are also populated by modified stuffed animals. **The nastiness gets worse: killing, maiming, and humiliations that almost always involve the dousing or smearing of goo.** This application of wax or colored polymer is a form of

contact, an evidence of relation between the individual characters and Hegarty the artist. Suicide, murder, body bags, and genital mutilations! Rage is afoot, and it's a little funny. A stuffed somebody (bear, bunny, ducky?) has an exploding hole and exit wound through his chest that sprays a pattern of red goo across the wall. A procession of red plastic piggy banks with their brains scooped out leads a squad of other modified cuddlies.

Hegarty makes a world of political allegory and psychoanalytic symbols. Banks commit aggressions and workers suffer; super-ego father figures issue phallic threats. The stakes are high because we live in times Hegarty refers to as "low and dishonest." Power needs to be understood; it needs to be played with and worked over. Laurence Hegarty is a practicing psychotherapist. He calls himself "some sort of species of Marxist." He loves the movies and was raised an Irish Catholic. His aging female cat's name is Stalin.

What's the thematic link between Hegarty's large group of cardboard movie cameras, airplanes, and rockets? They are all

purveyors of glances and other payloads of attention or harm. Hegarty cares about paying attention. What is it to "pay" attention, especially in the context of art presentation? He uses Cynthia Broan Gallery as a metaphor. The gallery workers are conscripted to interrupt their labors and periodically pull strings that reach into the space to animate the sculptures. Hegarty's work is for sale, of course (check out the prices). The unsold figures from his last show with this gallery are reused as stuffing for the bodybags. A drawing with a hole cut into it opens to a slot in the wall at the beginning of the exhibition. A handwritten note asks for payment to see the show. If we deposit money into the hole it drops though the wall back to our feet. He returns the cash, but not before highlighting the transaction; it now means something even if we *don't* pay. He has refused our money but has given us a theme.

The dictionary's first origin for the meaning of "pay" is "to cover with pitch, from *pix, picis*, to daub, besmear, or cover with tar, tallow, resin or other protective material." Hegarty was paying serious attention, in this sense, to those

animal plushies, but his action seems the opposite of protection. The dictionary's second origin for "pay" is "to please, to satisfy, from *paier, paer,* or *pacare*, to pacify." Now it's getting sexy. Hegarty has both his polemics and his more private pleasures. We hope everybody connected to this work will profit. **I'm being paid to write these words, and I officially urge you to buy some of Hegarty's art.** It could appreciate in value and you will certainly be appreciated. The money we all make should be invested wisely. Is our only choice, though, to put our assets back into a system we may not want to participate in or that we deplore? Can we separate our interests from others? Hegarty reproduces social forces within himself before casting them into his dramaturgy. He refers to real barbarisms by enacting harmless ones. Payback could become paydirt.

What do artists want spectators for? Why do artists need us, and what is expected of us? Perhaps the audience provides an environment, an interpretation-cultivating habitat for artworks to flourish. Hegarty's sculptures are like actors; they gesture, they wear masks, make-up, and costumes. They exist for us and beg to be understood. Hegarty lines them up into processions across the floor, up the wall, or into rows on shelves, as if enacting the pageantry of a secular religion. They form sentence-like strings in which each object functions like a word. The juxtapositions sometimes emphasize similarity of form or sometimes less obvious relations; hats, maps, rockets, banks, and bombs recur. The adjacencies can feel contingent, as though the objects could just as well be arranged differently without changing the overall sense. Sometimes object repetitions accumulate into taxonomies with the sense of a collection. The differences between objects encourage metaphors and expand themes. Brecht wrote that "the great modern subjects must be seen in the light of mime, they must have the character of gestures." Hegarty attaches gloves to some of his stuffed animals to increase their capacity for this silent nuanced language, so they can act like figures in a painting, by Tiepolo, for instance. Brecht adds that acting

shouldn't be about the transmission of feelings but should be "witty, ceremonious, ritual." The actor should "demonstrate" his or her role. Hegarty, with his troupe of cultural heroes and symbol-playthings, heartily agrees.

On a wooden flag-object Hegarty writes out Pablo Neruda's poem *Franco in Hell*, which concludes, "May an agonizing river of gouged-out eyes slide over you watching you endlessly." (Is this a custom punishment for popular artworks and celebrities?) Neruda's rage is embraced within Hegarty's contemporary psycho-political context. Bad deeds have been, and continue to be perpetuated against helpless people for bad reasons; art occasionally seeks justice.

Hegarty makes new things and transforms old ones. His work focuses on exchanges, like aggression, commerce, play, attention, or love, that are performed between people. He stages intersubjectivities and their relation to the institutions of public life: politics and the socially enmeshed individual. His work comes to grips with what William Gass

said of Robert Coover's fiction: "commercial deceit, political lies, and religious myths the better to strangle them." The dictionary eventually defines "pay" in the way we mostly use it, "to give what is due." Hegarty honors his debts to those he venerates and delivers blows to those who have it coming.
2006

Drew Dominick

IN HIS PIECE *Gearmoter Grinder*, 1995, Drew Dominick treats the spectator as a helpless target. When anyone approaches the gallery's entrance he or she causes two heavy-duty rotary grinders hanging by electrical cords from the ceiling to turn on. The grinders begin to lurch, swing, skid and drag their way back and forth across the gallery, marking up the white walls and floor while threatening spectators. If one decides to enter, a third grinder begins its motion by the door to block the means of exit. The three grinders are set at different speeds, inflecting and slowly adding density to the skids and gouges. Amid the rise and fall of whining motors and draping wires, these grinders enact a repeating variety of gestures, from gentle sweeping arcs to twisting leaps. By the fourth week of the exhibition, these repetitive actions marked three large blackish ovals on the floor and dug deep holes into the wall. Dominick created a mosh pit of convulsive machine dancing that requires a cautiously watchful attention while urging a detached appreciation of aestheticized violence. Even though our presence is required for the drama to begin, the work treats us with aggressive indifference.

Denis Diderot, inaugurating what Michael Fried would call a tradition of anti-theatricality, wrote that the highest value that a picture can achieve is reached when it creates a sense that the viewer does not exist, when the figures within a picture take no notice of the spectator. Dominick operates both theatrically and anti-theatrically by both needing the spectator to turn the work on then roughly treating him or her as being inconveniently in the way.

1995

Andreas Slominski

"WARNING!" says a sign at the entrance to an Andreas Slominski's exhibition. "NO DOGS, NO YOUNG CHILDREN, DO NOT TOUCH. Exhibition consists of SET TRAPS." It's true. It wouldn't be funny if someone's hand, pet, or little junior strayed into one these freedom-terminators. Nevertheless, Slominski's traps have the do-it-yourself beauty of assemblage sculpture. Each is made to be as attractive as possible to the little vermin, badgers, or birds it was designed to capture or kill; it is not always clear what fate each piece has planned for its victim. *Trap for Birds of Prey*, 1999, is perhaps the most straightforward; a dead rodent lies on a log surrounded with spikes positioned to impale the pouncing predator. Our identification roves as we consider the arrested fates of the victims and the ingenious craft that went into planning them; Slominski's pieces put the animal lover in us in conflict with the art lover.

Slominski's straightfaced role divides between tricker of animals and artworld trickster but inhabits the latter most profoundly. His playful tinkering with the convention of the readymade adds unexpected life to that well-rehearsed gesture. It doesn't seem important to know whether these traps are inventions, off-the-shelf products, or variations on traditional forms so much as it is to enjoy their accomplished functionality and often hilarious semiosis; *Trap for Young Rats* is in the form of a bus while *Bird Trap* has its bait seeds placed on the trapdoor lid of a can of pitted olives. Some, like *Wood Fowl Trap*, are quite ingenious; a T-shaped perch is placed at the top of a tall cylinder made of green barrels. The perch is hinged to drop the unsuspecting bird into a space whose diameter is too tight for it to fly out; a door at the bottom makes it easy to remove the helpless prisoner.

Commercial galleries can have the pregnant silence of a museum of musical instruments. Slominski's art appears poised and capable of executing precisely timed one-note performances. His instruments await with taut immobility a cue that will most likely never come as they perversely and literally embody Jaques Attali's definition of music as ritual murder.

1999

Peter Land

THEODOR ADORNO DESCRIBED THE OPENING of Beethoven's "Pastoral" symphony as "the bliss of dawdling, dillydallying as utopia." Beethoven's evocation of idyllic rural pleasures fittingly provides a soundtrack for the opening of Peter Land's video projection *The Lake*, 1999. Land, in traditional Danish hunting garb, strolls through the forest with his rifle. He gazes about, presumably looking for game, as bird sounds mingle with Beethoven's music. After taking a swig from his hip flask, Land gets into a rowboat at the edge of a small pond, paddles out to the center and fires a shot into the bottom of his boat. The shot cuts off Beethoven and begins Land's slow submersion into the pond. The artist sits impassively while his boat eventually sinks, leaving nothing but his feathered hunting hat floating on the surface. The birds continue their ambient chirping while the video finishes with a sequence of shots of the sun-drenched forest, now purged of Beethoven and Land.

Large drawings, in storybook illustration manner, accompany *The Lake* and add new layers to its comic allegory. Land's ritual self-sacrifice in the video is elucidated by the drawings as more slapstick than myth; giant rodents give directions, the path is littered with empty liquor bottles, and signs indicate "the point of no return," "black hole," or "the path to death." The drawings begin to look like an anti-drinking editorial. In its more streamlined video form, Land's narrative evokes Jacques Attali's nutty-sounding description of music as the "simulation of ritual murder, the monopolization of the power to kill." Developing Adorno's connections between music and social organization Attali makes the case that music's historical relation to noise is prophetic of coming modes of social organization. Land sentimentally purges the landscape of traditional musical composition. He performs what Attali ascribed to sacrificial rites, "the transformation of anxiety into joy." If Land's bird music is prophetic, it anticipates a jocular end to everything manmade.
1999

Céleste
Boursier-Mougenot

FILL AN INFLATABLE BACKYARD pool, float a bunch of variously sized bowls and glasses on the surface and stir. The music that results will be both absorbing and a clumsy plagiarism of Céleste Boursier-Mougenot's *untitled (series #2)*, 1999. The do-it-yourself, kitchen-meets-back yard, appearance of his work obscures its precise calibrations and highly particular conditions. The water in the artists's five blue pools is heated to optimize the resonance of five identical sets of tuned bowls circulating on pumped currents. Gentle collisions cause the bowls to chime their independent tones in the aleatory chorus.

A striking range of music is generated by Boursier-Mougenot's construction: unlikely arpeggios, eccentric chords, and unexpected phrases bubble from the cascading flow of incident. Things quiet momentarily into stuttering fragments only to swell again into anxious crescendos or percussive clusters. A drift of bowls parades down the center of each pool to divide at the far end into two processions moving around the perimeter in opposite directions. Collisions occur all over the

water's surface but intensify where the two ceramic herds converge back at the pump. Each pool contains one large bowl whose low tone undergirds the microtonal chambermusic blossoming throughout the space. Chairs placed informally around the room furnish the gallery as a social space and encourage considerations of the artwork as a microcosm of community.

At first, Boursier-Mougenot's music has an idyllic windchime quality that becomes increasingly complex as one immerses into its slowly fretful turbulence. Teasing musical developments appear and recede. A percussive modernist angularity haunts *untitled*'s gentle new-age surface while its genial pop-installation mood is darkened by the dangerous potential of electrical wires running into the pools. The piece's charm is a lure; its celestial blue openness is a trap that viewers willingly enter in order to enjoy Boursier-Mougenot's siren song—hopefully not at the risk of electrical shock.
1999

Lewis deSoto

PAUL VALÉRY WRITES, "As the steamship plunges down and sinks slowly, with all its resources, its machines, its lights, its instruments... Thus in the night and in the nether parts of oneself, the mind descends to sleep with all its equipment and its possibilities." Lewis deSoto's robot ocean liner *Ship*, 1998, likewise steams into its own dreamy night of floating analogies and personal associations. deSoto's person-sized black boat cruises the waterless ocean of the darkened gallery like a silhouette, its tiny windows lit from within. The ship is camouflaged in the color of night and spews a self-enveloping fog from its bottom. It acts lost but is guided by a sonar system that prevents it from hitting walls or becoming trapped in corners. The liner's itinerary wanders the empty room with hesitating changes of direction and lumbering slowness while dragging a power cord leash. Its glowing interior lights and independent decision making lends the Titanic-like boat a sense of somnolent agency. If the mind is a steamship, as in Valéry's analogy, deSoto figures it always in the dark, awake during business hours but dead at the pull of a plug. This oceanliner mind is a floating hotel, stowing transient beings within its luxurious hull. Sleep, here, is not a catastrophe of will but an achievement of surrender and drift.
1998

Motor Grundeis

Andreas Slominski *Trap or Young Ha*

Peter Land *title* 1999

Ursula Mougenot, *Untitled (series no.*), 1999

Lewis deSoto, *Ship*, 1998

Keith Tyson

WHEN WE'VE HAD A STROKE of good luck—or when our luck runs out –we take it personally, as though we were responsible. Analogously, some artists work in ways that cause us to wonder how much credit they deserve. Keith Tyson takes these hopes and anxieties seriously in the form of works developed from the proposals of an "Artmachine." This "machine" is evidently designed to recombine material from an inventory of art possibilities in order to generate new ones. Tyson performs the executive task of realizing these proposals without being completely responsible for their meaning. He presents himself as having gambled for his themes by entrusting their unpredictable determination to programmed operations; the resulting work often has the feel of a non sequitur or an accident; but like Freudian slips, these are accidents that were meant to happen.

Tyson's voice of chance speaks in the patois of contemporary art by customizing these accidents within conventionalized genre. No matter how the "machine's" operations are modeled their realization within the artworld insists upon a Tyson signature. Technically charted wall labels classify the works according to "iteration," "title," "format," and "status." In addition, their surface nonsense is both constrained and highlighted by an "Artmachine Iteration Number" that maps the work onto a hidden system in which chaotic significations are formulated and classified. *Artmachine Iteration Number AMCHII•The KFC Notebooks and the UCT*, 1995, is a cast of all the food items on the Kentucky Fried Chicken menu in lead, placed on a counter before an outdated computer monitor that graphically animates the growth of a virus. The work, with sound track and photos, outlines a biological contamination conspiracy narrative. Tyson's "Artmachine" is implicated if we apply the paranoiac interpretation reflexively.

Five Stages Canonic Combo Casino, 1996, posts within it a hilarious list of generative titles. *Casino* is a multiple that will be altered once a year for the next four years; each rendition will add another theme selected from the numbered list. The current state, *#85 Hesperides (wrapping pack)*, finds the gallery walls, ceiling and floor covered in a grid of one foot, blue tape squares. Long cylinders wrapped in plastic padding con-

nect various squares around the room, while two gold balls and a skull invoke the golden apples of the ancient Greek story. How will *#30 A Bright Clear Speck of Brilliance* alter the work in 1998 or *#64 Ambient Canal* in 1999. Tyson is committed to taking his chances.

1996

The Richard Rosenblum collection of scholar's rocks

SCHOLAR'S ROCKS, OR GONGSHI, are a thousand-year-old Chinese traditional form in which seemingly untouched rocks are fitted to a highly crafted, custom-fitted, pedestal to highlight their inherent characteristics and trigger associations. Like images seen in clouds, the hollows, perforations, complex surfaces and profiles can seem like miniature worlds or landscapes. The Richard Rosenblum collection, exhibited at the Asia Society, demonstrate the depth and range of this tradition as well as its connection to various genres of picture-making. The rocks were originally "harvested" to fulfill particular virtues like *shou* (scale), *tou* (the appearance of penetrability), or *zhou* (texture). Nature was the artist, but sometimes a few adjustments were needed to help the rocks to look natural.

There are differences of opinion over whether or not certain scholar's rocks have been worked. Some have been completely carved, some indiscernibly enhanced and others untouched. The finely wrought artifice of the bases, however, urges us to pause over details of the piece as if they were intended. A Taoist belief holds that there is a mountain somewhere containing a perfect representation of the cosmos, and that stalactites inside the mountain give off a nourishing "milk of contentment." Scholar's rocks, often prized for their effect of wetness, solicit our desire to imaginatively ingest them. It is no surprise, then, that those bosomy Taoist stalactites are used to explain the fleshy bulges on Souzhou-style bases.

1996

Ellen Altfest

ELLEN ALTFEST ASKS us to slow down, to crawl, to feel our way across the variegated surfaces of her depicted objects until we experience them as materialized hallucinations. The dense skin of her paintings invites us to travel into nether-spaces of bewildering complexity where we become lost in a thoroughly mapped world right in front of our eyes.

When is seeing like blindness? When everything must be touched into existence, part by part, as when one makes a detailed depiction. Altfest looks at her motif then looks away to perform precise labors in the fading memory of that perception, over and over again. How many touches does it take to make a tumbleweed? Thousands upon thousands! No tumbling anymore, however, for Altfest's desert wanderer as she first immobilizes it in the corner of her studio and then, for all eternity, renders it on the canvas. But our eye continuously tumbles through the weed's tangled geodesics to find purchase in its many areas of perplexing coherence. Altfest's work is an exercise of extreme and deliriously inefficient will seeking both accuracy and metaphor. The tumbleweed, like all her subjects, suggests a brain, a world, or an animate being, before inevitably cycling back to its origin as nothing special. Ellen Altfest's paintings celebrate the way objects become engulfed by their surroundings. Her disciplined vigilance encourages an ecstasy of matter and vision.

2005

James Siena

JAMES SIENA'S ENAMEL PAINTINGS CRACKLE with a nervous radiance. Almost any description of his paintings, drawings, and prints, though, misses some important aspect of his deceptively simple practice. It can be variously said that he makes folk Op Art or rule-based process paintings or perhaps a form of psychedelic technomorphic handicraft patterning. His work is always the result of monkishly repetitive task labors performed in obedience to rules the artist imposed on himself. Some examples: lines may not touch, line segments only connect to each other once, or the image must be made from one unbroken line. The resulting resemblances to traditional patterns, maps, diagrams, or drug-culture idioms seem to be more of a semiological byproduct than a primary aim of his method. We add the associations while he sticks to the rules.

What is the relationship between Siena's generative axioms and the resulting image, with its precise sum of approximations, depersonalized eccentricity and cartoon rationality? A dumb stare into each picture's agitated buzz results in a reordering of our visual priorities and habitual ways of navigating a painting. It's easy to follow the reasonable itinerary of Siena's labyrinthine line as it limns an adjacent one, encircles or nests within another. It's impossible to become lost, but the path often leads to bewilderment at the startling surplus of effects derived from these simple means. Our looking is surely faster than the speed of his making but the hours of his focused marking urge us to retard at our gaze and ponder the gravity of those labors.

Everything happens within the limits of the work's four sides; lines turn back to the interior when they come to the picture's edge. We are not looking at cropped sections of a broader expanse but something emphatically generated internally. Rather than being windows onto another world, each image has the autonomy of an icon. Siena's space is generally very shallow but the interior is compressed, active and sometimes warped by perspectival illusion. The small gouache *Global Key, Diagonal Version*, 2006 is all triangles, starting with an original division of the painting from upper left to lower right; each triangle is then subdivided until there is no more room. *Global Key* performs with triangles what other works do with loops, boxes, or zigzags: the raising of casual contingency to a level of densely packed necessity.

In dozens of drawings and paintings Siena uses a meandering line to make intestine-like forms whose bodily associations are explicitly elaborated in two small gouache drawings called *a girl inside her own vagina*, 1994, and *a boy surrounded by his penis*, 1994. The nesting operations Siena frequently employs in the abstract work become a metaphor for self-enclosed solitude. Inside and out are interchangeable as the ideographic figures unravel and squeeze the ever-diminishing interstices around them. In Siena's new portraits this folding morphology is applied to the faces of old people. His baggy geriatrics inhabit their challenged condition with a variety of horror, acceptance and baffled anger. It's sad and funny, but is this what happens to a person after a lifetime of working like James Siena?

2008

Keith Tyson, *Artme-
chine Iteration Number
AMCHII•CCXXXVII Five
Stage Canonic Combo
Casino (detail)*, 1996

Horizontal Rock with Grottoes

Ellen Altfest, *Tumbleweed*, 2005

James Siena, *Global Key, Diagonal Version, 2006*

Felix Culpa

THE COMPUTER'S SCREEN IMAGE HAS NO MATERIAL PRESENCE; the RGB image, unlike a painting, has a bodiless, infinitely reproducible immortality. Its passage into matter is often understood as something of a fall from the cleaner world of digitally encoded spirit. Print outputs are secretions from an information ideal that bleed and fade. The image's incarnation as matter begins to flesh out different relationships with our body as we are now able to touch, modify or destroy the thing. Why should one convert the immaterial screen image into an object? There are plenty of commercial reasons as well as neurotic ones: accumulation and a desire for souvenirs or relics, power over the past.

If memory can never be protected from our inclination to lie or retouch, then computer-imaging is a happy accessory to this crime. To retouch is also to participate in the image fiction; one can clarify what was hazy or erase what was unpleasantly too distinct; the plasticity of memory is augmented. Elements can be added, moved or distorted, caressed or vandalized. In the retouch imagination one fingers not just the image but also the digital terms that constitute it. Computer images have a mutable immateriality like mental images. I would like my paintings to character-ize this space as both resistant and inviting.

When drawing at the computer (unlike a painting) one's hand is not in the field of vision; it is working nearby with the mouse. On the screen is a surrogate/ambassador hand, anes-thetized and ever-clean, acting in a responsive environment. Scanning, like photography, is a refigured seeing. Digital tools promise prosthetic enhancements as well as disfiguring mutila-tions. The computer becomes an auxiliary organ to incorporate images; digitalization becomes digestion as images are broken down, reproduced, and expelled. Output becomes end-product. The accumulation and retention of data produces value; saved images build compound interest.

Paintings are both things and images. They are a stilled flow, hardened muck, output through hu-man wetware. In computer imaging, like painting, one can establish intimacy and distance through a language of erasure, grafting, cutting, and pasting.

But with computer imaging dream logics and historical vernacu-lars can be folded into the process with a keystroke. Ghosts haunt the screen space in the form of a low-opacity paste. Implantation, contamination, rupture, delirious confusion, and the grotesque can be purchased as plug-in filters.

Using computer metaphors to make paintings augments the creative capacities of the ancient prac-tice while, perhaps, enmeshing it more deeply into the standardized grid of technocratic discipline. A turbulent network of exchanges has stimu-lated new anxieties and excitations about relations between the technological and biological, the unique and the reproducible, autonomy and the loss of freedom. In spite of the inclination to virtuality the computer has already introduced evolutionary and mutational deviations into the life of objects. It has exercised, in my studio, a welcome mutational influence.

1991

David Humphrey, *Sisters*, 1991

David Humphrey, *Christmas 1962*, 1991

Fritz Welch

PLINY DESCRIBED THE ORIGIN OF PAINTING as having occurred when a lover traced her beloved's shadow on a rock. Modern projectors have given this practice an extraordinary range and longevity. Fritz Welch sustains the lover's part of this tradition, even though his images are on a gallery wall and his beloved may be hard to identify. Welch's images have extended genealogies that pass as much through reproductive technologies and advertising vernacular as through his attentive hands and brain. His schemas incorporate and personalize the characteristic breakdown that results from repeatedly copied images. Welch turns the loss of resolution into an opportunity to exercise invention in the psychedelic mode. He draws swirling graphite blossoms within the schematic, high-contrast shadow zones; his graphite swirls and eddies stay within the blackened parts of the image, rendering them as if they were objects themselves, floating across the gallery's sheet-rocked whiteness. The marks act independently of their depiction-function and radiate a dense graphite presence, a negative glow, of smudges left by the working process.

Biomorphic modern-art organisms breed in Welch's low-res vernacular habitats. Insect logos and mutating machines are inflected by imaging stutters, glitches, and slurs. But up-close, the artist's obsessive hand slows down the image and lovingly renders these effects as a fertile turbulence. *Driven*, 1996 pictures a symmetrically doubled car crash, perhaps a car crashing into its double as a Welch insect pulls a cloud of decomposing images between the split cars. *Congenital T-Shirt*, 1996 pictures an analogous Siamese-twinning of the object. A doubled white T-shirt is imprinted with anamorphically stretched images of a fly. But Welch's labors are as passing shadows, since his wall drawings will be painted over when his installation is replaced by some other artist's work.

1996

Alexi Worth

IF photography and painting have become a middle-aged couple, the accumulated tensions within their relationship count as good theater for Alexi Worth. His new, emphatically hand-made paintings don't mimic the appearance of photographs or use photomechanical tools like armies of modern and contemporary artists, but rather address the relationship thematically with more personally stylized conventions. Worth weaves a consideration of lenses, reflections, and the desire to capture an image into the psycho-social subject matter of people and their need for contact with others.

The black disk pictured in *Lenscap*, 2006, nearly fills the picture, leaving just enough space to show the five oversize fingers that hold it. Peeking through from the background is a much smaller hand pulling an apple from a tree; it turns out to belong to Eve, copied from Titian's painting *Adam and Eve*, 1550. She is shown committing the first crime while also providing a delicious metaphor for Worth's musings on vision, blindness, and intersubjectivity. The lenscap occludes what is behind but the thin coat of black paint used to represent it reveals, more than any other part of the painting, the rugged tooth of the canvas. Worth's lenscap indicates the painting's point-of-view to be that of a camera while also spotlighting the work's character as a handmade material object.

Whenever an object or person blocks our view in a Worth painting, something thematically important is revealed; often it's about us, the Spectator. Many paintings feature shadows as protagonists. *Rag and Palette*, 2006, shows an artist, seen from behind, casting a shadow across the face of his painted female subject. The two figures are closely aligned to suggest a hybrid person, a fusion of depicter and depicted, even as they face in opposite directions. Worth casts the Pygmalion story, in the complicated lights of psychotherapy and feminism, as an ambivalent power dynamic. Both *Model in Shadow*, 2006, and *Head and Shoulders*, 2006, picture a seated woman with the shadow of an off-frame man thrown across her. The shadow equates the spectator with the painter in his studio, both standing before the painting and its distracted female subject. In these works Worth spins a variation on Pliny the elder's account of the invention of painting, in which a young woman traces the shadow of her departing beloved. This oft depicted and frequently discussed origin story joins depiction and proto-photography, icon and index, with the glue of desire, understood as the

incompatible impulses of longing and possession. Worth's paintings playfully invoke these themes while finding ingenious ways to visually scramble the distinctions between people. In *Double Sip*, 2006, a person with a wine glass raised in front of his or her face is seen from the point of view of someone doing the same. The lens-like distortions of glass and liquid make a patterned swirl of pressing fingers, shadows, and a wish for connection. Cheers!
2006

Louis Lussier

A CAMERA doesn't discriminate between shadows and objects. To its brainless eye, light and dark are just two halves of a single image. We decide what is a thing and what is not, automatically filtering shadows out as unimportant. Louis Lussier's photographs redirect our brain's object-oriented habits into the obscure depths of shadows so that we can imagine what is hidden. Silhouettes, reflections and blurs replace objects in Lussier's dematerialized world of noirish cities and indistinct men. His "Grey Matter" series is saturated with mysterious moods and symbolist potential.

Untitled "Looker," 1995, like much of Lussier's work, is a doubled image in numerous ways; interior and exterior, right and left diptych panels, multiple exposures and unlocatable reflections shuffle our attention between different viewpoints. The effect undermines the appearance of solidity and renders objects spectral and subjective. Radiant florescent and incandescent bulbs float in *Looker*'s nocturnal plasma but fail to illuminate the surroundings; the bulbs hover like the glow of an idea. If a shadow can be understood as a hole in the light, then Lussier inverts this by making light appear to be a hole in shadow. He withdraws the object from sight in order to allow a melancholic shade to spread his themes of solitude and anonymity.

Leonardo da Vinci wondered whether shadows were not merely the absence of light, but might also be an active opponent to it, what Michael Baxandal describes as "radiating from denseness as light radiates from a light source." Lucier uses this principle as a springboard to dive into penumbral netherworlds of image making. His work entertains the possibility that appearances do *not* deceive, that presences lurk in the shadows.
1995

Hiroshi Sugimoto

A DESIRE to capture the fugitive passage of light through a lens has often been figured within photographs as an impossible or morbid longing. Hiroshi Sugimoto's continuing series of photographs of vacant movie theaters and drive-ins highlights the complexity of this desire. Sugimoto projects a complete film onto the screen during his camera's long exposure. The movie wipes itself out to become a beaming white square, a source of illumination for the detailed features of each of the many movie houses he has photographed. These radiant blank screens and evacuated theaters, recorded with generic unblinking objectivity, face each other in taut interdependence. The camera's point of view approximates the projector's, but does not register the moving image. The point of view is not from the position of the film-going audience, but rather from the source of technological vision within the photographic fiction and the source of light for these images. Sugimoto produces a metaphysical void wherein all movies are the same. He shifts attention away from this light-annihilated center to the precisely detailed margins of American movie-house and drive-in architecture.
1998

Troy Brauntuch

TROY BRAUNTUCH'S WORKS often begin by telling us he knows a secret and proceed to say that he won't tell us what it is. His paintings are images from sources we are likely to know only generically, through advertising or photo-journalism. He reduces the source picture's brightness, enlarges its size, and eliminates the accompanying text and context.

The amount of time between when the original photo was taken and now is magnified by Brauntuch's laborious transcription and enlargement. The nocturnal moodiness of his treatment suggests that these are elegies for that lost moment. The image has escaped from its source; its original purpose has been cut loose into a netherworld of voiceless, mystified detachment. Dumb facts are animated with an almost narcotic or oneiric breath.

The hand-made, labor-intensive character of Brauntuch's work contrasts with the seamless unity of photographic effect. Given its radical lack of imagination or spontaneity, his method becomes an image of labor itself. The disembodied eye, either fogged-in or fenced-out, is mirrored in the alienated hand serving it. A small *Untitled*, 1992 image zooms in on Brauntuch's fence-vision. This nearly abstract picture is simply divided by two slightly overlapping grids. Brauntuch suggests analogies between the canvas weave, a tennis net, a chain-link fence, dot-matrix reproduction and the drawing mark itself.

1992

Fritz Welch, *Driven*, 1996

Alexi Worth, *Lenscap*, 2006

Louis Lussier, *Untitled "Regarder"*, 1995

Hiroshi Sugimoto, *Tri-City Drive-In, San Bernardino*, 1993

Troy Brauntuch,

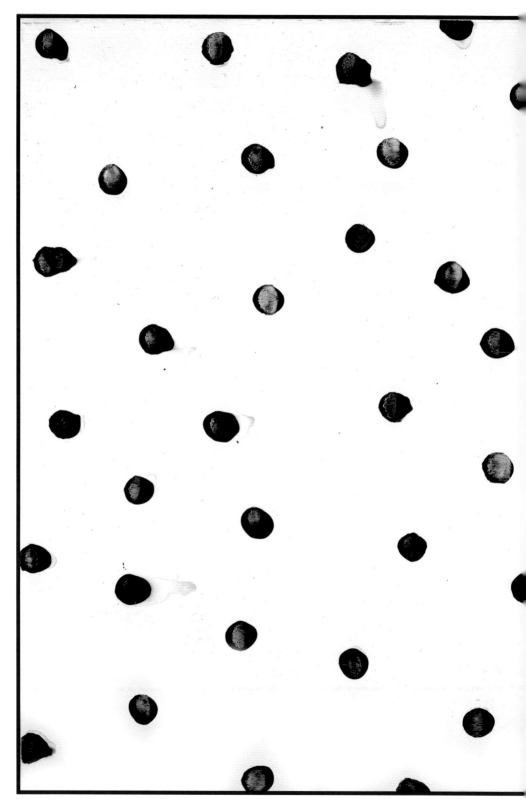

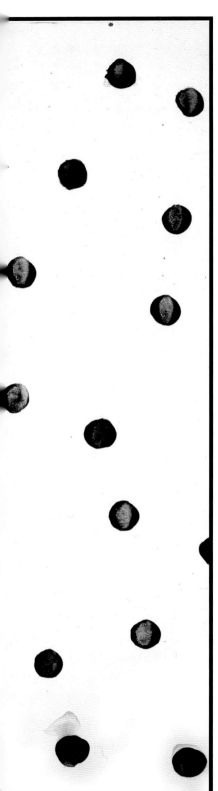

Jacqueline Humphries, 1989

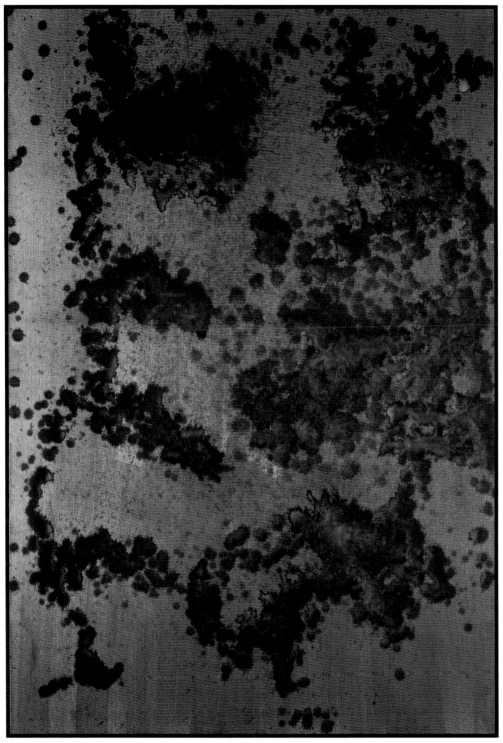

Andy Warhol, *Oxidation Painting*, 1978

Gerhard Richter, *Seascape*, 1998

The Abject Romance of Low Resolution

And under the sinister splendor of that sky the sea, blue and profound, remained still, without a stir, without a ripple, without a wrinkle – viscous, stagnant, dead.

Joseph Conrad, *Lord Jim*

THE EVOLUTION OF HIGHER AND HIGHER LEVELS OF REPRODUCTIVE TECHNOLOGY has created a hierarchy of image resolutions that gives lower and budget reproductions an increasing potential for affective or critical treatments by artists. Low definition has acquired an ability to appear more convincingly "real," because its crudity is understood as directness. A low-resolution image, like a badly taken photograph, or an image produced after many generations of cheap copying, has the capacity to solicit the viewer's participation in a production of its sense. That degree of filling-in-the-details required to "recognize" or "define" the low-resolution image draws the viewer closer to a realm of memory and association. Like certain stained walls and cloud formations, these vague images create an increased susceptibility to the unintended or subjective, exercised by the peculiarities of the maker and viewer. To zoom in on an image is to move down toward the resolution threshold, to the point where the medium refuses to cooperate, where it asserts its identity as something completely different, approaching nonsense.

The historical development of image-making technologies is an important modifier of living memory. One can recognize the era of almost any picture by its stylistic and technological character. In modern times the rapid succession of consumer-directed technologies (camera, home movies and video) gives each generation its own characteristic self-representation. Outmoded technologies linger as an abject support to the high self-esteem of "state-of-the-art." Every era has its own hierarchy of image making, usually reflected in the economically conditioned character of higher and lower levels of resolution or "quality." An era's production of images, especially at the economic low end, usually follows the same route as garbage and human waste, into the nearest disposal site. One can often learn more from what is thrown away, what is considered not worth looking at, than from what is officially preserved.

Sigmund Freud writes in his *Preface to John Bourke's Scatological Rites of all Nations*, "Civilized men today are clearly embarrassed by anything that reminds them too much of their animal origin. They deny the very existence of this inconvenient trace of the earth, by concealing it from one another, and by withholding it from the attention and care which it might claim as an integrating component of their essential being. The wiser course would undoubtedly have been to admit its existence and to dignify it as much as its nature will allow." Images are the end products of cultural life. They become waste after they move down the promotional, entertainment, or information chute. Artists have evolved a tradition of fulfilling Freud's suggestion to dignify all manner of shit as much as "its nature will allow." One could include here much Modern painting, including Pop art that has been preoccupied with scrutinizing what it considers its own reduced material condition. These artists bestow a dignity to that condition by eliminating from the practice anything not considered its "nature." Freud indirectly characterizes this postured defiance of dominant culture when he continues: "Children are, indeed, proud of their own excretions and make use of them to help in asserting themselves against adults."

The incontinent production of images in our time has been relentlessly observed. Imagery has become fast, higher quality, and cheaper to produce as a result of technological innovations. Andy Warhol is generally appreciated as having illuminated this condition by his entropic recycling of mass-produced images. The *Oxidation Paintings*, in which he pissed directly onto a sensitized canvas to produce a corrosive image of the spill, can be understood as a bodily identification with this aspect of mass media. The resulting automatist abstraction, when understood in the context of his whole practice, represents the nadir of low-resolution reproduction.

Conrad's description of sky and ocean could figure the way painting has existed under the "sinister splendor" of photographic mass media. Gerhard Richter's photo related oil canvases, *Sea Piece (Brown, Smooth)*, 1969, for instance—more than Warhol's dry silk-screened works—evoke the "viscous, stagnant, dead" state of paint in this analogy. The numb aloofness of Richter's work is often appreciated as a critical commentary on the effects of consumer-oriented representation. The idea of "low resolution" suggests a low resolve, or indolence. By absorbing the codes and appearance of photography into the practice of painting, Richter rhetorically mutes his individual "voice" while expanding its capacity to speak of the nature of representation. Richter and Warhol, in different ways, affect a passivity in relation to their sources that is rendered in the images' degradation on the canvas.

The way an image copied or magnified many times breaks down into chaotic nonsense resembles the relation between figure and ground that Clement Greenberg saw as the structural grammar of Modernist painting. This relation could be considered a symbolic elaboration of the process of primary ego-differentiation. The struggle between a desire to lose one's boundaries and fearfulness of this loss, the promise of fulfillment and the threat of dissolution, is the painter's romance of a return to origins, as well as the drama of a degrading reproduction. The quest of the figure (paint) to merge with the ground (canvas) fulfills a regressive fantasy to picture an undifferentiated infantile state; a nostalgic sublime. Indeed, newborn babies are unable to differentiate themselves from their surroundings while their desires are normally met. Jacqueline Humphries' abstractions act out a variation of this drama in blunt gestures. Her repetitive, viscous marks, as in *Four Corners*, 1989, suggest an extreme close-up of dysfunctional dot-matrix reproduction. Low resolution here translates as languid irresolution. The dumb simplicity of dissolving gestures registers a low-intensity resolve to simply mark the surface without the burden of representation. Humphries' work celebrates painting's condition as a petri dish of primal slime.

Painting has always struggled to rise through the viscous and undifferentiated quality of its material substance. Mastery is generally understood as a perfect adaptation of the materials to the consciousness of the maker. The hyper-low resolution viscosity of wet paint is an abject mirror and support of this consciousness's exercise of will. The partially defined and the unresolved are suspended in the stubborn muck of paint. Indeed, painters use it to assert themselves. Paint records what is involuntary for the painter in addition to his or her volition. My own paintings, like *Top of the Stairs*, 1991, seek to thematize this incontinence of memory. The amplified incompleteness of old family pictures provides a ground for imaginative and retrospective retouching. The work perhaps enacts an abject romance on the therapeutic couch.

André Bleikasten describes an undignifying civilized horror at the involuntary present in William Faulkner's novel *Sanctuary*. He writes, "Bodies are not sanctuaries. No presence, no mystery dwells in them—unless it be that of their generation and death. What dignity could one find in these leaking sacks of skin? Bodies do not know how to contain and control themselves. Everything urges them to spill their slimy little secrets."

1992

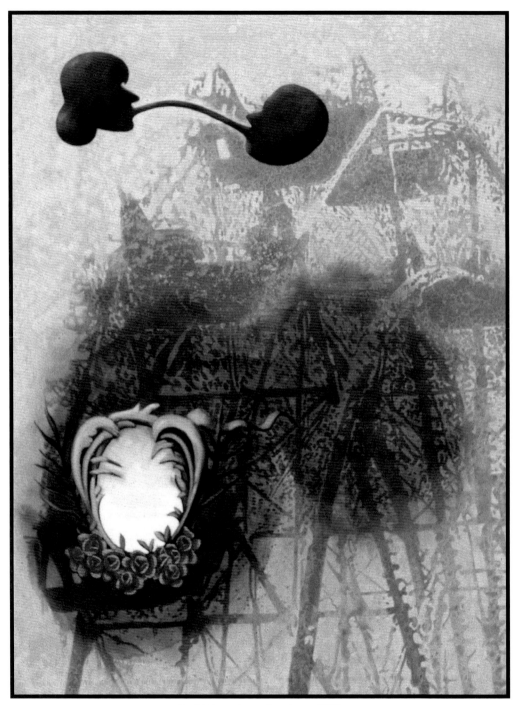

David Humphrey, *Pasttimes*, 1989

Nancy Shaver and James O. Clark

THE SIGHT OF A GALLERY littered with trash has become a commonplace. In fact, the formless, overlooked, pathetic, ad-hoc, and banal are at risk of retaining their banality through over-use by artists. Making art from discarded materials with no cultural pedigree is a process that has acquired a surprisingly long and fruitful genealogy. One routinely finds work attempting to establish a new low for what can be accepted as art. Nancy Shaver and James O. Clark are two artists who work in a zone a few steps above this bottom.

Art historian T. J. Clark, in his essay "Clement Greenberg's Theory of Art," discusses what he considers an overlooked aspect of Greenberg's account of modernism that he calls "practices of negativity." By this he means "some form of decisive innovation, in method or materials or imagery, whereby a previously established set of skills or frame of reference... are deliberately avoided or travestied in such a way as to imply that only by such incompetence or obscurity will genuine picturing get done." Shaver's and Clark's works are distinctly modern in this sense. With a modest rhetoric of sincerity, their work threatens to collapse back into its pre-art status as discarded junk. The material's noisy history of past uses is orchestrated with different degrees of formality, into an obscure meaning close to nonsense. T. J. Clark attempts to renovate Greenberg's Marxism by suggesting that this treatment of the artist's materials has critical value as an "attempt to capture the lack of consistent and repeatable meanings in the culture." While this may be true in a general sense, Shaver and Clark's work inclines toward a more intimate address that emphasizes personal idiosyncrasies.

Nancy Shaver is the more casual of the two. In her show at Curt Marcus Gallery, she assembled thirty-seven artworks, ranging from portrait drawings to minimally altered found objects. There is something unkempt about the found objects and her drawing that gives the whole an exhausted melancholic quality. The faded past of her materials and imagery acknowledges that communication is limited to the incremental adjustment of prior uses.

The painted marks and colors that cover these jars, vases, and paper are presented as mute evidence of personal handling. They are like mementos whose history of affectionate attention forms a patina of personal claim to preserved memory. By painting them, she absorbs these objects into her speech while also creating a subtle mood of loss. This ambivalent claim is staged in *Shaver* 1991, where her name is crudely written across the back of a distressed glass case. In the center of the case sits a bound packet of torn notes and postcards and a broken pitcher. The drawing *Self Portrait as Vase* 1996 is a muted declaration that these are objects leading a threshold existence between what is part of her identity and what is not. The marked "X" which appears frequently in the drawings could signify a blunt authorizing signature or a variable for an undetermined or canceled self. What T.J. Clark calls the "the lack of consistent meaning" in culture we find echoed in Shaver's work as an anxiety *not* to produce meaning. The rumpled silence of her work is sustained by the variety of old jars and vases that punctuate the show. Their contents are gone, sealed-off or undisclosed. Her gestures are what Clark would call "speech stuttering and petering out into etceteras and excuses."

James O. Clark, in his show at Max Protetch, is more buoyantly expressive with his trash. The work, with its awkwardly protected argon and fluorescant lights, embodies a delight that could illustrate this garage inventor's illuminated breakthrough: a light turning on over his head. If these objects were alive the lights would be their heart or life force. Clark's use of discarded materials at first suggests "practices of negativity," but the dynamic formality and playfulness is more assertively positive. Many of Clark's sculptures appear to be electrical objects that have been repaired, re-repaired and adapted to new uses. They seem to have defied entropy by an accumulation of ad-hoc maneuvers. There is a kind of absurd overelaborated recycling mentality that seeks to waste nothing, yet includes materials far in excess of the ostensible purpose: to wire a light. This excess is the "voice" of Clark's work. *Hamadryad*, 1991, for example, features in its metal interior a small multi-colored light resting on the bristles of a brush that is submerged in wax. The curious minty odor that radiates from inside triggers associations beyond the utilitarian history of the materials. A pressure gauge, a metal bow and four wheels rendered useless by an enigmatic piece of colored plastic braced to the bottom further elaborates Clark's symbolic tendencies. *TLC* 1978-1991 contains a yellow argon light floating in a large helium-filled plastic envelope above the tank and assorted electronics that anchor it; the grimy industrial support system rests tenderly on a pink lace-decorated cushion. Clark's work remains traditionally modern in its aspirations to an integrated, synthesized personal vision.

1991

David Batchelor

HUNTER-GATHERER AND COLOR THEORIST David Batchelor makes festive trees out of cheap plastic objects. His smaller tabletop sculptures are haiku essays on the wounded beauty and animist potential of everyday objects.

2007

Tomoko Takahashi

TOMOKO TAKAHASHI BLOTS OUT all written content from hundreds of pieces of paper in her piece *Drawing Room*, 1998. She has stapled to the walls personal notes, tickets, maps, faxes, envelopes, advertising, and packaging materials to form a narrative of cancelled words. *Drawing Room* is simultaneously a score and a performance. Takashi invites us to relax our attention and trust her obsessive verve. We have no reason to doubt that these reams of matter are authentic relics, rescued at the moment of exiting the artist's life. She sequences this would-have-been rubbish into a chamber music of abstract rhythms by sorting it into subgroups, tangents and blossoms of related materials. A pattern of black markings stresses the logic of each document's layout while canceling its content to establish a nervous, polyrhythmic pulse between the horizontal marks and the paper's increasingly tipped axes.

Takahashi's marks are sketchy, so it is easy to identify what kind of document she has covered over: a London Metro ticket, personal correspondences and statements or toothbrush and battery packaging. Words sometimes squeeze through the hail of cross-outs like oracles: "seminars," "ultra," "Miss T," "Snappy Snaps," "relief." One intuits a pattern of commuting, career attentions, snacking, and headaches. Items are grouped

by category in parallel alignment at first. Lines and squares marked on the wall form a diagrammatic schema. A pattern develops along the wall for a while before swelling into a tsunami of nonaligned materials. A turbulent mass hangs in the rear corner of the space before drifting upward across the back wall toward an air vent. It then encircles a doorframe and vestibule, where increasingly colored materials accumulate.

Takahashi's paper trail finally drops low to the ground and returns to the entrance, crumpled and jammed into a small gap between the wall and floor. The time of viewing rubs against the time she apparently spent while gathering these artifacts to make her timeline of trash. Takahashi uses ephemeral materials, things that were born to die, in order to trace a life measured by their use.

1998

Tom Fruin

TOM FRUIN HARVESTS THE FRUITS OF WASTE, MOSTLY DRUG BAGS but also candy bar wrappers, flattened beer cans and other, what he calls "addictive, recreational and non-essential" consumables. Fruin honors these discarded product-skins, that once offered guilty pleasures, by sewing them together to make translucent tapestries. He suspends them from the wall to highlight both the leftover traces of their sometimes outlawed contents and the exquisite delicacy of their patchwork construction. Like stained glass, they splash their varied colors onto the wall behind while projecting an image of collective appetites

Fruin provides opportunities to marvel at the brazen copyright illegality of heroin brand names like HBO, Gucci, or McDonald's and the gallows humor of other brands like RIP or Death Row. Fruin takes early morning field trips to various parks and housing projects to harvest an always-renewed crop of colored baggies and small printed wrapping papers. His pieces are often organized as graphs or maps of these excursions to show layered patterns of behavior and fortuitous beauty. His own behavior includes the various roles of field worker, cataloger, anthropologist and humble seamstress but his pieces also disclose the behavior of others, like the product's manufacturer, distributor and consumer who ripped his or her way to the prized goodies. Fruin's research discloses drug-choice geographies (pot at this bench, coke by that tree) and the inscrutable patterns of marketing and consumption within a broader social context of neighborhoods and parks. Packaging that began as a cheery lure was eventually discarded by the consumer as implicating evidence. Fruin organizes those promises, aversions and spent satisfactions into a patterned chorus of radiant harmonies and urban rhythm.

2002

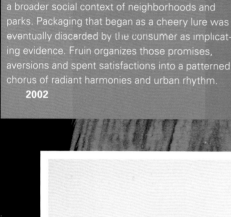

Nancy Shaver, *Dust to Dust*, 1991

James O. Clark, *Hamadryad*

David Batchelor, *Unplugged (remix)*, 2007

Tomoko Takahahi, *Drawing Room*, 1998

Tom Fruin, *Jacob Riis Houses: Northeast Corner*, 2008

On Modern Art

And is it not true that even the small step of a glimpse through the microscope reveals to us images which we would deem fantastic and overimaginative if we were to see them some-where accidentally, and lacked the sense to understand them.

Ian Dawson, *#24 Tilt Trucks*, 2002

Tilt Trucks and Free Fliers

"I WANT TO SAY JUST ONE WORD to you, just one word. Are you listening?… Plastics." This is the secret to a brilliantly successful future emphatically given to a disbelieving Ben, Dustin Hoffman's disoriented character in *The Graduate*, by a well-meaning friend of his parents. Ben's incipient counter-cultural values came, and went, and have come again, in a world now more dramatically polymerized than anything those characters in 1967 ever imagined. Ian Dawson, though, takes the older man's advice seriously, in a deviant way. He transforms a post-war consumer utopianism into a high-art anarchism, both protesting and celebrating the state of things.

The encyclopedia describes *thermoplastic* as a polymer in which molecules are held together by "weak secondary bonding forces" that soften when exposed to heat and return to a solid condition when cooled. This is what gives plastic its plasticity, its capacity to be molded into any shape. Dawson uses a blowtorch to melt and bond plastic bowls, chairs, wastebaskets, hangers, and milk cartons. The objects slur together to make artworks alive with arrested movement. The blowtorch is a surrogate for the artist's hand; its scorching touch reshapes material according to the artist's spontaneous and chance-embracing intentions.

Dawson's creative destructions subtly elaborate the various industrial and geological back-stories of plastic. In the beginning dead plants and animals became crude oil under profound terrestrial pressure and geothermal heat. Later, companies made toys and plastic hangers from the processed remains of those organisms so that the artist could restore some nature to them in the form of accelerated entropy. Dawson efficiently converts his new plastic goods into scrap in an extravagant production of waste. He adds, however, a rich genealogy and wealth of offbeat references to artists like John Chamberlain, Robert Smithson, Yves Klein, and Salvador Dali. Refined materials become raw material for elaborated refinements. Safety orange, industrial blue, and tutti-frutti rainbows of cheap color, selected by the manufacturers to signal fanciness or functionality, are re-used by Dawson for painterly effect and compositional brio. The colors reveal and conceal each other with all the dynamic sluicing and improvisational panache of an action painting.

Dawson also makes sculpture of crumpled paper. This work, like the melted sculptures, is constructed from destroyed machine-made products. The papers begin with various geometric patterns and diagrams printed on them, and are then crumpled into balls and assembled into piles. The works make a reference to topology by enacting processes best described by that science. How can the various break points and angled edges of a crumpled sheet be predicted or described? Topology is interested in the relation of math to objects. Dawson's paper sculptures solicit those considerations by making volumes constructed from a single plane. He converts an image into a thing by crunching its two dimensions into three. It would require a brain-stretching act of imagination to picture the original pattern from our always-partial view of each crumpled sheet. The regular pattern printed on the paper both highlights and camouflages the chaotic geometry of the crumple as it rises into a pile. Action is layered upon abstraction layered onto actual things; behavior collides with thought and organized matter. If Dawson's plastic pieces gesture toward the floor, his paper sculptures seem to rise toward the ceiling. Together they fill the gallery's architecture with highly artificial stalactites and stalagmites.

So much depends on the laws of physics. Dawson is a process artist in the way he applies initial operations to the materials and then lets nature do the rest; he rolls the dice. In a set of drawings using conventional marbleizing techniques, the vagaries of chemical circumstance become a snapshot of fluid dynamics; chemistry generates the image. Dawson's magic is familiar but can still astonish with lurid and nuanced effects. The images look like celestial or microbiological objects seen under enhanced magnification. The surface plane of the paper intersects with the irregularity of the marbleizing brew to make plasmic images ready for publication in a science publication.

Dawson's sculptures encourage analogies; they can be seen as tiny islands or giant blossoms. They are like Chinese scholar rocks, gongshis, in the way they evoke a sense of landscape in microcosm. The clefts, precipices, holes, and hollows of Dawson's sculptures resemble science-fiction geological formations and can be considered according to the elaborate gongshi taxonomy of sources and attributes. His objects are suggestive the way a mottled and stained wall was for Leonardo: a chaotically dispersed perceptual field that one can project into or imaginatively enter. The allover field solicits our brain's habit of projecting coherence. The unintegrated becomes integrated according to cognitive-perceptual habits, like when we recognize figures in the clouds. Dawson's willed incoherence performs what Robert Smithson would call in a different context "entropy bootlegging." Both artists repackage the effects of dissolution for our delectation and their own emphatic assertions.

In 2003 Dawson worked with plastic tilt-trucks and multicolored free flier dispensers. Both objects are designed to transport goods from one place to another, but Dawson has interrupted their missions to purvey his own more ephemeral cargo. MOD, the com-pany that manufactures the tilt trucks, promises in its literature that their trucks are "ruggedly built," for "long service under the toughest kind of punishment." MOD wasn't anticipating Ian Dawson. He purchases his material new, taking these humble instruments out of circulation to be recycled into altered art-states. He takes them halfway to total dissolution; if the heat were to continue these pieces would eventually become puddles. The energy that held the plastic in its form is undone for a moment to suspend the objects between two states. The originals are sometimes transformed beyond recognition, their identities unfastened along with their molecular structure. Dawson queries the stability of things the way a Dutch master might use the image of a snuffed candle or overturned goblet in a still-life painting.

Objects become more conspicuous when they cease to function. Broken things flare into consciousness to interrupt the smooth flow of our routine. Dysfunctional objects lose the happy invisibility they had when they worked properly. Artworks, likewise, help us to trip on the overlooked. But art also encourages us to see through things, to their history, cultural context, or to the artist. We are led, hopefully, to re-look at the objects around us with skewed vision. Those things, as a consequence, might be felt to look back at us.

2003

David Humphrey, *Pounder*, 2007

Describable Beauty

ONE OF THE INGLORIOUS REASONS I BECAME AN ARTIST was to avoid writing, which, thanks to my parents and public school, I associated with odious authoritarian demands. I found the language of painting, in spite of all its accumulated historical and institutional status, happily able to speak outside those constraints. Of course language and writing shade even mute acts of looking. The longer and more developed my involvement with painting became, the more reading and writing freed themselves from a stupid superego. Writing about art could be an extension of making it. But there persists in me a lingering desire to make paintings that resist description, that play with what has trouble being named.

I was recently asked to speak on a panel about beauty in contemporary art and found myself in the analogous position of speaking about something that I would prefer resisted description. **Describing beauty is like the humorlessness of explaining a joke.** It kills the intensity and surprise intrinsic to the experience. I found, however, that descriptions can have more importance than I originally thought. The rhetorical demands of defining beauty often lead to ingenious contradictions or sly paradoxes. It's amazing how adaptable the word is to whatever adjective you put before it: radiant, narcotic, poisonous, tasteless, scandalous; shameless, fortuitous, necessary, forgetful, or stupid beauty. I think artists have the power to make those proliferating adjectives convincing based on what Henry James called the viewer's "conscious and cultivated credulity." A description can have the power to prospectively modify experience. To describe or name a previously unacknowledged beauty can amplify its possibility in the future for others; it can dilate the horizon of beauty and hopefully of the imaginable. To assume that experience is shaped by the evolution of our ingenious and unlikely metaphors is also helpful to artists; it can enhance our motivation and cultivate enabling operational fictions, like freedom and power. We are provided another reason to thicken the dark privacy of feeling into art.

Loving claims are frequently made for beauty's irreducibility, its untranslatability, its radical incoherence. André Breton rhapsodized that "convulsive beauty will be veiled erotic, fixed explosive, magical circumstantial or will not be." Henry James defined the beautiful less ardently as "the close, the curious, the deep." I think that to consider beauty as the history of its descriptions is to infuse it with a dynamic plastic life; it is to understand beauty as something that is reinvented over and over, that needs to be invented within each person and group.

Beauty's problem is usually the uses to which it is put. Conservatives use beauty as a club to beat contemporary art with. Its so-called indescribability and position at a hierarchical zenith makes beauty an unassailable standard to which nothing ever measures up. This indescribability, however, is underwritten by a rich tangle of ambiguities and paradoxes. **For critics more to the left, beauty is a word deemed wet with the salesman's saliva.** They see it used to flatter complacency and reinforce the existing order of things. Beauty is here described as distracting people from their alienated and exploited condition and encouraging a withdrawal from engagement. This account ignores the disturbing potential of beauty. Even familiar forms of beauty can remind us of the fallen existence we have come to accept. When beauty stops us in our tracks, the aftershock triggers reevaluations of everything we have labored to attain. Finding beauty where one didn't expect it, as if it had been waiting to be discovered, is another common description. Beauty's sense of otherness demands, for some, that it be understood as universal or transcendent; something more than subjective. Periodic attempts are made to isolate a deep structural component of beauty; articulated by representations of golden sections, Fibonacci series, and other images of proportion, harmony and measure; a boiled-down beauty.

Even in the most unexpected encounters with the beautiful, however, there coexists some component of déjà vu or strange familiarity. To call that experience universal or transcendent performs a ritual act of devotion. It protects the preciousness of one's beauty experience in a shell of coherence. I think there are strong arguments for beauty's historical and cultural breadth based in our neural and biologically evolved relation to the world, but arguments for artistic practices built on that foundation often flatten the peculiar and specific details that give artworks their life. The universalizing description also overlooks the work's character as a rhetorical object, subject to unanticipated uses within the culture. It draws people toward clichés and reductive stereotypes that are then rationalized as truths and archetypes.

If I have any use for the idea of beauty, it would be in its troubling aspect. I was describing to a friend my mother's occasional fits of oceanic rage during my childhood, and she told me I should approach beauty from that angle. Like mothers, I suppose, beauty can be both a promise and a threat. All roads eventually lead back to family matters. Perhaps this path to beauty begins to slant toward the sublime; to that earliest state of relatively blurred boundaries between one's barely constituted self and the tenuously attentive environment. Attendant experiences of misrecognition, identification, alienation, and aggressivity during early ego development become components of the beauty experience. The dissolving of identity, the discovery of unconscious material in the real, a thralldom of the senses underwritten by anxiety, are a few of my favorite things. If there is a useful rehabilitation of beauty in contemporary art, I think it would be to understand it as an activity, a making and unmaking according to associative or inventive processes. Beauty would reflect the marvelous plasticity and adaptability of the brain.

I'm tempted to go against the artist in me that argues against words and throw a definition into the black hole of beauty definitions; that beauty is psychedelic, a derangement of recognition, a flash of insight or pulse of laughter out of a tangle of sensation; analogic or magical thinking embedded in the ranging iconography of desire. But any definition of beauty risks killing the thing it loves.

1996

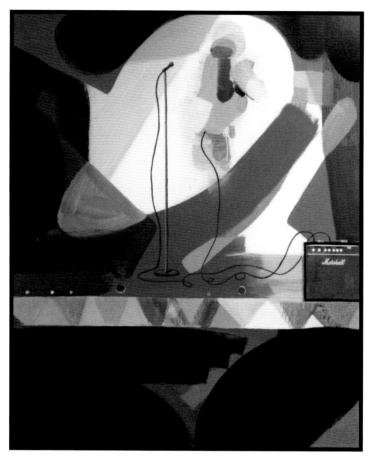

David Humphrey, *Marshal*, 2008

David Humphrey, *Party Girl*, 2000

Cover. David Humphrey, *Plein Air*, 2008, acrylic on canvas, 60 x 72 inches. Photo: Matthew Monteith. © David Humphrey, courtesy the arist and Sikkema Jenkins & Co.

Page 9. David Humphrey, *Made for Each Other*, 2009, acrylic on canvas, 52 x 36.2 inches. Photo: Matthew Monteith. © David Humphrey, courtesy the arist and Sikkema Jenkins & Co.

Page 10. David Humphrey. *Roman Nocturne*, 2008 acrylic on canvas, 36.2 x 52 inches. Photo: Matthew Monteith. © David Humphrey, courtesy the artist and Sikkema Jenkins & Co.

Page 12. David Humphrey, *Witness*, 2008, acrylic on canvas, 36.2 x 52 inches. Photo: Matthew Monteith. © David Humphrey courtesy the artist and Sikkema Jenkins & Co.

Page 14. David Humphrey, *Joined*, 2008, acrylic on canvas, 36.2 x 52 inches. Photo: Matthew Monteith. © David Humphrey, courtesy the artist and Sikkema Jenkins & Co.

Page 22. Joel Meyerowitz, *Crowd on Street, New York City*, 1976. © Joel Meyerowitz, courtesy Edwynn Houk Gallery.

Page 22. David Humphrey, *Artist With Tree*, 1980, oil on canvas, 22 x 18 inches. © David Humphrey courtesy the artist and Sikkema Jenkins & Co.

Page 23. *Summer of Solitude*, from *Crowds*, edited by Jeffrey T. Schnapp and Matthew Tiews, Stanford University Press, 2006.

Page 25. *Hi My Name is Artwork*, M/E/A/N/I/N/G Online #1, www.writing.upenn.edu/epc/meaning/01/davidhumphrey.html

Page 24. David Humphrey, *Self Portrait*, 2000, oil on canvas, 54 x 44 inches. © David Humphrey, courtesy the artist and Sikkema Jenkins & Co.

Page 26. David Humphrey, *Thanks!*, 2004, acrylic on canvas, 60 x 72 inches. © David Humphrey, courtesy the artist and Sikkema Jenkins & Co.

Page 27. David Humphrey, *Studio*, 1996, oil in canvas, 54 x 44 inches. © David Humphrey, courtesy the artist and Sikkema Jenkins & Co.

Page 31. Dana Schutz, *How we would give birth*, 2006, oil on canvas, 60 x 72 inches. Courtesy the artist and Zach Feuer Gallery. *Art in America*, June/July, 2007.

Page 31. R. Crumb, *Quissac, Nov. 13, '03*, 2003, ink on placemat, 10 1/2 x 8 3/4 inches. Courtesy the artist, Paul Morris, and David Zwirner, New York.

Page 32. Peter Saul, *Man Looking for a Bathroom*, 2000, acrylic on canvas, 62 1/2 x 66 1/2 inches. Courtesy the artist and David Nolan Gallery. *Art issues* #66, January/February, 2001.

Page 32. James Esber, *Self-Portrait of the Artist as a Foursome*, 2000, acrylic on canvas, 75 x 68 inches. Courtesy the artist and Pierogi. *Art issues* #66, January/February, 2001.

Page 34. Amy Sillman, *Shield*, 1987, oil on canvas 72 x 60 inches. © Amy Sillman, courtesy the artist and Sikkema Jenkins & Co. *Bomb Magazine*, Issue #72, Summer, 2000.

Page 36. Amy Sillman, *Blizzard*, 1997, oil on canvas, 60 x 50 inches. © Amy Sillman, courtesy the artist and Sikkema Jenkins & Co. *Art issues* #53, Summer, 1998.

Page 36. Team SHaG, *Lonley Dog*, 2002, mixed media on canvas, 11 x 9 inches. Courtesy Amy Sillman, David Humphrey and Elliot Green.

Page 36. Team SHaG, *All But*, 2002, oil on canvas, 56 x 46 inches. Courtesy Amy Sillman, David Humphrey and Elliot Green.

Page 37. Henry Darger, *Untitled (Calmaminia Strangling Children for Revenge of Defeat in Battle)*, c. mid 20th century, watercolor and pencil on paper, 24 x 37 inches.Courtesy the artist and Edlin Gallery.

Page 37. Kerry James Marshall, *Everything Will be Alright I Just Know it Will*, 2004, screenprint, 30 x 44 inches. Courtesy of Jack Shainman Gallery.

Page 37. *Life and Limb*, curated by David Humphrey for Feigen Contemporary 2005.

Page 39. Dana Hoey, *A Lesson For Bobo*, 1995, c-print, 40 x 30 inches. Courtesy the artist and Friedrich Petzel Gallery. *Art issues* #50, November/December, 1997.

Page 39. Richard Onyango, *Drosie in the Hotel Intercontinental*, 1990, acrylic on canvas, 63 x 47 1/4 inches. Courtesy Salvatore Ala Gallery, Milan.

Page 39. Odd Nerdrum, *Blind Wanderer*, 1992, oil on linen, 106 x 120 inches. Photo: Dorothy Zeidman. *Art issues* #27, March/April, 1993.

Page 41. Catherine Murphy, *Pendant*, 2005, oil on canvas, 42 x 47.75 inches. © Catherine Murphy, courtesy Knoedler & Company. *Art in America*, October, 2008.

Page 42. Chris Ofili, *Confession (Lady Chancellor)*, 2007. Photo: David Humphrey. *Art in America*, February 2008.

Page 43. *Nineteen Penises*, curated for Visual AIDS Web Gallery, February, 2006.

Page 43. *Like a Man*, for M/E/A/N/I/N/G forum, 1993.

Page 44. David Humphrey, *Bear Boy*, 2006,acrylic on canvas, 54 x 44 inches. © David Humphrey, courtesy the artist and Sikkema Jenkins & Co.

Page 44. Michael Harwood, *Barberini Faune, Glyptothek*, 1988, silver gelatin print, 9 1/2 x 6 1/2 inches. Courtesy the artist.

Page 45. David Humphrey, *Preoccupied*, 1998, oil on canvas, 72 x 60 inches. © David Humphrey, courtesy the artist and Sikkema Jenkins & Co.

Page 45. Michael Mitchell, *Untitled*, 1999, graphite on paper, 9 x 12 inches. Courtesy the artist.

Page 45. David Humphrey, *Phone Boy*, 1998, oil on canvas, 80 x 64 inches. © David Humphrey, courtesy the artist and Sikkema Jenkins & Co.

Page 48. Nikki S. Lee, *The Exotic Dancers Project*, 2000, fujiflex print. © Nikki S. Lee, courtesy Sikkema Jenkins & Co. Previously unpublished.

Page 48. Elmgreen and Dragset, *Prada Marfa*, 2005. Produced by: Art Production Fund and Ballroom Marfa, location: Marfa, Texas, photo: Lizette Kabré, previously unpublished.

Page 49. Tom Friedman, *Hot Balls*,1992. © Tom Friedman, courtesy Gagosian Gallery. *Art issues* #28, May/June, 1993.

Page 52. Merry Alpern, *Shopping #36*, 1999, cibachrome print. © Merry Alpern, courtesy Bonni Benrubi Gallery. *Art issues* #59. September/October, 1999.

Page 52. Shizuka Yokomizo, *Stranger*, 1999, c-print 50 x 4 $^1/_2$ inches. Courtesy the artist. *Art issues* #67. March/April, 2001.

Page 52. Kevin Landers, *Untitled*, 1999, c-print, 20 x 16 inches. Courtesy XL gallery. *Art issues* #59, September/October, 1999.

Page 53. Kevin Landers, *Untitled (McDougal is Dead)*, 1999, c-print, 20 x 16 inches. Courtesy the artist and Elizabeth Dee Gallery. *Art issues* #59, September/October, 1999.

Page 55. Eugene Von Bruenchenhein, *Untitled*, c. 1940's – 1950's, black and white photograph, 8 x 10 inches. *Art issues* #35, November/December, 1994.

Page 55. Amy Adler, *Once In Love With Amy*, 1997, unique cibachrome print, 48 x 70 inches. Courtesy the artist. *Art issues* #50, November/December, 1997.

Page 56. Julie Heffernan, *Self Portrait as Radiant Host*, 2000, oil on canvas, 82 x 83 inches. Courtesy P.P.O.W. Gallery.

Page 56. *Fizzy Nimbus*, catalog essay for *Julie Heffernan: Everything That Rises*, University Art Museum Univeristy at Albany, 2006.

Page 62 - 63. Hannah Wilke, *Intra-Venus #5*, June 10, 1992 and May 5, 1992, 1992-93, Performalist Self-Portrait with Donald Goddard, chromagenic supergloss diptych, 71 $^1/_2$ x 47 $^1/_2$ inches each. Courtesy Donald and Helen Goddard and Ronald Feldman Fine Arts. *Art issues* #33, May/June, 1994.

Page 64. Don Ed Hardy, *Man-o-War or Man-o-War Rising*, photo by Trina von Rosenvinge, 1991. dimensionas variable. Courtesy the artist. *Art issues* #25. November/December, 1992.

Page 64. Alix Pearlstein, *Egg Yang*, 1995, video still. Courtesy the artist. *Art issues* #40, November/December 1995.

Page 67. Mary Heilmann and Elizabeth Cannon, *Crimson and Clover*, 1995, installation view. Courtesy Mary Heilmann, Elizabeth Cannon and Cristinerose Gallery. *Art issues* #40, November/December 1995.

Page 67. Tanya Marcuse, *Bridal Suite Nº6*, 1995, platinum/palladium print, 5 x 4 inches. Courtesy the artist. *Art issues* #40, November/December 1995.

Page 68. *Hair Piece*. *Art issues* #9, February 1990.

Page 70. Jeanne Dunning, *Head 2*, 1989, laminated cibachrome mounted to Plexiglass, 28 $^1/_4$ x 18 $^7/_8$ inches. Courtesy the artist.

Page 70. David Humphrey, *Hair Piece*, 1990, oil on canvas, 72 x 60 inches. © David Humphrey courtesy the artist and Sikkema Jenkins & Co.

Page 71. Frida Kahlo, *Self-Portrait with Cropped Hair*, 1940, oil on canvas, 15 $^3/_4$ x 11 inches. Museum of Modern Art, New York.

Page 71. Curtis Mitchell, *Untitled (Hair)*, 1989, hair braided rug, 4 x 65 x 105 inches. Courtesy the artist.

Page 72. Mike Kelly, *Double Lapping Tongue Brunette*, 1989, acrylic on paper, 102 x 81 cm. Photo: Douglas M. Parker, courtesy Rosamund Felsen Gallery and Jablonka Gallerie

Page 72. Patty Martori, *Untitled*, 1988, steel, human hair, 31 $^1/_8$ x 72 $^1/_2$ x 21 $^1/_2$ inches. Courtesy Pat Hearn Gallery.

Page 73. Sue Williams, *See Price List*, 1989, acrylic on canvas, 42 x 58 inches. Courtesy David Zwirner Gallery.

Page 75. Naomi Fisher, *Untitled (heliconia)*, 2000, cibachrome mounted on aluminum, 50 x 40 inches. Courtesy of the artist. *Art issues* #64, September/October, 2000.

Page 78. Catherine Howe,*The Spaniel*, 2000, oil on linen, 66 x 48 inches. Courtesy the artist from the catalog essay *Who's Talking?* for solo exhibition at Littlejohn Contemporary, 2003.

Page 82. Robert Greene, *Together*, 1997, oil on board, 27 $^1/_4$ x 25 inches. Courtesy Robert Miller Gallery. *Art issues* #53, summer 1998.

Page 82. Paul McDevitt, *Still Life – A Flightless Pair*, 2004, colored pencil on paper & ink on paper, 11 x 14 inches. Courtesy the artist and Stephen Friedman Gallery Miser and *Now* magazine issue #7.

Page 83. Sally Ross, *Untitled (yellow flowers)*, 1998 oil on canvas, 36 x 44 inches. Collection of Dina Ghen. *Art issues* #49, September/October, 1997.

Page 86. Richard Phillips, *Portrait of God (after Jeff Bernstein)*, 1998, oil on canvas, 101 x 72 inches. © Richard Phillips, courtesy Gagosian Gallery. *Art issues* #56, January February, 1999.

Page 87. John Currin, *The Never-Ending Story*, 1994, oil on canvas, 38 x 30 inches. © John Currin, courtesy the artist and Gagosian Gallery. *Art issues* #33, May/June 1994.

Page 88. Frank Holliday, *As I Lay Dying*, 1996, oil on canvas, 38 x 36 inches. Courtesy the artist. *Art issues* #61, January/February 2000.

Page 88. Susanna Coffey, *Self-Portrait (Mirrored Glasses, Chrystie St.)*, 1997, oil on canvas, 12 x 11 inches. Courtesy the artist. *Art issues* #48, Summer 1997.

Page 88. Chris Ofili, *The Naked Soul of Captain Shit and the Legend of the Blackstars*, 1999, acrylic, collage, glitter, resin, map pins, and elephant dung on canvas, 96 x 72 inches. *Art issues* #61, January/February, 2000.

Page 93. Gillian Carnegie, *Belle*, 2006, oil on board, 9 x 13 inches. © Gillian Carnegie, courtesy the artist and Andrea Rosen. *Art in America*, November, 2007.

Page 93. Lucien Freud, *Blond Girl on a Bed*, 1987, oil on canvas, 16 x 20 inches. James Kirkman Ltd., London. *Art issues* #33, May / June 1994.

Page 94. Henri Mattise, *Odalisque in Grey Culottes*, 1926-1927, 21 x 25.5 inches. © Succession H. Matisse/ARS, NY. Photo: C. Jean. Musee de l'Orangerie, Paris, France. Photo Credi: Réunion des Musées Nationaux/Art Resource, NY.

Page 94. Rene Magritte, *The Key of Dreams*, 1930, oil on canvas, 32 x 23.6 inches. Private collection, © ARS. Photo credit: Photothèque R. Magritte-ADAGP/Art Resource, NY. *Art issues* #26, January/February 1993.

Page 94. John Wesley, *Fruit Tree*, 1996, acrylic on canvas, 44 x 59 inches. Courtesy the artist and Fredericks and Freiser Gallery. *Art issues* #53, Summer 1998.

Page 94. *When I Think About You I Touch Myself*, curated by David Humphrey for the New York Academy of Art, 2005.

Page 96. David Humphrey, *Sierra Love Team*, 1977, oil on canvas, 54 x 44 inches. © David Humphrey courtesy the artist and Sikkema Jenkins & Co.

Page 97. Kurt Kauper, *Cary Grant #2*, 2003, oil on birch panel, 47 inches diameter. Courtesy the artist.

Page 98. David Humphrey, *Bathers*, 1996, oil on canvas, 30 x 22 inches. © David Humphrey, courtesy the artist and Sikkema Jenkins & Co.

Page 99. GB Jones, *Untitled*, 1991, pencil on paper 12 x 9 $^{1}/_{2}$ inches. Courtesy Feature Gallery Inc. *Art issues* #32, March/April, 1994.

Page 99. Moise Kisling, *Large Red Nude*, 1949, oil on canvas, 37 x 65 inches. Petite Palais, Musee d'art Moderne, Geneva.

Page 100. Lynda Benglis, *NOW*, 1973, video still 10 minute video loop. © Lynda Benglis, courtesy Cheim & Read.

Page 100. George Quaintance, *Portrait of Glen Bishop*, 1956, oil on canvas, 32 x 25 $^{1}/_{16}$ inches. Collection of Norburt Sinski and George Dudley.

Page 102. Dana Schutz, *Reclining Nude*, 2002, oil on canvas, 48 x 66 inches. Courtesy Zach Feuer Gallery.

Page 104. Jo Hormuth, *Massage Therapist Frame (Scooping Technique)*, 1999-2000, cast epoxy, acrylic enamel, 15 x 24 x 2.5 inches. Courtesy the artist and Gallery Kusseneers, Antwerp. *Art issues* #62, March/April 2000.

Page 105. Medardo Rosso, *Portrait of Henri Rouart*, 1889 – 90, bronze, 50 x 28 x 20 inches. Courtesy Galleria Nazionale d'Arte Moderna, Rome. *Art issues* #49, September/October, 1997.

Page 105. Julian Trigo, *Untitled*, 1994, acrylic & charcoal on canvas, 58 x 78 inches. Courtesy the artist. *Art issues* #34, September/October, 1994.

Page 106. *Squeezy*, statement to accompany a solo exhibition; Lace Bubbles and Milk, digital media by David Humphrey at Pittsburgh Filmmakers, 2002.

Page 106. David Humphrey, *Squeezy*, 2000, plaster, paint, stuffed bears and video, 12 x 17 x 12 inches. © David Humphrey, courtesy the artist and Sikkema Jenkins & Co.

Page 107. David Humphrey, *Bunnies*, 2006, 36 x 36 x 27 inches, celluclay, hydrocal and fake fur, © David Humphrey, courtesy the artist and Sikkema Jenkins & Co.

Page 108. *Wet Clay*, presentation on a panel at NCECA Conference; Columbus, Ohio, 1999.

Page 109. David Humphrey, *Kitties*, 1997, glazed ceramic and celluclay, 7 x 7 x 5 inches. © David Humphrey, courtesy the artist and Sikkema Jenkins & Co.

Page 109. David Humphrey, *Crypig*, 2001, glazed ceramic and celluclay, 12 x 13 x 9 inches. © David Humphrey, courtesy the artist and Sikkema Jenkins & Co.

Page 109. David Humphrey, *Dogpack*, 1998, glazed ceramic and celluclay, 12 x 13 x 9 inches. © David Humphrey, courtesy the artist and Sikkema Jenkins & Co.

Page 109. David Humphrey, *Booty Bank*, glazed ceramic and celluclay, 6 x 9 x 9 inches. © David Humphrey, courtesy the artist and Sikkema Jenkins & Co.

Page 109. David Humphrey, *Hunter and Quarry*, 1999, glazed ceramic and celluclay, 9 x 12 x 6 inches. © David Humphrey, courtesy the artist and Sikkema Jenkins & Co.

Page 109. David Humphrey, *Dogstack*, 1997, glazed ceramic and celluclay, 12 x 7 x 7 inches. © David Humphrey, courtesy the artist and Sikkema Jenkins & Co.

Page 111. Mike Ballou, *orange cave (audience member)*, 1999, hot glue and enamel paint, 3.5 x 5 x 1.25 inches. Courtesy the artist. *Art issues* #57, March/April, 1999.

Page 114. George Stoll, *Untitled Sponge Painting*, 1998, burned balsa wood and alkyd, 4.5 x 6 x 1.3 inches. *Art issues* #56, January/February, 1999.

Page 114. James Hyde, *Massive Pillow*, 1999, acrylic on linen with crumpled newspaper, 70 x 86 x 50 inches. Courtesy the artist. *Art issues* #62, March/April, 2000.

Page 115. Mamma Andersson, *Leftovers*, 2006, acrylic and oil on panel, 48 x 62 $^7/_8$ inches. Courtesy David Zwirner and Galleri Magnus Karlsson, Stockholm. *Art In America*, November, 2006.

Page 115. Elizabeth Campbell, *House (A Standardized Affectation of Telepresence)*, 2000, (detail), mixed-media installation, 144 x 240 inches. Courtesy the artist. *Art issues* #67, March/April, 2001.

Page 118. Tal R, *Drawing Room*, 2006, oil on canvas, 98.5 x 98.6 inches. Courtesy Contemporary Fine Arts, Berlin. Photo: Jochen Littkemann. *Art in America*, March, 2007.

Page 118. Thomas Trosch, *The Pink Lady*, 1999, oil on canvas, 31 x 40 inches. Courtesy the artist and Fredericks and Freiser Gallery. *Art issues* #62, March/April, 2000.

Page 119. Andrew Masullo, *3003*, 1994, oil on canvas, 10 x 8 inches. Courtesy of the artist and Feature Inc. *Art issues* #35, November/December, 1994.

Page 119. Gabrielle Orozco, *Yogurt Caps*, 1994, (detail), four yogurt caps, dimensions variable. Photo: Tom Powell. *Art issues* #35, November/ December, 1994.

Page 120. Jill Giegerich, *Untitled*, Inventory # JG-1991-15, resinite sandpaper, copper, brass, plastic, fiberglas, wood, wax, plywood, 94 $^1/_2$ x 57 x 31 inches.

Page 121. *Soma Zone*, catalog essay for survey exhibition of Jill Giegerich at the Armory Center for the Arts, Pasadena, 2002.

Page 124. *Dumbstruck*, catalog essay for *Unnameable Things*, curated by Clint Jukkala for Gallery One, New Haven, 2008.

Page 126. David Humphrey, *Detail from Matisse's Morrocans*, 2007, acrylic and colored pencil on mylar, 12 x 9 inches. © David Humphrey, courtesy the artist and Sikkema Jenkins & Co.

Page 127. Carrie Moyer, *Rope Dancer*, 2007, acrylic on canvas, 48 x 92 inches. Courtesy CANADA, LLC.

Page 127. Chuck Webster, *Deep Beneath My Fingers*, 2007, oil on panel, 70 x 60 inches. Courtesy ZieherSmith Gallery.

Page 127. Chris Martin, *Untitled*, 2002-4, oil on canvas, 26 $^1/_{18}$ x 29 $^1/_{18}$ inches. Courtesy the artist and Mitchell-Innes & Nash.

Page 128. Martin Ramirez, *138 Untitled*, c. 1948 – 1963, crayon and pencil on pieced paper. Courtesy the American Folk Art Museum, promised gift of Margaret Robson. *Best of 2007, Artforum*, December 2007.

Page 129. Anonymous photograph of Tarmo Paso and Martin Ramirez at DeWitt State Hospital in Auburn California c. 1950s.

Page 132. Carl Ostendarp, *A Kick in Time*, 1994, casein, latex paint on linen, 106 x 140 inches. Courtesy the artist and Elizabeth Dee Gallery. *Art issues* #37, March/April, 1995.

Page 132. Fiona Banner, *Bodoni*, 1999, pencil on paper, 92.5 x 59 inches. Courtesy of the artist. Photo: Murray Guy Gallery. *Art issues* #58, Summer 1999.

Page 133. Remy Zaugg, *A Selfportrait The Town A Window*, 1990/93, acrylic on canvas, 3 panel: 5 x 39; 5 x 25; 5 x 26 inches. Photo: D. James Dee. *Art issues* #34, September/October, 1994.

Page 133. Marcus Raetz, *Todo-Nada*, 1998, Cast brass with black patina, waxed on cardboard pedestal, casting: 3 x 38.6 x 4.6 inches, base: 59.75 x 12.5 x 6.75 inches. Courtesy Brooke Alexander. *Art issues* #58, Summer, 1999.

Page 137. Chuck Close, *Bill Clinton*, (detail). 2006, oil on canvas, 108.5 x 84 inches. Artinfo.com, 2008.

Page 137. Ricci Albenda, *People*. (primary painting), 1996, acrylic on canvas, 32 X 47 inches. Courtesy Andrew Kreps Gallery. *Art issues* #43, Summer, 1996.

Page 140. Willem De Kooning, *Untitled VII*, 1985, oil on canvas, 70 x 80 inches. Purchase and gift of Milly and Arnold Glimcher. © ARS, NY, The Museum of Modern Art, New York. Photo credit: Digital Image Photo credit: The Museum of Modern Art/Licensed by SCALA / Art Resource, NY. *Art in America*, "Willem de Kooning at L&M and Gagosian", April, 2007.

Page 141. Milton Resnick, *Judgement of Paris*, 1991, gouache on paper, 12.25 x 18 inches. © Estate of Milton Resnick, courtesy Cheim & Read. *Art issues* #25, November/December, 1992.

Page 141. Jorg Immendorff, *Untitled*, 2006, oil on canvas, 70.75 x 59 inches. Courtesy Michael Werner Gallery, New York and Berlin. *Art In America*, "Jorg Immendorf at Michael Werner", September, 2007.

Page 142. David Humphrey, *Ike's Bridge*, 2006, acrylic on canvas, 72 x 86 inches. © David Humphrey, courtesy the artist and Sikkema Jenkins & Co.

Page 143. *Ike and Me, Cultural Politics*, Vol. 4, Number 3, November 2008.

Page 144. Dwight D. Eisenhower, *The Deserted Barn*, 1958, oil on canvas, 16 x 20 inches. Private collection.

Page 144. Dwight D. Eisenhower, *The Covered Bridge*, 1958, oil on canvas, 16 x 20 inches. Private collection.

Page 145. David Humphrey, *Ike's Woods*, 2006, acrylic on canvas, 72 x 86 inches. © David Humphrey, courtesy the artist and Sikkema Jenkins & Co.

Page 145. Eisenhower at his easel, Dwight D. Eisenhower Library, Abilene, Kansas

Page 147. Jeffrey Vallance, *The Traveling Nixon Museum*, wood case with objects, 20 x 22.5 x 7.25 inches. Courtesy of the artist and Rosamund Felsen Gallery. *Art issues* #17, April/May, 1991.

Page 148. Hildred Goodwine and the Caballeros Desert Museum, *New Observations*, #128.

Page 149. Hildred Goodwine, *Cup O' Sugar*, oil on canvas, 1973, 18 x 24 inches.

Page 152. Douglas Blau, *The Conversation Piece*, 1993, (detail), various framed pictures, dimensions variable. Courtesy the artist. *Art issues*, #58, Summer 1999.

Page 153. Rachel Harrison, *Reno*, 1999, wood, polystyrene, acrylic, photograph, 67 x 28 x 28 inches. Courtesy Green Naftali gallery. *Art issues* #59, September/October, 1999.

Page 155. Kate Kuharic, *Super Bowl Sunday*, 2003, oil on linen, 36 x 24 inches. Courtesy P.P.O.W. gallery, catalog essay for solo exhibition at PPOW gallery 2004.

Page 156. *A Brighter Urge*, catalog essay for *A Brighter Day*, curated by Elyse Goldberg for James Cohan Gallery, NY, 2006.

Page 158. Roxy Paine, *Vertical Sequence 4*, 2006. polymer, oil, lacquer, wood, glass. 43 x 17 x 17 inches. © Roxy Paine, courtesy James Cohan Gallery.

Page 159. David Alltmejd, *The Settler*, 2005, wood, paint, Plexiglas, mirror, foam, resin, synthetic hair, lighting system, shoes, wire, molding clay, beads, glitter, glue, 40 x 46.3 x 90.6 inches, base dimensions: 18 x 120 x 78 inches. © David Altmejd, courtesy Andrea Rosen Gallery.

Page 159. Jenny Holzer, *Selections from Survival: What Urge Will Save Us…I*, 2005, Danby Imperial marble footstool, 17 x 23 x15.75 inches, edition of 10. © Jenny Holzer, courtesy the Artists Rights Society and Chiem & Read.

Page 160. Alison Elizabeth Taylor, *Desert Forest*, 2006, wood inlay, polymer 39 x 60 inches. © Alison Elizabeth Taylor, courtesy James Cohan Gallery. Photo: Christopher Burke, The West Collection.

Page 161. McDermott & McGough, *The Vilest Way*, 2005, oil on linen, 90 x 114 inches. © McDermott & McGough, courtesy Cheim & Read.

Page 164. Barnaby Furnas, *Red Sea*, 2006, urethane on canvas, 11.6 x 26 feet, courtesy the artist and Marianne Boesky Gallery. *Art in America*, January 2007.

Page 164. Inka Essenhigh, *Virgin and Volcano I*, 1998, oil on canvas, 78 x 72 inches. © Inka Essenhigh, courtesy of the artist and 303 Gallery. *Art issues* #57, March/April, 1999.

Page 163. Jane Fine, *Battlefield III*, 2003, acrylic and ink on wood panel, 42 x 57 inches. Courtesy the artist and Pierogi, catalog essay for solo exhibition at Pierogi gallery 2006.

Page 168. Alexis Harding, *Flexible or Fixed*, 2007, oil and gloss paint on mdf panel, 72 x 72 inches. Courtesy Mummery + Schnell, London, Artinfo.com, 2008.

Page 168. Eva Lundsager, *Old Wound Aches*, 1994, oil on wood, 19 x 19 inches. Courtesy the artist and Greenberg Van Doren Gallery. *Art issues* #37, March April, 1995.

Page 169. John Pfahl, *The Fatal Brink*, 1996, from the series "Niagara Sublime", fujicolor print, 20 x 24 inches. Courtesy the artist and Janet Borden Gallery. *Art issues* #49, September/October, 1997.

Page 169. Elliott Puckette, *Wake*, 1997, ink, gesso, kaolin on wood, 40 x 60 inches. Courtesy the artist and Paul Kasmin Gallery. *Art issues* #49, September/October, 1997.

Page 172. Kenneth Goldsmith, *Soliloquy*, 1996 344 pages, 30 x 23 inches each. *Art issues* #48, Summer, 1997.

Page 172. Charles Long, *My Colorful Family*, 1998, rubber and wood, 108 x 48 x 7 inches. © Charles Long. Courtesy the artist and Tanya Bonakdar Gallery. *Art issues* #54, September/October, 1998.

Page 173. Richard Prince, *Untitled*, 1998, silk-screen, paper and pigment on foamcore, 96 x 72 inches. Courtesy Barbara Gladstone Gallery. *Art issues* #54, September/October, 1998.

Page 173. Drew Beattie & Daniel Davidson, *There's Summer and Fall Between Now and Then #16*, (detail), 1991-1992, mixed media on paper, 14 x 11 inches. Courtesy the artists. *Art issues* #29, September/October, 1993.

Page 179. John Coplans, *Self-Portrait (Back no. 16)*, 1992, silver print, 73 x 48 inches. Courtesy the estate of John Coplans. *Art issues* #25, November/December, 1992.

Page 179. John Mandel, *Untitled*, 1990, graphite on paper, 20 inches x 24 inches. Courtesy the artist. *Art issues* #16, February/March, 1991.

Page 179. David Diao, *Studio Visits*, 1991, acrylic and vinyl on canvas, 42 x 36 inches. Courtesy the artist. *Art issues* #21, January/February, 1992.

Page 179. Richard Pettibone, installation view. Courtesy Michael Kohn Gallery. *Art issues* #12, Summer, 1990.

Page 184. Steve McQueen, *Deadpan*, 1997, video still. Coutesy Museum of Modern Art, New York. *Art issues* #52, March/April, 1998.

Page 184. Jonathan Borofsky, *Ballerina Clown*, 1989, aluminum, steel. Gear motor, aluminum mesh, urethane, fiberglass, 30 x 17.5 x 5 feet. Collection: Harlen Lee Associates, Venice, CA © Jonathan Borofsky, courtesy the Paula Cooper Gallery. *Art issues* #10, March/April, 1990.

Page 184. Daniela Steinfeld, *Affengeil*, 1999, from Studio Series, c-print, mounted on Forex, 40.9 x 24 x 32.2 inches. Courtesy of the artist. *Art issues* #65, November/December, 2000.

Page 185. Dennis Oppenheim, *Battered Tears*, 1994, hard foam, fiberglass resin, videotape, video monitors, pigments, 14 x 16 x 6 feet. Courtesy the artist, collection: Museum van Hedendaagse Kunst, Gent, Belgium. Photo: Erma Estwick. *Art issues* # 36, January/February, 1995.

Page 186. Rodney Graham, *Vexation Island*, 1997, video still. Courtesy the artist and 303 Gallery. *Art issues* #52, March/April, 1998.

Page 186. Tony Oursler, *Getaway #2*, 1994, video projector, VCR, videotape, mattress, cloth. Performance by: Tracy Leipold, irregular dimensions (overall approx. 14 x 76 x 124 1/2 inches). Courtesy the artist and Metro Pictures. *Art issues* #36, January/February, 1995.

Page 187. Anne Chu, *Charming Girl*, 2003, wood, fabric and wire, 42.5 x 59 x 90 inches. Courtesy the artist and 303 Gallery. *Bomb Magazine* #87, Spring, 2007.

Page 189. Guillermo Kuitca, *Ein Deutsches Requeim*, 1995, mixed media on canvas, 71 x 92 inches. Courtesy of the artist and Sperone Westwater. *Art issues* #41, January/February, 1996.

Page 190. Laurence Hegarty, *Low Dishonest Times*, 2006, mixed media, dimensions variable. Courtesy of the artist. *Paydirt*, catalog essay for solo exhibition at Cynthia Broan Gallery, NY, 2005.

Page 196. Drew Dominick, *Gear Motor Grinders*, 1995, installation view. Courtest Jose Frere Gallery. *Art issues* #41, January/February, 1996.

Page 196. Andreas Slominski, *Trap for Young Rats*, 1999, metal, wood and bait, 24 x 8 x 9 inches. Courtesy the artist and Metro Pictures. *Art issues* #60, November/December, 1999.

Page 196. Peter Land, *The Lake*, 1999. Courtesy Galleri Nicolai Wallner, Copenhagen. Photo: Peter Land. *Art issues* #60, November/December, 1999.

Page 198. Céleste Boursier-Mougenot, *Untitled (series #2)*: 2, 1999, inflatable plastic pool, pump, water, 31 assorted bowls, 7 stem glasses, immersion heaters, Clorox, 22 $^1/_2$ x 100 x 100 inches. © Céleste Boursier-Mougenot, courtesy of the Paula Cooper Gallery. *Art issues* #60, November/December, 1999.

Page 198. Lewis deSoto, *Ship*, 1998, metal, motors, smoke machine, computer controllers and lights, 22 x 16 x 70 inches. Courtesy of Bill Maynes Inc., New York and Brian Gross Fine Art. *Art issues* #65, November/December, 2000.

Page 200. Keith Tyson, *Artmachine Iteration Number AMCHII•CCXXXVII*, Five Stage Canonic Combo Casino, 1996, (detail), mixed media, dimensions variable. *Art issues* #44, September/October, 1996.

Page 200. *Horizontal Rock with Grottoes*, C18, 7.26 x 12.5 x 5.5 inches, from the Richard Rosenblum collection. *Art issues* #44, September/October, 1996.

Page 200. Ellen Altfest, *Tumbleweed*, 2005, oil on canvas, 42 x 52 inches. Courtesy the artist and Bellwether, New York. Press release for solo exhibition at Bellwether 2005.

Page 201. James Siena, *Global Key, Diagonal Version*, 2006, gouache on paper, 10.7 x 8.3 inches. © James Siena, courtesy Pace Wildenstein photograph by Kerry Ryan McFate, courtesy Pace Wildenstein, previously unpublished.

Page 202. *Felix Culpa*, presented at a panel at The New School University, New York organized by Lenore Malen, 1993.

Page 203. David Humphrey, *Sisters*, 1991, oil on canvas, 86 x 60 inches. © David Humphrey, courtesy the artist and Sikkema Jenkins & Co.

Page 203. David Humphrey, *Christmas 1962*, 1991, oil on canvas. © David Humphrey, courtesy the artist and Sikkema Jenkins & Co.

Page 206. Fritz Welch, *Driven*, 1996, graphite on wall, dimensions variable. Courtesy the artist. *Art issues* # 45, November/December, 1996.

Page 206. Alexi Worth, *Lenscap* , 2006, oil on canvas, 40 x 30 inches. Private collection, courtesy of DC Moore Gallery. *Art in America*, December, 2006.

Page 207. Louis Lussier, *Untitled "Regarder"*, 1996, black-and-white silver print on fiberbase paper, 38 x 72 inches. *Art issues* # 45, November/December, 1996.

Page 207. Hiroshi Sugimoto, *Tri-City Drive-In, San Bernardino*, 1993, silver Gelatin Print, 47 x 58.75 inches. © Hiroshi Sugimoto, courtesy Gagosian Gallery. *Art issues* #32, March/April, 1994.

Page 207. Troy Brauntuch, *Untitled*, 1992, conte on linen, three panels: 71 x 52 inches each. Photo: James Franklin. *Art issues* #24, September October, 1992.

Page 208. Jacqueline Humphries, *Four Corners*, 1989, oil on canvas, 72 x 72 inches. © Jacqueline Humphries, courtesy Greene Naftali.

Page 210. Andy Warhol, *Oxidation painting*, 1978, Urine, metallic pigment in acrylic medium on canvas, 76 x 52 inches. © The Andy Warhol Foundation for the Visual Arts/ARS, NY. Photo Credit: The Andy Warhol Foundation, Inc./Art Resource, NY .

Page 211. Gerhard Richter, *Seascape*, 1998, oil on canvas, 9 feet 6 $^1/_8$ inches x 9 feet 6 $^1/_8$ inches. San Francisco Museum of Modern Art, anonymous donor.

Page 212. *The Abject Romance of Low Resolution*, Lusitania, Vol. 1, No. 4, 1992.

Page 214. David Humphrey, *Pasttimes*, 1989, oil on canvas, 72 x 60 inches. © David Humphrey, courtesy the artist and Sikkema Jenkins & Co.

Page 218. Nancy Shaver, *Dust to Dust*, 1991, glass bottles, paper, armatures, 6.25 x 9 x 21 inches. Courtesy Feature Inc. *Art issues* #20, November/December, 1991.

Page 218. James O. Clark, *TLC*, 1978-91, helium, mylar laminated with polyethylene, foam, lace, fabric, metal. wire, electronics and argon light, 135 x 65 x 34 inches. Photo: Dennis Cowley, courtesy the artist. *Art issues* #20, November/December, 1991.

Page 218. David Batchelor, *Unplugged (remix)*, 2007, found object. Photograph David Humphrey, courtesy Wilkinson Gallery, London, Artinfo.com, 2008.

Page 219. Tomoko Takahashi, *Drawing Room*, 1998, installation view. *Art issues* #54, September/October, 1998.

Page 219. Tom Fruin, *Jacob Riis Houses: Northeast Corner*, 2008, found drugbags, paper, orange thread, 8.5 x 7 inches. Courtesy of the artist, press release for solo exhibition at Stux Gallery 2002.

Page 222. Ian Dawson, *#24 Tilt Trucks*, 2002, plastic, 168 x 294 x 120 inches. *Tilt Trucks and Free Flier*, catalog essay for Ian Dawson at Grand Arts, Kansas City, 2003.

Page 226. David Humphrey, *Pounder*, 2007, acrylic on canvas, 60 x 72 inches. © David Humphrey, courtesy the artist and Sikkema Jenkins & Co.

Page 228. *Describable Beauty*, New Observations, No. 113, 1996.

Page 230. David Humphrey, *Marshal*, 2008, acrylic on canvas, 54 x 44 inches. © David Humphrey, courtesy the artist and Sikkema Jenkins & Co.

Page 231. David Humphrey, *Party Girl*, 2000, oil on canvas, 54 x 44 inches. © David Humphrey, courtesy the artist and Sikkema Jenkins & Co.

Page 239. David Humphrey, *Man With a Tiger*, 2008, acrylic on canvas, 36.2 x 52 inches. Photo: Matthew Monteith. © David Humphrey, courtesy the artist and Sikkema Jenkins & Co.

Page 239. David Humphrey, *Interspecies Embrace*, 2009, acrylic on canvas, 36.2 x 52 inches. Photo: Matthew Monteith. © David Humphrey, courtesy the artist and Sikkema Jenkins & Co.

BLIND HANDSHAKE would not exist without the help of others, first of all Gloria Kury, whose invitation to do a book with Periscope Publishing came as a lovely surprise. She encouraged the idea that the project should have a strong graphic component and urged me to find a collaborator, who turned out to be the extraordinary Geoff Kaplan. His ideas, inventions and design responses are an integral part of *Blind Handshake*; they enact the complicated sociability between writing and art making that I have labored to describe. I also owe a great deal to the American Academy in Rome where Geoff and I crafted the book's final shape. My year there as a fellow was the best way to make new things and obtain perspective on old ones while navigating the Academy's charged space of scholarship and interdisciplinary high jinx.

My neurotic aversion to writing has been gratefully dissolved by the various editors who have solicited words from me over the years: Gary Kornblau for *Art issues*, Mira Shor and Susan Bee for *M/E/A/N/I/N/G*, Betsy Sussler for *Bomb* and Nancy Princinthal for *Art in America*. Barry Schwabsky, Martim Avillez, Jeffrey Schnapp and Joy Garnett have also provided unusual opportunities for me to write. When an artist asks for a catalog essay I'm flattered and frightened but grateful for a chance to live with their work more deeply. Nell McLister, my editor, who has produced both art criticism and artworks, was the perfect person to help navigate and clarify the monstrous pile of words I've accumulated. Thank you Monica de la Torre for suggesting her! I am eternally grateful to Nika Sarabi for her tireless help with every part of this book. And thanks, most of all, to my darling wife Jennifer Coates who has been involved with every aspect of my work and to whom I dedicate this book.

David Humphrey, *Man With a Tiger*, 2008

David Humphrey, *Interspecies Embrace*, 2009